REAL CIVIL SOCIETIES

Dilemmas of Institutionalization

edited by
Jeffrey C. Alexander

SAGE Studies in International Sociology 48
Sponsored by the International Sociological Association/ISA

SAGE Publications Ltd
6 Bonhill Street
London EC2A 4PU

SAGE Publications Inc
2455 Teller Road
Thousand Oaks, California 91320

SAGE Publications India Pvt Ltd
32, M-Block Market
Greater Kailash – I
New Delhi 110 048

British Library Cataloguing in Publication data

A catalogue record for this book is available from the British
Library

ISBN 0 7619 5820 7

ISBN 0 7619 5821 5 (pbk)

Library of Congress catalog record available

Typeset by Type Study, Scarborough, North Yorkshire
Printed in Great Britain by Biddles Ltd, Guildford, Surrey

Contents

Notes on Contributors

Göran Ahrne is Professor of Sociology at Stockholm University; he is also associated with SCORE (Stockholm Center for Organizational Research). His main research area is organization theory and the state. His most recent book in English is *Social Organizations: Interaction Inside, Outside and Between Organizations*, published by Sage in 1994. He has recently published several articles on the organization of the state.

Jeffrey C. Alexander is Professor of Sociology at the University of California – Los Angeles. Since his multi-volume *Theoretical Logic in Sociology* (1982–83), he has published numerous books and articles, most recently *Fin-de-Siecle Social Theory: Relativism, Reductionism, and the Problem of Reason* (1995) and *Neofunctionalism and After* (1998). In recent years he has concentrated increasingly on the problems of culture and civil society. He is the co-founder (with Piotr Sztompka) of the Research Committee on Social Theory of the International Sociological Association.

Ronald Jacobs is Assistant Professor of Sociology at the University of Albany, State University of New York. His work, which has appeared in the *American Journal of Sociology, Sociological Theory* and *Media, Culture and Society*, focuses on the relationship between civil society and the media. He has just finished a book, *Race, Media, and the Crisis of Civil Society: From Watts to Rodney King*, which will be published by Cambridge University Press.

Víctor Pérez-Díaz is Professor of Sociology at Complutense University and Director of the ASP Research Center in Madrid. His main research interest is civil society and the public sphere, political economy and democratic transitions. He is author of *The Return of Civil Society* (Harvard University Press, 1993) and *Spain at the Crossroads* (Harvard University Press, forthcoming).

Michael Pusey is Professor of Sociology at the University of New South Wales, Sydney, Australia; he is also a fellow of the Academy of the Social Sciences in Australia. He is currently researching the impact of economic restructuring on the Australian middle class and preparing a national interview survey on the quality of life in Australia. His books include *The Dynamics of Bureaucracy* (1975), *Control and Knowledge* (1980), *Jürgen Habermas* (1987) and *Economic Rationalism in Canberra* (1991).

Elisa P. Reis is Professor at the Federal University of Rio de Janeiro (IFCS/UFRJ), and is the current President of Brazil's National Association for the Social Sciences (ANPOCS). Her work concentrates mostly on sociological theory and on political sociology. She chairs a large research program on social inequality. Her most recent publication in English is *Citizenship and National Identity* (Sage, New Delhi, 1997).

Luis Roniger of the Department of Sociology and Anthropology at the Hebrew University of Jerusalem is a comparative-historical sociologist. Among his books are *Patrons, Clients, and Friends* (with S.N. Eisenstadt, Cambridge University Press, 1984), *Hierarchy and Trust in Modern Mexico and Brazil* (Praeger, 1990), and *The Legacy of Human Rights Violations in the Southern Cone* (with Mario Sznajder, forthcoming).

Philip Smith is Senior Lecturer and Director of Postgraduate Studies in Sociology at the University of Queensland. He has published widely in the area of social and cultural theory, with a particular emphasis on the role of discourses within civil society and their relationship to the dynamics of exclusion and violence. Recent publications include an edited volume entitled *The New American Cultural Sociology* (Cambridge) and numerous journal articles on codes and narratives in civil discourse.

Piotr Sztompka is a Professor of Sociology at the Jagiellonian University at Krakow, Poland. His interests focus on sociological theory, and particularly the theories of social change. He has written a number of books on this area, including most recently *Society in Action: The Theory of Social Becoming* (Polity Press, 1991) and *The Sociology of Social Change* (Blackwell, 1993).

David Zaret is Professor of Sociology at Indiana University. He is completing a book on the origins of the public sphere in early modern England, which analyses change in communicative practices and its implications for the origins of democratic conceptions of the political order.

1

Introduction
Civil Society I, II, III: Constructing an Empirical Concept from Normative Controversies and Historical Transformations

Jeffrey C. Alexander

In 1990, when I first returned to Eastern Europe after the fall of the old regimes, I submitted a short essay to the Hungarian political weekly *Valosog* about the shock of encountering 'real' as opposed to 'ideal' civil society. Quoting briefly from that piece, which evidently was never published, can provide a bit of 'historical' atmosphere for the theoretical remarks which follow.

Just when intellectuals in Poland and Hungary were celebrating the return of civil society as an ideal, they have encountered it as a social fact. It's like a cold shower the morning after.

Almost single-handedly, Eastern European intellectuals reintroduced 'civil society' to contemporary social theory. Until they started talking and writing about it, it had been considered a quaint and conservative notion, thoroughly obsolete. Locke thought the civil realm necessary for freedom, of both the political and economic kind; the American Founding Fathers and Tocqueville alike believed that the independence of this realm formed the basis for everything good and right.

Once industrial displaced commercial capitalism, however, civil society took on a different, decidedly more ambiguous hue. Marx criticized it as merely formally free: 'civility' allowed privacy and selfish greed. Progressive intellectuals since then have wanted to eliminate civil society and set up a substantively good (read socialist and public) society in its place.

Eastern European intellectuals experienced that effort to create the good society first hand; they wanted to return to formal freedoms instead. To find a theory that embraced liberty without social guilt, they returned to the 18th century, when civil society was conceived in a positive way.

It was with these old fashioned ideas that the anti-communist revolutions were led, by intellectuals who made alliance with the few charismatic figures they could find. They articulated the inchoate frustrations of their nations, creating the 'people' in the very process of making the revolution in their name.

Now that they have carved out a civil society, however, intellectuals are not at all sure they want it. Neither are the charismatic leaders or the 'people' themselves. They are learning that civil society means more than civilian and anti-military. It also means citified, not only civil and cordial but also capitalist, thoroughly bourgeois. Kant translated civil society as *Bürgerliche Gesellschaft*. Literally, this meant a burgher, citydweller's society; it was also a synonym for the capitalist middle class.

In these new civil societies, market relations have assumed central importance. Pragmatic bargaining and the pushing and shoving of done deals are the orders of the day. Respecting formal rules, not pursuing some utopian conception of the good, is what holds such a society together. In postcommunist societies, it is about all one can hope for today, or have any right to expect. In this real civil society, intellectuals, charismatic leaders, and even 'the people' themselves may soon be out of a job.

When the intellectuals of Eastern Europe came to power, they thought they could have it all – enlightenment, capitalism, and democracy itself. The practical task of social reconstruction makes these social ideals difficult for the intellectuals to sustain. The utopian ideology they bring to their task, however, reduces even further the possibility of success...

In the good old bad days, opposition intellectuals coined the term 'real socialism' to dramatize how socialism in practice departed from the dream. It is time to start talking about 'real civil society'. (Alexander, 1990)

Virtually every important concept in the social sciences is the result of a striking kind of secularization process, a process that takes an idea from practical experiences, from the often overwhelming pressures of moral, economic, and political conflicts, to the intellectual world of conceptual disputation, paradigm dispute, research program, and empirical debate. Even after they have made this transition, of course, such concepts retain significant moral and political associations, and they remain highly disputed. What has changed is the terrain in which they are discussed, compromised, and struggled over. The intellectual field, after all, has a very distinctive specificity of its own.

We can recognize how this process resulted in the creation of such apparently 'classical' social science concepts as class, status, race, party, religion, and sect. More recently, we can observe a similar process of secularization with the emergence of concepts like gender, sexuality, and identity. The subject of the present volume is a concept, civil society, that is undergoing 'secularization' at the very moment we write. For a second time this idea has emerged into intellectual discourse from the ongoing tumult of social and political life. Once again, it must be conceptually refined so that it can be subject to more disciplined moral disputation and empirical social science.

The contributors to this volume push this secularization process forward in varied and important ways. In this introduction, I will try to do my part, suggesting that civil society has been conceived in three ideal-typical forms which have succeeded each other in historical time. After situating these ideal types historically, and evaluating them theoretically, I will introduce an analytical model of the relationship between civil society and the other kinds of institutional spheres which compose society. I will suggest that only by understanding the 'boundary relations' between civil and uncivil spheres can we convert civil society from a normative into a 'real' concept which can be studied in a social scientific way.

Civil Society I: Inclusiveness as Sacralization

It is well known that in its modern, post-medieval, post-Hobbesian form, 'civil society' entered into social understanding only in the late seventeenth century, with the writings of figures like Locke and Harrington (see Seligman, 1993). Developed subsequently by the Scottish moralists, especially Ferguson and Smith, by Rousseau, and by Hegel, and perhaps employed energetically for the last time by Tocqueville, 'civil society' was an inclusive, umbrella-like concept referring to a plethora of institutions outside the state. Definitely it included the capitalist market and its institutions, but it also denoted what Tocqueville called 'voluntary religion' (non-established Protestant covenantal denominations), private and public associations and organizations, all forms of cooperative social relationships that created bonds of trust, public opinion, legal rights and institutions, and political parties.

It is vital to see that in this first period of its modern understanding, civil society I (CSI) was endowed with a distinctively moral and ethical force. As Hirschman (1977) has shown in *The Passions and the Interests*, the civilizing qualities associated with civil society most definitely extended to the capitalist market itself, with its bargaining, its trading, its circulating commodities and money, its shopkeepers and its private property. Identified by such terms as *le doux commerce*, the processes and institutions of the capitalist market were benignly conceived – at least by the progressive thinkers of the day – as helping to produce qualities associated with international peace, domestic tranquility, and increasingly democratic participation. Capitalism was understood as producing self-discipline and individual responsibility. It was helping to create a social system antithetical to the vainglorious aristocratic one, where knightly ethics emphasized individual prowess through feats of grandeur, typically of a military kind, and ascriptive status hierarchies were maintained by hegemonic force. Hirschman shows, for example, that Montesquieu can be understood as providing high ethical praise for capitalism in its early phase. Benjamin Franklin's

famous and influential *Autobiography*, filled with vain self-regard
and identifying public virtue with the discipline and propriety of
market life, might be said to provide an equally important example
of a more popular, more bourgeois, but perhaps not less literary
kind.

The decidedly positive moral and ethical tone attributed to
market society underwent a dramatic transformation in the early
middle of the nineteenth century. The development of capitalism's
industrial phase made Mandeville's famous fable of capitalism's bee-
like cooperation seem completely *passé*. As Hirschman tells this
story, the pejorative association of capitalism with inhumane instrumentality, domination, and exploitation first emerged among radical
British political economists like Hodgkins in the 1820s and 1830s.
Marx encountered this Manichean literature in the early 1840s and
he provided it with a systematic econonomic and sociological theory.
His voice, while by far the most important in theoretical terms, was
in historical terms only one voice among many. The emerging hatred
of capitalism, its identification with all the evils of feudal domination
and worse, was expressed among a wide and growing chorus of
utopians, socialists, and republicans. It is noteworthy that the new
industrial capitalists and their liberal economic spokesmen did not
shy away from this new view of capitalism as an anti-social force.
Brandishing the doctrine of *laissez-faire* in a rather anti-Smithean
way, their motto seemed to be, 'society be damned!' There exists no
better representation of this growing self-understanding of the
antagonism between an evil, egoistical 'market' on the one hand,
and 'society' in the moral and collective sense on the other, than
Polanyi's *The Great Transformation* (1957), a book which served in
the post-war period to perpetuate the very theoretical misunderstandings I am problematizing here.

Civil Society II: Reductionism as Profanation

In social theory this dramatic transformation of the moral and social
identity of market capitalism had fateful effects on the concept of
civil society. As Keane (1988) was the first to point out, the
connotations of this fecund concept now became drastically nar-
rowed. Shorn of its cooperative, democratic, associative, and public
ties, this second version of civil society (CSII) came to be pejora-
tively associated with market capitalism alone. Marx's writings
between 1842 and 1845 reflect and crystallize this reduction in a
remarkable clear and influential way. Not only is civil society now
simply a field for the play of egoistical, purely private interests, but it
is now treated as a superstructure, a legal and political arena

produced as camouflage for the domination of commodities and the capitalist class. For Marx, industrial capitalism seemed only to consist of markets, the groups formed by markets, and states. Society in the collective and moral sense was dissolving. Only the submerged and repressed cooperative ties established by working class production, Marx believed, could provide the basis for collectively binding social organization.

It is not surprising that in this social and intellectual situation, in the middle of the nineteenth century, civil society as an important concept in social theory shortly disappeared. If it was no more than an epiphenomenon of capitalism, it was no longer necessary, either intellectually or socially. In the context of the ravages of early industrial capitalism, social and intellectual attention shifted to the state. Substantive rather than formal equality became the order of the day. Issues of democratic participation and liberty, once conceived as inherently connected to equality in its other forms, became less important. Strong state theories emerged, among radicals and conservatives, and bureaucratic regulation appeared as the only counterbalance to the instabilities and inhumanities of market life. In the newly emerging social sciences, mobility, poverty, and class conflict become the primary topics of research and theory. In social and political philosophy, utilitarian and contract theories assumed prominence, along with the neo-Kantian emphasis on justice in terms of formal rationality and proceduralism at the expense of ethical investigations into the requirements of the good life.

The legacy of this century-long distortion of the capitalism/civil-society relationship has had regrettable effects. Identifying society with the market, ideologists for the right have argued that the effective functioning of capitalism depends on the dissolution of social controls. Secure in the knowledge that civil society is the private market, that economic processes by themselves will produce the institutions necessary to promote democracy and mutual respect, they have disbanded public institutions that helped crystallize social solidarity outside the marketplace without moral qualms. Yet if, for the right, the capitalism/civil-society identification suggested abolishing society, for the left it suggested abolishing markets and private property itself. If civility and cooperation were perverted and distorted by capitalism, the latter would have to be abolished for the former to be restored. In this task, the big state became the principal ally of the left, and progressive movements became associated not only with equality but with stifling and often authoritarian bureaucratic control.

In the last decade, as is well known, revolutionary social and cultural events have created the circumstances for a renewed intellectual engagement with civil society. Big state theory has lost its prestige, economically with the falling productivity of command economies, morally and politically with the decline of state communism and bureaucratic authoritarian regimes. Within social science there is now more interest in informal ties, intimate relationships, trust, cultural and symbolic processes, and the institutions of public life. In political and moral philosophy, there has been a return not only to democratic theory but – under the influence of renewed interest in Aristotle, Hegel, and pragmatism – to hermeneutical investigations into the lifeworld ties of local culture and community.

Civil Society III: Analytical Differentiation as Realism

These theoretical developments, and the social processes they inform and reflect, have allowed us to understand civil society in a clearer manner than before. More precise and more specific than the all-inclusive umbrella idea of CSI, more general and inclusive than the narrowly reductionist association of CSII, there is growing recognition of, and interest in, civil society as a sphere that is analytically independent of – and, to varying degrees, empirically differentiated from – not only the state and the market but other social spheres as well.

With the emerging understanding provided by civil society III (CSIII), it is more clear than ever before that earlier conceptions mistakenly linked not only individualism (its emergence) but also the collective sense of social obligation (its decline) with market society. Individualism (see, for example, Taylor, 1989) has a long history in Western societies, as a moral force, an institutional fact, and a set of interactional practices. It has a non-economic background in the cultural legacy of Christianity, with its emphasis on the immortal soul, conscience, and confession; in Renaissance self-fashioning; in the Reformation's new emphasis on the individual relation to God; in the Enlightenment's deification of individual reason; in Romanticism's restoration of expressive individuality. Institutions that reward and model individuality can be traced back to English legal guarantees for private property in the eleventh century; to the medieval parliaments that distinguished the specificity of Western feudalism; to the newly independent cities that emerged in late medieval times and played such a powerful historical role until the emergence of absolutist states. The economic practices of market capitalism, in other words, did not invent moral (or immoral) individualism. They should be viewed, rather, as marking a new specification and institutionalization of it, along with other newly emerging forms of social organization, such as religious sect activity, mass parliamentary democracy, and romantic love.

Just as individualism in its moral and expressive forms preceded, survived, and, indeed, surrounded the instrumental, self-oriented individualism institutionalized in capitalist market life, so did the existence of 'society'. As Margaret Somers (1993) has shown, civil ties and the enforcement of obligations to a community of others were part of the fundamental structure of many British towns centuries before the appearance of contemporary capitalist life. The notion of a 'people' rooted in common lineage, of the community as an ethnos, formed the early basis for an ethically binding, particularist conception of nationhood from at least the fifteenth century, as the writings of Liah Greenfield (1992) and Rogers Brubaker (1996) suggest. The egoistical, impersonal, and morally irresponsible practices of early industrial capitalism were not checked by some kind of 'protectionist' movement that grew mysteriously out of nowhere, as Polanyi seems to argue in his description of the reaction to 'market society'. To the contrary, this protectionist movement, acting in the name of 'society', emerged precisely because there already existed strongly institutionalized and culturally mandated reservoirs of non-market, non-individualistic force in Western social life. It was from these sources that, as Patrick Joyce (1991) has most recently shown, there emerged protests against capitalism on behalf of 'the people'.

As this brief historical discussion suggests, civil society and capitalism must be conceptualized in fundamentally different terms. Civil society should be conceived (Alexander, 1997) as a solidary sphere in which a certain kind of universalizing community comes gradually to be defined and to some degree enforced. To the degree this solidary community exists, it is exhibited by 'public opinion', possesses its own cultural codes and narratives in a democratic idiom, is patterned by a set of peculiar institutions, most notably legal and journalistic ones, and is visible in historically distinctive sets of interactional practices like civility, equality, criticism, and respect. This kind of civil community can never exist as such; it can exist only 'to one degree or another'. One reason is that it is always interconnected with, and interpenetrated by, other more and less differentiated spheres which have their own criteria of justice and their own system of rewards. There is no reason to privilege any one of these non-civil spheres over any other.[1] The economy, the state, religion, science, the family – each differentiated sphere of activity is a defining characteristic of modern and postmodern societies. We are no more a capitalist society than we are a bureaucratic, secular, rational one, or indeed a civil one.

Rather than try to reduce the contemporary social system to the identity of one of its spheres, I would suggest that we acknowledge social differentiation both as a fact and as a process and that we study the boundary relationships between spheres. The contributors to this volume share my particular interest in the boundary relations between what might be called the civil and non-civil spheres. I believe, in fact, that the social history of 'capitalism' can be illuminated in precisely these terms.

Boundaries between Civil and Non-Civil Spheres: The 'Capitalism' Problem Revisited

One can speak of civil and non-civil boundary relationships in terms of facilitating inputs, destructive intrusions, and civil repairs. Boundary tensions can seriously distort civil society, threatening the very possibility for an effective and democratic social life. These distorting forces are destructive intrusions; in the face of them, the actors and institutions of civil society can make repairs by seeking to regulate and reform what happens in such non-civil spheres. Yet such subsystem interpenetration can also go the other way. Some of the goods and the social forms produced by other spheres actually facilitate the realization of a more civil life. Conservative theorists and politicians, not to mention the elites in these non-civil spheres themselves, are inclined to emphasize the facilitating inputs of non-civil spheres to the creation of a good social life. Those on the liberal and radical left are more inclined to emphasize the destructive intrusions that these interpenetrations entail, and the repairs that must be made as a result. Neither side of this argument can be ignored in the effort to theorize the relation between civil society and other kinds of social institutions in a general way.

That the economic sphere in its capitalist form facilitates the construction of a civil society in important ways is a historical and sociological fact that should not be denied. When an economy is structured by markets, behavior is encouraged that is independent, rational, and self-controlled. It was for this reason that the early intellectuals of capitalism, from Montesquieu to Adam Smith, hailed market society as a calming and civilizing antidote to the militaristic glories of aristocratic life. It is in part for this same reason that societies which have recently exited from communism have staked their emerging democracies on the construction of market societies in turn. Yet, quite apart from markets, industrialization itself can be seen in a positive vein. By creating an enormous supply of cheap and widely available material media, mass production lessens the invidious distinctions of status markers that separated rich and poor in more restricted economies. It becomes increasingly possible for masses of people to express their individuality, their autonomy, and their equality through consumption and, in so doing, to partake of the common symbolic inheritance of cultural life. Facilitating inputs are produced from the production side as well. As Marx was among the first to point out, the complex forms of teamwork and cooperation that are demanded in productive enterprises can be considered forms of socialization, in which persons learn to respect and trust their fellow partners in the civil sphere.

In so far as the capitalist economy supplies the civil sphere with facilities like independence, self-control, rationality, equality, self-realization, cooperation, and trust, the boundary relations between these two spheres are frictionless; structural differentiation thus seems to produce integration and individuation in turn. It is clear to all but the most diehard free marketers, however, that an industrializing, market economy also has put roadblocks in the way of civil society. In the everyday language of social science, these blockages are expressed purely in terms of economic inequalities, that is, as class divisions, housing differentials, dual labor markets, poverty, and unemployment. These facts only become crystallized in social terms – as social problems produced by the dynamics of public opinion and social movements (Alexander, 1996) – because they are viewed as destructive intrusions into the civil realm. Economic criteria are, as it were, interfering with civil ones.

The stratification of economic products, both human and material, narrows and polarizes civil society. It provides a broad field for the 'discourse of repression' (see Chapter 6), which pollutes and degrades economic failure. Despite the fact that there is no inherent relationship between failure to achieve distinction in the economic realm and failure to sustain expectations in civil society – the lack of connection being the very point of the construction of an independent civil realm – this connection is continually made. If you are poor, you are often thought to be irrational, dependent, and lazy, not only in the economy but in society as such. The relative asymmetry of resources that is inherent in economic life, in other words, becomes translated into projections about civil competence and incompetence. It is often difficult for actors without economic achievement or wealth to communicate effectively in the civil sphere, to receive full respect from its regulatory institutions, and to interact with other, more economically successful people in a fully civil way (Sennett and Cobb, 1972). Finally, material power as such, power garnered only in the economic realm, too often becomes an immediate and effective basis for civil claims (see Walzer, 1983). Despite the fact that the professionalization of journalism has separated ownership and effective editorial control, through their power to purchase newspapers as private property, capitalists of different political stripes can and do fundamentally alter some of the communicative institutions that are central to civil society.

Yet to the degree that civil society exists as an independent force, economically underprivileged actors have dual memberships. They are not just unsuccessful or dominated members of the capitalist economy; they have the ability to make claims for respect and power on the basis of their only partially realized membership in the civil realm. On the basis of the implied universalism of solidarity in civil society, moreover, they believe these claims should find a response. They broadcast appeals through the communicative institutions of civil society; organize such social movements demanding socialism or simply economic justice through its networks and public spaces; and create voluntary organizations, such as trade unions, that demand fairness and freedom of expression to wage employees. Sometimes they employ their space in civil society to confront economic institutions and elites directly, winning concessions in face-to-face negotiations. At other times, they make use of regulatory institutions, like law and the franchise, to force the state to intervene in economic life on their behalf. While these efforts at repairs often fail, they often succeed in institutionalizing 'workers' rights'. In this situation, civil criteria might be said to have entered directly into the economic, capitalist sphere. Dangerous working conditions are prohibited; discrimination in labor markets is outlawed; arbitrary economic authority is curtailed; unemployment is controlled and humanized; wealth itself is redistributed according to criteria that are antithetical to those of a strictly economic kind.

The kinds of tense and permeable boundary relationships I have described here cannot be conceptualized if capitalism and civil society are conflated with one another – as they are in CSI and II. Only if these realms are separated analytically can we gain some empirical purchase not only on the wrenching economic strains of the last two centuries but on the extraordinary 'repairs' that have been made to the social fabric in response. There is no doubt, indeed, that in the boundary relations of capitalist economy and civil society the interplay of facilitating input, destructive intrusions, and repairs will continue in the future. In the process, new economically related civil issues, workplace democracy for example (Bobbio, 1987), will become the focus of public spotlight.

**Non-Economic Boundary Relations between Civil and
Uncivil Spheres**

I have tried to separate civil society and capitalism, however,
not only better to conceptualize economic strains but to challenge the identification of 'capitalism' with 'society', that is, to
challenge the very notion that the society we live in can be understood under the rubric of capitalism. Markets are not, after all, the
only threats, or even the worst threats, that have been levied
against democratic civil life. Each of the other non-civil spheres has
also fundamentally undermined civil society in different times and
different ways. In Catholic countries, Jews and Protestants have
often been construed as uncivil and prevented from fully entering
the civil life. For most of the history of civil societies, patriarchal
power in the family transferred directly into the lack of civil status
for women. Scientific and professional power has empowered
experts and excluded ordinary persons from full participation in
vital civil discussions. Political oligarchies, whether in private organizations or in national governments themselves, have used secrecy
and manipulation to deprive members of civil society of access to
information about crucial decisions affecting their collective life.
The racial and ethic structuring of primordial communities has
distorted civil society in terrible ways.

In fact, the identification of capitalism and civil society is just one
example of the reductive and circumscribing conflation of civil
society with a particular kind of non-civil realm. Indeed, in the
course of Western history the anti-civil intrusions I have referred to
above have been so destructive that the social movements organized for repair, and the theorists who articulate their demands,
have sometimes come to believe that these blockages are intrinsic
to civil society itself. Socialists have argued that civil society is
essentially and irrevocably bourgeois; that, as long as there are
markets and private property, participants in the economic realm
can never be treated in a respectful and egalitarian way. In a
homologous manner, radical feminists have argued that civil societies are inherently patriarchal, that the very idea of a civil society is
impossible to realize in a society that has families which allow men
to dominate women. Zionists, similarly, have argued that European
societies are fundamentally antisemitic. Black nationalists have
claimed that racism is essential, and that the civil realm in white
settler societies will always, and necessarily, exclude blacks.

On the basis of arguments I have presented here, I would suggest
that these radical arguments for emancipation from civil society
are neither empirically accurate nor morally compelling. They

generalize from particular historical instances of highly distorted and oppressive boundary relations, drawing the illegitimate conclusion that the civil sphere must always be distorted in this particular way. On this faulty basis, they project utopian societies, communism for example, which deny the necessity for a universalistic civil sphere, utopian projects which claim to abolish boundary conflicts altogether. What they really deny, however, is the pluralism, complexity, and inevitably conflict-ridden nature of democratic social life. The separation of capitalism and civil society points, then, to the need to recognize the relative autonomy that exists between civil society and other kinds of social spheres, a relative autonomy which sometimes manifests itself in highly destructive interpenetrations but can also allow highly effective repairs.

About This Volume

There are two genres in the rapidly growing contemporary literature on civil society, and it is fair to say, I think, that neither has really succeeded in illuminating CSIII.

One genre (for example, Keane, 1988; Calhoun, 1992; Seligman, 1993; Hall, 1995) devotes itself primarily to purely theoretical treatments of the idea of civil society, either celebrating the return of CSI or pessimistically declaiming, usually in the tradition of CSII, the impossibility of sustaining a civil society today. The present collection differs from these efforts by being frankly empirical in a sociological sense. Rather than voting yes or no on the 'idea' of civil society, the contributors to this volume convert the abstract idea into an operational sociological concept, and they use it to examine the messy to-and-fro, pulling and pushing that occurs when the normative idea is institutionalized. In doing so, these chapters illustrate the potential social scientific utility of CSIII. They show how the revival of 'civil society', as both social realm and normative conception, produces a vital new empirical tool for analyzing the structural and cultural processes of actually existing societies. *Vis-à-vis* more utopian treatments, on the one hand, the contributors to this volume exhibit a more cautious and often skeptical attitude about the possibility of realizing the ideals of civil society as such. *Vis-à-vis* the more skeptical philosophical attacks on the very idea of civil society, on the other hand, these contributions demonstrate that, to one degree or another, important elements of the utopian promises of civil society have, in fact, been incorporated into actually existing social systems.

There is, however, a second and very different genre of civil society literature, one which employs the concept to examine particular and specific contemporary developments in this or that 'transitional' society. While these treatments, typically by political scientists (for example, Stepan, 1985; Diamond, 1992), certainly contribute to the secularizing process I described at the beginning of this introductory essay, they suffer from a decided lack of attention to the broader theoretical issues of contemporary debate. Indeed, they tend to employ the archaic, all-inclusive approach of CSI. Precisely because it offers a way of broadly contrasting democratic and undemocratic societies, such an umbrella concept often suffices as Víctor Pérez-Díaz suggests in Chapter II, below, for the comparative purposes of transition studies. Its usefulness does not, however, extend to the task of comprehending the dynamics of differentiated and conflicting social spheres after democracy in the political sphere has become institutionalized. In this collection, by contrast, while the sociological contributors engage in a great deal of empirically specific analysis, and do refer to issues of the transition, they apply 'civil society' in a manner that remains sensitive to the broader theoretical issues of contemporary debate and are continuously concerned with the limitations on, and possibilities for, the continued viability of a civil sphere in complex and conflictual differentiated systems.

In Part I, the contributors to *Real Civil Societies* discuss how the hierarchies and other exigencies of economic, political, and organizational life make it difficult to institutionalize the highly universalistic, often utopian norms and structures of civil societies. While Elisa Reis, Michael Pusey, and Luis Roniger concentrate on the particular empirical cases of Latin America and Australia, they also use civil society as a comparative concept to consider the implications of their findings in general theoretical terms.

After forcefully laying out the extraordinary scale of economic inequality in Brazil and Latin America more generally, Reis asks how such verticality could not fail to make the democratic and egalitarian ideals of civil society more difficult to realize in practice. She suggests, indeed, that the political invocation of civil society in the Brazilian context often serves to mask existing social inequalities by evoking markets and civil liberties rather than the need for an egalitarian and interventionist state. Nonetheless, Reis not only employs the civil society concept in a deeply evocative way but suggests that the reach of civil discourse can in principle be broadened. In fact, Reis argues that it *must* be if it is to become a less ambiguously progressive force for deepening democracy in a substantive sense. If Brazil, and other Latin American countries, are going to escape from what Edward Banfield called 'amoral familism', Reis argues, there will have to be the renewal of social struggles for real civility.

The analyses of Roniger and Pusey complement and elaborate the points Reis has made. Pusey makes use of the civil society concept to highlight the human and social deficits of the 'Thatcherite' free market economics that Australian Labor and Conservative governments alike have pursued over the last two decades. On the one hand, Pusey's discussion demonstrates that the complex, decoupled nature of the subsystems of contemporary society makes archaic any notion of civility as a seamless overarching principle of social integration and coherence. On the other hand, he shows how the idea of civil society, properly conceptualized in a truly sociological way, can provide criteria for critical empirical and moral evaluation *vis-à-vis* the activities, both hierarchical and instrumental, that emanate from society's other, non-civil spheres.

The same dual strategy is followed by Roniger. After showing that the historical idea of civil society emerged as an alternative to the hegemonic patron–client principle of traditional society, Roniger goes on to suggest that, nevertheless, patronage is a phenomenon that is impossible to eliminate from even the most democratic and civil of contemporary societies. He shows how patronage hierarchies and the institutions that grow around them challenge the egalitarian and participatory ideals and practices of civil societies. Yet, Roniger also demonstrates that, under certain social conditions, patron–client networks can articulate positively with 'modernity' and 'democracy', contributing to the fuller realization of a civil society by allowing democratic processes to control the informal organizations of society.

Göran Ahrne's highly original theoretical discussion, which concludes this first part on 'Uncivil Hierarchies', carries these points through in regard not to a particular case study but in relation to organizations as such. Ahrne points out the remarkable parallels between emerging debates about civil society and the long-standing arguments that have taken place inside organizational theory. Demonstrating that the latter are organized around similar utopian goals – participation, democracy, and community – Ahrne shows that the important advances in organizational sociology, from Michels to Selznick and Lipset to the neo-institutionalism of today, have come from studying how empirical pressures and processes force a departure from these normatively highly valued outcomes. On the basis of this example, he challenges social scientists involved in the civil society debate to stop using utopian discourse and to start using social science theory and ideas. Even the highly imperfect realization of civil society ideals, Ahrne warns, depends on putting institutional arrangements into place that can offset the kinds of forces that, organizational studies have shown, derail democracy, participation, and equality.

If Part I of *Real Civil Societies* is designed to thematize the challenges that social hierarchies pose to the idealization of civil society that is so rampant in contemporary discussions, Part II, 'Bifurcating Discourses', is designed to achieve the same kind of 'reality testing' in the cultural realm. Democratic theorizing has virtually always described the thrust toward civil society as emanating from a monological normative discourse that is positive, progressive, emancipating, and utopian – in short, sacred in a secular sense. In my own approach, by contrast (see Chapter 6), I have tried to demonstrate that this civil discourse, whether theoretical or popular, has always contained within itself a contradictory theme that is negative, reactionary, repressive, dystopian – in short, profane. These internal cultural dichotomies, I suggest, have provided the basis for classifying and justifying the exclusion of various groups – racial, ethnic, gender, national, and religious – in the course of the centuries-long existence of real civil societies.

In their contributions, Philip Smith and Ronald Jacobs build upon this framework even while elaborating, applying, and revising it in significant and original ways. Smith relativizes civil society discourse by showing how much it has in common with the dichotomous cultural structures of the fascist and communist movements that challenged it. At the same time, however, he demonstrates that a small number of dramatic semiotic inversions in communist and fascist codes, and a significantly different emphasis in some of their binary pairs, both represent and contribute to the world-historical conflicts between these movements.

For his part, Jacobs makes a major contribution by demonstrating how the dichotomizing semiotic structure of civil society allows it so easily to assume a racialist form. He documents this theoretical observation through an interpretive reconstruction of the principal African-American and white majority newspapers in Los Angeles during the civil disturbances in the city's south central area during the 1960s and 1990s, in the Watts and Rodney King 'riots', respectively. Jacobs shows how the binary model of democratic and anti-democratic discourse, systematically related to different narrative forms, can provide a model for tracing the intricate back-and-forth dynamics of the intense struggles for hegemony and legitimation that ensued between police, politicians, community groups, and communicative institutions during these crisis periods.

'Arbitrary Foundings', Part III of *Real Civil Societies*, demonstrates that, contrary to the idealized, teleological discourse of CSI, the historical origins of civil societies are thoroughly contingent. Although some of the particular historical actors who struggle to create democracy may be fully committed to a civil society program, others will just as strongly be opposed. Even groups who are committed to the ideals of civil society, moreover, may not be prepared, either culturally or institutionally, to carry these ideals out in their actual practices.

Piotr Sztompka shows that this realistic paradox seems very much to be the case in contemporary post-communist Poland. Sztompka suggests that, by reason of its historical foundations in the struggle against the pseudo-public of state communism, the contemporary discourse of Polish civil society has been unsuccessful in gaining the trust it needs to perform effectively its solidarizing and legitimating tasks. Because citizens remain highly suspicious of the public sphere, real civil society often remains a hollow shell behind which privatistic and fragmenting institutional processes and interactional practices continue to play themselves out.

Zaret's bold historical reconstruction of the process by which public opinion came to play a decisive role in the English democratic revolution further underscores how contingent are the foundings of real civil societies. He shows that printing was a technical innovation introduced for purely commercial reasons. In other words, in contrast to the more teleological renderings of the emergence of public opinion offered by the 'grand theories' of civil society, the actual reasons for public opinion's appearance were more humble – not explicitly related to the project of the bourgeois class, Puritan religion, or democratic revolution. Yet, when public opinion did emerge, Zaret shows, it immediately began to play a decisive role, allowing the radical moral discourses of Puritanism and democracy to be widely disseminated and, eventually, internalized by conservatives and revolutionaries alike. Drawing a contemporary lesson from his historical case study, Zaret suggests that, contrary to many postmodern jeremiads, the contemporary extensions of printing in commercial mass media today – whether in television or cyberspace – cannot be understood as, in themselves, playing an inherently blocking or facilitating role in the creation of more civil societies.

Pérez-Díaz takes this contingent approach to the origins of real civil societies in an extremely interesting direction by applying it to the problem of the European Community. Employing the civil society concept to offset current preoccupation with the economic and political dimensions of unification, Pérez-Díaz argues that neither cross-national markets nor supranational units like voluntary associations or bureaucracies are sufficient to create the solidarity and trust upon which the construction of a democratic European Community depends. What must be added to these ingredients, if a compelling identity of 'Euro-citizen' is to be sustained, is a vivid,

European public sphere. The creation of such a civil sphere depends, however, on greatly intensifying the level of pan-European public discussions. Whereas dialogues about compelling contemporary issues – such as economic policy or official scandals – are presently carried out within the framework of individual nation-states, Pérez-Díaz argues that they must be upgraded to a European frame of reference. Yet this reframing will only occur, he shows, if new kinds of narratives are created. National separateness is fueled by stories tying the salvation of individual states to interstate antagonism, narratives that gained intensity from early modern times until the end of World War II. In the watershed post-war era, policies for European unification first arose, along with new origin myths that linked the birth of 'Europe' to the heroic overcoming of earlier catastrophes. Only if this kind of mythology is expanded and elaborated, Pérez-Díaz insightfully points out, will it succeed in capturing the imaginations of intellectual elites and the masses of lay citizens alike, and only if they are inspired in this imaginative way will there develop the collective effervescence upon which the creation of a truly European public sphere depends.

Conclusion

The aim of this collection is twofold. Its first ambition is to draw the attention of 'working sociologists' to the concept of civil society. Its second aim is to show how this concept must be redefined if it is to make the transition from a normative and political idea to a concept that plays an important role in theoretical and empirical social science alike. It is rare for a conference-based volume to achieve the intellectual coherence of this collection, and rarer still for it to contain contributions of such high competence and originality. This attests, I believe, to the importance of the concept 'civil society' to the future of the social sciences.

Notes

1 In this regard, I cannot entirely agree with the characterization of my theoretical position that Víctor Pérez-Díaz offers in the compelling essay that concludes this volume, 'The Public Sphere and a European Civil Society' (Chapter 11). Differentiating 'minimalist' approaches to civil society as a distinctive subsystem (which he identifies as the position of me and Habermas) from 'maximalist' approaches that apply 'civil society' to entire social systems, Pérez-Díaz argues that the latter approach has the advantage of suggesting necessary linkages between a democratic public sphere and the spheres of economy, state, family, and ideology. By contrast, he suggests, minimalist approaches overemphasize the relative importance of the public sphere, denigrating the role of other subsystems and playing up

community and participation in a utopian way. As my discussion above suggests, however, analytically differentiating 'civil society' (CSIII) does not necessarily involve privileging it *vis-à-vis* the social or moral contributions of other spheres. What it does involve is specifying the distinctive contribution of the civil sphere. Not only can the specificity of contemporary 'boundary conflicts' be explained in this way but the contingencies of the construction of civil society can be effectively modeled. For, as Pérez-Díaz's own empirical discussion of the birth pangs of a European civil society illustrates, the presence of capitalist markets and democratic state structures does not guarantee that a viable public sphere will emerge. CSIII is the only approach that can model a *variety* of relations between civil and non-civil spheres. This is not to say that the umbrella notion of civil society – Pérez-Díaz's 'maximalism' – is never warranted. For the purposes of criticizing authoritarian states, the demand for a 'civil society', can effectively mobilize actors against a 'state society'. Analytically, however, this broad usage actually refers to a social system that contains a relatively autonomous civil sphere in the sense of CSIII.

References

Alexander, Jeffrey C. (1990) Real Civil Societies. Unpublished manuscript.

Alexander, Jeffrey C. (1996) 'Collective Action, Culture and Civil Society: Secularizing, Updating, Inverting, Revising and Displacing the Classical Model of Social Movements', in M. Diani and J. Clarke (eds), *Alain Touraine*. London: Falmer. pp. 205–34.

Alexander, Jeffrey C. (1997) 'The Paradoxes of Civil Society', *International Sociology*, 12 (2): 115–33.

Bobbio, Norberto (1987) *The Future of Democracy*. Minneapolis, MN: University of Minnesota Press.

Brubaker, Rogers (1996) *Nationalism Reframed: Nations and the National Question*. Cambridge: Cambridge University Press.

Calhoun, Craig (1992) *Habermas and the Public Sphere*. Cambridge, MA: MIT Press.

Diamond, Larry (1992) 'Introduction: Civil Society and the Struggle for Democracy', in L. Diamond (ed.), *The Democratic Revolution: Struggles for Freedom and Pluralism in the Developing World*. London: Freedom House.

Greenfeld, Liah (1992) *Nationalism: Five Roads to Modernity*. Cambridge, MA: Harvard University Press.

Hall, John A. (1995) *Civil Society: Theory, History, Comparison*. Cambridge: Polity.

Hirschman, Albert O. (1977) *The Passions and the Interests: Political Arguments for Capitalism before its Triumph*. Princeton, NJ: Princeton University Press.

Joyce, Patrick (1991) *Visions of the People: Industrial England and the Question of Class, 1840–1914*. Cambridge: Cambridge University Press.

Keane, John (1988) 'Remembering the Dead: Civil Society and the State from Hobbes to Marx and Beyond', in J. Keane, *Democracy and Civil Society*. London: Verso. pp. 31–68.

Polanyi, Karl (1957) *The Great Transformation*. Boston: Beacon.

Seligman, Adam (1993) *The Idea of Civil Society*. New York. Free Press.

Sennett, Richard and Cobb, Jonathan (1972) *The Hidden Injuries of Class*. New York: Vintage.

Somers, Margaret R. (1993) 'Citizenship and the Place of the Public Sphere: Law, Community, and Political Culture in the Transition to Democracy', *American Sociological Review*, 58 (5): 587–620.

Stepan, Alfred (1985) 'State Power and the Strength of Civil Society in the Southern Cone of Latin America', in P.B. Evans, D. Rueschemeyer and T. Skocpol (eds), *Bringing the State Back In*. Cambridge: Cambridge University Press.

Taylor, Charles (1989) *Sources of the Self: The Making of Modern Individualism*. Cambridge, MA: Harvard University Press.

Walzer, Michael (1983) *Spheres of Justice*. New York: Basic.

PART 1

UNCIVIL
HIERARCHIES

2

Banfield's Amoral Familism Revisited: Implications of High Inequality Structures for Civil Society

Elisa P. Reis

This chapter applies Banfield's (1958) notion of 'amoral familism' to a reflection on problems of solidarity and social integration within contexts of acute social inequality. Relying on the concept as defined in *The Moral Basis of a Backward Society*, I argue that today's public sphere seems somehow to be shrinking in Brazilian cities and in other major Latin American centers as well, in certain ways resembling the phenomenon that Banfield described in a small rural village in southern Italy.

The first section of this chapter reviews Banfield's discussion and points to its theoretical and practical implications. The second focuses on the contemporary trends towards social exclusion currently observed in Latin America and on the consequences these may have for the building of social identity. The third and final section presents some brief observations concerning the problems of integration and solidarity within Latin America and advances a few tentative conclusions of a general theoretical nature.

Ethos, Interests, and Social Solidarity

When Banfield carried out his study in southern Italy during the 1950s, he was struck by how the local villagers' sense of identification was restricted to their immediate families. While his main interest was in exploring the issue from a socio-psychological perspective, Banfield rightly called attention to the shrinking of the borders of the community. He coined the term 'amoral familism' to describe a situation in which social solidarity and the feeling of belonging did not extend beyond the home environment. Describing 'habits of the heart', he was primarily concerned with the implications of an ethos that prevented these people from acting in concerted ways for the common good. Amoral familism thus designated an ethos that excluded collaboration outside the restricted family circle.

Banfield summarized the attitude in these words: 'Maximize the material, short-run advantage of the nuclear family; assume that all the others will do likewise – this seems to be the rule Montegranesi follow when they act' (1958: 83). As a consequence, he observed, the only motive for showing concern with public affairs was the prospect of short-run material gain (1958: 84).

Although he did not write very explicitly about this subject, we may infer from Banfield's ethnographic research that amoral familism was a sort of 'maladjustment' to the new times. Caught between the old and new ways, the local population abandoned their basic feelings of mutual trust, defensively retreating into the limits of their intimate circles. While the traditional 'natural' community of former days was already a thing of the past, the more modern habit of associating in order to advance common interests – an approach that was to bring much progress elsewhere – had not yet taken root in this region.

Banfield identifies the decline of the traditional extended family as one of the key elements responsible for the contraction of feelings of solidarity (1958: 10 and 144–5). In drawing a comparison with the typical American village of St George, Utah, Banfield suggests that what took place in Montegrano was not a progressive affirmation of individualism that would permit a concomitant spread of civic solidarity ties; to the contrary, the Italian village's retreat into the realm of the immediate family as the natural community seemed to suggest that these people were caught between tra-ditional old social ties and modern new voluntary initiatives to promote social projects.

Considering the historical and intellectual context in which *The Moral Basis of a Backward Society* was written – at a time when both development models and hopeful expectations abounded – one may get the impression that Montegrano was an anomaly, or at least that it was experiencing the momentary pains of a transitional situation. The assumption was that the passage from tradition to modernity was loaded with tensions and occasional adjustment problems, but that sooner or later modern logic would triumph and the progressive art of associating into a civic community would take over as the legitimate social norm.

As Banfield indicated, left to its own private familistic logic, amoral familism would ultimately make social life impossible. Without generalized cooperation, societies are condemned to reproduce a Hobbesian nightmare. In Banfield's view, it was only because the larger Italian state enforced the public order that social life remained possible within this community. In other words, the social fabric was preserved because state authority made up for the deficit in civic solidarity and provided minimal public goods (1958: 155–6).

Moreover, Banfield held optimistically to the hope that the associative ethos already institutionalized in other Italian regions would have a demonstration effect among those immersed in familism. He therefore assumed that the greater prosperity enjoyed within regions where wider associative initiatives had been adopted would convince Montegranesi of the advantages of relinquishing amoral familism. In this sense, he contended that the influence or direct leadership of people from northern Italy, together with educational programs, would probably contribute to overcoming moral and psychological obstacles to association.

In short, although Banfield did not advance any simplistic mechanical predictions, he somehow expected that in due time the village would overcome this backwardness. He felt that the values and beliefs typical of amoral familism would not disappear overnight, but that the diffusion of economic and cultural modernity, combined with deliberate developmental efforts directed by outside leadership, would foster gradual change in the prevailing social morality.

Accepting the logic underlying modernization theory, Banfield seemed to feel that Montegrano, and similar transitional villages, would eventually move beyond the narrow limits of the family as the moral universe. Moreover, from this theoretical perspective, the assumption was that solidarity would extend much beyond the scope of traditional social networks. The universalization of modernity would push the boundaries of the community beyond the household, and a civic feeling would bind people together around public as well as broader private concerns. The idea that the Italian state would champion the effort to draw the remaining backward villages into the national community was also derived from the theoretical assumption that integration into the community of citizens would be a natural outcome of the spreading of modernization.

It is clear that Banfield was concerned not with individual choices but rather with the moral structure circumscribing decisions. Instead of focusing on the rationale for not joining public initiatives, he concentrated on the morality that equated the boundaries of the solidarity unit to those of the closed family circle. As indicated in his introduction to *The Moral Basis*, what the author had in mind was 'a study of the cultural, psychological, and moral conditions of political and other organizations' (1958: 9). In this sense, we could say that what mattered to him were the pre-contractual elements of solidarity.

In other words, instead of focusing on the choices made by actors, Banfield placed priority on those elements of the perceived situation which made the local inhabitants perceive collaboration in public initiatives as too costly.

In reflecting upon the situation described by Banfield, it is clear that his key interest was in understanding an ethos, or, as he cites from W.G. Sumner, 'the sum of the characteristic usages, ideas, standards and codes by which a group is differentiated and individualized in character from other groups' (1958: 10). While discussing prevailing values, however, Banfield also captured the dilemma of collective action in a nutshell: people in Montegrano saw no incentive for their joining collective efforts. When interviewed, they often indicated that they did not believe there would be any payoff to participating in public initiatives. In this sense, the cultural, psychological, and moral parameters identified by Banfield constituted as legitimate an analytical perspective as would be a focus on the choices indeed made by the actors who thought it more convenient to secure immediate benefits for their nuclear families.

In other words, the picture drawn by Banfield suggests that a generalized lack of trust made members of the community perceive a retreat into the private realm as their most rational choice. According to his interpretation, it was because people felt it more urgent to secure their own, and their close relatives', immediate material interests that they were unable to defer gratification so as to gain greater benefits through political and/or corporate initiatives. If people refused to participate in public initiatives, it was because they had automatically calculated the opportunity costs of associating.

Banfield's analysis of the inability to move from the private to the public realm which is typical of amoral familism is not free of ambiguities. While his stated effort was to treat amoral familism as a causal variable that blocks socioeconomic development, sometimes Banfield portrayed it as the result of stagnant economic conditions. In my view, exploring this very ambiguity may help us move beyond monocausal models of social explanation. Thus, instead of nudging causal arrows in one direction or another, we should take advantage of the analytical resource offered by an exploration of the impact that structural factors have on people's choices, be these factors economic or cultural (Hays, 1994). In other words, prevailing morals can be seen as parameters in the same sense that economic conditions can: they define the contours where choices are made.

So while Banfield was focusing on some sort of irrational resistance to association displayed by the population (whereas association might have improved everyone's lot), he also allows us to conclude that an acute scarcity of resources can erode pre-contractual solidarity and spawn an empire of selfish egoism. Still, there must be something else to the question, for not all situations of scarcity lead to restrictive solidarity. Common hardship may instead fuel intense solidarity among fellow victims. It is thus important to search for additional conditions which could explain why feelings of mutual trust fail to develop in particular scarcity situations.

It is precisely this sort of derivation linking resource scarcity to the absence of incentives for participating in collective initiatives that I would like to explore here. My aim is to call attention to the implications of similar forms of amoralism in societies characterized by high inequality structures. To what extent can we expect the mutual trust that characterizes communal feelings to become generalized within national societies where there are very acute disparities in the population's life chances? If the notion of fellow citizen does not find resonance in people's daily lives, why should we expect them to develop a common identity and a willingness to join in efforts to advance common projects?

These observations may at first glance seem trivial, or may appear to be mere resurrections of certain classical statements about class cleavages and inevitable confrontations which have recently acquired a reputation as old-fashioned and as conducive to flawed predictions. Yet widespread poverty and inequality together constitute one of today's most pressing social problems (Wacquant, 1994), particularly within the Third World, where the magnitude and scope of deprivation reach dramatic proportions (Lechner, 1990; O'Donnell, 1994; Weffort, 1990). Under these circumstances, study of persistent – and sometimes even rising – poverty and inequality pose a great challenge to sociologists. It is in this sense that an effort to rethink the concept of amoral familism with respect to the basic problem of the social order may help enhance our sociological understanding of what precisely is going on where poverty and inequality are the rule.

In regard to Latin American societies in particular, which have seen developmental projects frustrated and hopes for modernization crushed, what are the chances that we may witness some progress in the art of associating? Despite the contemporary spreading of middle-class associations and the flourishing of social movements (see, for example, Boschi, 1987; Cardoso, 1983; Eckstein, 1989; Slater, 1994; Viola et al., 1989), the truth remains that the large majority of those at the bottom have no incentives for participating in common initiatives. If the consolidation of the nation-state has apparently failed to foster the naturalization of a broadened notion of social identity among large numbers of people, just what are the incentives for moving beyond the current narrow limits of public space? What are the prospects that democracy will be effectively consolidated within societies that have failed to achieve wider social integration? Why is the idea of a 'national community' a mere abstract notion valued only in the traditional populist political market? Why do those who are worst off lack incentives for joining forces in order to secure better life chances?

There are no ready-made answers to the above worrisome questions, and it seems well worth relying on conceptual and theoretical resources in order to reflect upon such pressing contemporary problems as: acute poverty and enormous inequalities (in the case of Latin America see, for example, Cardoso and Helwege, 1992); widespread violence; generalized political corruption and unscrupulousness; and other manifestations of the absence of solidarity (Reis and Cheibub, 1993).

The Elusive Solidarity: Inclusion and Exclusion in Latin America

The construction of a public arena in Latin America, as in many other Third World societies, was historically associated with the process of development and modernization under the aegis of the state. Even the most ardent critics of modernization theory implicitly or explicitly incorporated a developmental perspective which conferred on the state responsibility, in positive and/or normative terms, for integrating the national territory, championing economic development, and forging a collective identity based on some notion of citizenship (Reis 1992; Reis and Cheibub, 1993).

True enough, national integration within Latin America has been fragile in many cases, economic growth often only intermittent and unbalanced, extended citizenship mostly a promise. Still, the national development project provided the basic elements for a 'compliance ideology' (Wilson, 1992), thereby supplying the conditions for attaining a minimal degree of generalized social solidarity. For Wilson, compliance ideology (or political culture) is the 'critical link between the individual and the social environment'. In his words, 'a compliance ideology is infused with conceptions of justice that involve broad definitions of the appropriate interests of individuals and of the community. In this sense, a compliance ideology is an ethos that always subordinates some interests that might otherwise be acted upon' (1992: 20).

For decades, variations of a development ideology within Latin American societies constituted the backbone of a compliance ideology in the above terms, or, in Gramscian terms, of a successful hegemony project. Combined with the assumptions of modernization theories, this ideology supplied the rationale for representative democracies and, more frequently, for coups and dictatorships. Under one or the other form of government, state planning and direct state investments served a twofold purpose: they provided the means by which adequate market conditions could be instituted for private entrepreneurs and for workers as well, while at the same time they laid down the conditions for incorporating the growing urban masses into the political arena.

That the state-capitalist model bore a strong elective affinity with the corporatist ethos prevailing in the region is an argument that has been widely discussed in the literature (see, for example, Morse, 1988; Schmitter, 1974; Stepan, 1978; Wiarda, 1973). Rather than add to the existing controversy over whether cultural, political, or economic factors prevail either logically or historically in explaining such an ethos, I would like to call attention to the fact that the interaction of these factors is what to a large extent explains the particular conception of civil society that took root in Latin America. This conception emphasized the direct relationship between citizens and the state authority while it segmented social demands and banned open competition between classes, groups, or any other cluster of social interests.

Despite the acute inequalities characterizing Latin America's social, political, and economic hierarchies, the progress of the national society under the aegis of the state provided the ideological grounds for holding society together. To be more precise, economic growth on the one hand, and a nationalistic ideal on the other, made possible some sort of social solidarity. Steady economic growth assured the continuous creation of new positions within the socioeconomic hierarchy; this in turn lent credibility to the promise of progressive incorporation of new citizens into the political community, and indeed made this incorporation plausible.

In other words, the process of defining a broader social identity, which took place alongside Latin America's process of modernization, was shaped by a nationalistic ideal championed by the state. Despite immense social disparities, the appeal to the community embodied in the notion of nation-state acted to prevent the emergence of competing social identities. No matter how disparate consumption patterns and actual life chances may have been, expectations for a better future for the whole nation formed the basis upon which feelings of common membership could be built. The idea of membership in a national community expressed the generalized belief that the nation's progress would distribute the fruits of modernization among growing numbers of people. According to this view, state-led development would guarantee both incorporation of those at the bottom and also the strengthening of a national community of interests.

It is in this sense that the concept of civil society as understood throughout most of Latin America has historically left little space for specific and autonomous social interests. As was the case in many other contexts, national development projects within the region, in so far as they stressed a communion of interests, contributed to delegitimizing the existence of diversified social interests and allowed societies to neglect acute problems of social integration (Calhoun, 1993). The failure of pluralism to take firm root in Latin America has been inversely related to the institutionalization of state corporatism both as a compliance ideology and as a public policy model (Reis, 1992).

The limitations of state-guided political integration were observed by a number of analysts who commented on Latin America's prevailing model of political incorporation (for example, Reis, 1982; Santos, 1979; Schmitter, 1971; Schwartzman, 1982; Stepan, 1978; Werneck, 1976). While these authors for the most part discussed recalcitrant authoritarianism in Latin America, in one way or another they all called attention to the fact that collective political identity within the region has been defined in consonance with an organic view of the nation-state which subordinates civil society to the state and uses populist discourse to dilute diverging social interests.

As to the problematic implications of state-led economic growth, only later did these become the object of widespread criticism. It was only after privatization and neo-liberalism had become successful political banners in post-industrial societies, and central planning widely discredited in former socialist countries, that the state's market role became an issue in Latin America.

In fact, the poor performance of most Latin American economies during the 1980s was probably a sufficient enough condition to cause the erosion of the state's legitimacy as entrepreneur. In any case, the argument condemning statism was originally derived from ideologies developed outside Latin America. That is to say, the ideological crisis of the nation-state as the basic cluster of solidarity was not peculiar to Latin America but was, rather, a much broader phenomenon with varying implications around the world.

Soon, however, the continent's deepening economic crisis forced budgetary cuts to be made and monetary stabilization policies put into effect, in many contexts making all too visible the state's loss of competence in fulfilling its now disputable economic roles as well as, in many cases, its most basic functions as keeper of law and order. The crisis of the state in Latin America has thus encompassed three critical dimensions: the economic, the administrative, and the ideological (O'Donnell, 1994).

While we could certainly separate the economic discussion from the one concerning collective identity, it is worth examining these two dimensions in conjunction in order to more fully assess the problem of social integration within the region. After all, the integration crisis affects not only the state, but the nation-state as well. Despite current ongoing criticisms of the state, the implications which Latin America's historically consolidated forms of statism may have on the evolution of social solidarity have yet to be consistently discussed. We have still not fully explored the consequences that the patterns of interaction between state and society that predominated within the region until just recently may have had on the definition of collective identities and, consequently, on the scope and forms of social solidarity. In other words, we have not fully investigated the consequences that such patterns may have on collective identity formation and, therefore, on Latin America's image of civil society.

To mention just one way in which the definition of collective identities in Latin America still bears the imprint of a historical organic communion of corporatist bent, let me recall that throughout the region most discourse regarding civil society links the notion directly to altruism and goodwill while casting enlightened self-interest as a form of illegitimate egoism. In other words, the discourse on civil society which is in tune with the prevailing ethos places greatest value on a communitarian ideal of strong Christian inspiration. That in itself would constitute no obstacle to the promotion of stronger and wider collective identities were it not for the fact that the actual consequence is the perpetuation of elitism, with populism as its corollary. The broad masses who must struggle desperately to assure their immediate survival find no incentive for associating because they cannot afford deferred gratification, while the prevailing ethos entrusts the enlightened elites with responsibility for caring for the poor.

The candid confession of one social scientist that 'what we call today civil society strongly resembles what we used to call the people' (Vilas, 1994: 11) makes visible the populist elements pervading the Latin American interpretation of civil society, even in this post-dictatorial era. What I mean to say is that because civil society discourse in Latin America has historically rejected the notion of specificity of interests in favor of some holistic image of society, the region has been fertile ground for elitism, with populism as its flip side, while the benevolence and charisma of those who campaign for the cause of good, with either secular or religious ardor, continue to form the ideological fulcrum of solidarity.

In the Brazilian case, an appropriate illustration of the above is found in the appeal to 'goodwill' that has pervaded discussions over inflation control, democratic consolidation, basic social needs, and almost every other pressing item on the political agenda. An equally eloquent example is that despite repeated calls for a social pact, none has ever come into being, for precisely the same reason that makes it appear so necessary: there is a lack of selective incentives which could bind together a diversity of autonomous yet interdependent interests. Similar examples could be cited from elsewhere around the region. The logic that sees private interests as binding together the social fabric is alien to the consent ideologies that define civil society in Latin America.

The good intentions and positive results of charitable and altruistic initiatives notwithstanding, we ought to carefully investigate what we mean by 'the national community', what positive incentives are offered for joining it, and what negative incentives may exist as well. Among the better-off, adhesion to collective efforts basically seems to be a 'religious' question, in either the stricter or the looser sense of the term, but when we think of the destitute masses what comes to mind is anomie and alienation. In my view, the conditions for consolidating democracy – an issue that has deservedly drawn attention among analysts – must include a careful discussion of the redefinition of civil society now in the making. While political science has debated what political institutions and political options are open to strategic actors in the consolidation of democracy, sociology should discuss collective identity formation and variations in the propensity to join collective initiatives of a public nature while discussing the future of democratization.

While very relevant in themselves, social movements and philanthropy do not necessarily enhance civic solidarity, nor do they automatically strengthen democracy. Despite the spread of voluntary associations rightly emphasized in the literature on Latin America (Calderon and dos Santos, 1989; Kowarick, 1987; Mainwaring and Viola, 1984), the fact remains that growing numbers of unintegrated people do not enjoy the objective conditions for attaining such integration, nor do they display any willingness to join collective efforts that would move them towards it. Though most philanthropic associations target these very people as their privileged constituency, the latter relate to such associations on a patron–client basis at best (Adler-Hellman, 1994). They seem to lack civic solidarity, preferring instead some restrictive definition of morality that resembles the amoral familism defined by Banfield.

Spontaneous association and generalized collaboration can in fact be observed among the destitute. We can identify myriad examples of self-help initiatives, family strategies, informal cooperative efforts with next-door neighbors entailing basic survival tasks or child-care, etc. However, the analogy with amoral familism holds precisely because these initiatives remain private and are defined in restrictive terms. Cut off from the public arena and reminding us of 'foster families', these forms of solidarity are not modeled in civic terms. What takes place could be better described as reciprocity on a personal basis. The opportunity costs entailed in generalizing such initiatives into collective enterprises would be too steep, for their participants neither trust anonymous interactions nor enjoy the availability of organizational resources.

Among better-off sectors, an inclination to define the community space in restrictive terms seem likewise to be on the rise. The greater the distance between social sectors, the more the plight of those at the bottom becomes an abstract concern for those on top. Theoretically, those who have something to lose closely associate violence, insecurity, and their own concrete daily fears with poverty and inequality, while in practice the state's inability to ensure order, security, and welfare motivates private protection initiatives. These private actions in turn contribute to reducing the public arena, further stretching social distances and reinforcing restrictive notions of solidarity.

In Latin America's large urban centers, the traditional differentiation in status has taken on new meanings. Although the links between widespread criminality and extreme poverty and inequality are far from clear, the combined effect of all three has been to strengthen ethnic- and class-based discrimination. The very widening of social distances has led people to fear the use of public spaces and to retreat into their own privacy, shunning social interaction outside their circle of peers. These dynamics not only contribute to widening the distances between classes; they also explain the generalized culture of fear permeating the whole society.

Exhortations to put into practice social fraternity and similar principles in an effort to fight poverty tend to obscure the fact that acute deprivation and too much inequality can act as deterrents to solidarity. The degree and extension of poverty, as well as the accentuated inequalities one currently observes in Latin America, pose one of the most serious obstacles to social solidarity in the region. If, following Alexander, we define *solidarity* as the subjective feelings of integration that individuals experience as members of social groups, and *inclusion* as 'the process by which previously excluded groups gain solidarity in the *terminal* community of a society' (1990: 269), we are led to conclude that the current tide against social integration is strong. The distance between social sectors has widened, aggravating the state of alienation in which the unintegrated find themselves. Large sectors of the population remain excluded, see no chances of being incorporated, and therefore display no feelings of solidarity towards the larger society.

One could conceive of inclusion as a conscious movement championed by those already included as a way of assuring social order. Discussing poverty nearly one century ago, Simmel (1908) described welfare initiatives as measures that respond basically to societal concerns, not to the intrinsic rights of the poor. From Durkheim's (1973) perspective, occasional social pathologies generate institutional devices to re-establish the solidarity balance. In a different vein, Polanyi (1957) offered a similar view when he defended the idea that society has a self-protective drive; he saw the 'hidden hand' of sociability as naturally creating forms of social inclusion for the underprivileged. None of these authors, however, thought that the success of such correction mechanisms would be automatic. Even from Durkheim's functional perspective, the possibility remains that pathological evolutions of social solidarity can generate societal entropy.

In this sense, I would like to suggest that the ways in which some social concerns have been dealt with in Latin America – and which can in qualified ways be seen as similar to amoral familism – have had perverse consequences as far as solidarity is concerned. Thus it is, for example, that many private efforts to compensate for the state's failure to ensure public order and security have in fact helped aggravate the problem. Widespread reliance on private police and bodyguards, payment of protection money, the creation of death squads, *de facto* privatization of public spaces through the blocking-off of streets, etc. all evince what has become, to paraphrase Huntington (1968), some sort of a 'social praetorianism' *within* the region: reliance on means of violence has become widespread, and competition over such means further demoralizes the public authority.

It becomes likelier that we will observe some amplified form of amoral familism the more that actors (individual and collective) perceive precautionary gains as their best alternative. Inflation provides an exemplary illustration here: to beat skyrocketing prices, individual actors seek to defend themselves both by stocking up on goods and by raising their own prices, two strategies that exacerbate the problem. As anti-inflation shock therapies in Brazil have made clear, despite a generalized principled willingness to join in the cooperative game of attempting to put the brakes on rising prices, there are not enough incentives to ensure that individuals will actually relinquish their defensive strategies. And as in the case where personal security problems are remedied by private action, the actor's individualized efforts to minimize private losses end up aggravating the problem.

In concluding these reflections on the problem of social solidarity in Latin America, let me summarize my argument by saying that the crisis of the nation-state must be understood within its proper historical perspective. That is to say, in order to comprehend how solidarity seems to be somehow contracting – belying anticipated universalistic social integration – we ought to take into account both Latin America's historical model of social incorporation and its present-day economic vicissitudes.

Latin America's historically institutionalized model of citizenship has contributed to fostering a collective identity built around a conception of the nation-state that places authority above solidarity. In this viewpoint, the nation-state encompasses all particularized interests as the symbolic expression of an organic body. The many variations of consent ideology – which has been called 'corporatist', 'Ibero-Mediterranean', 'Latin-Christian', etc. – have stressed the moral superiority of the general will embodied in the state, to the detriment of the active interplay of diversified interests.

Two major caveats must be taken into account, however. First, it is important to bear in mind that this sort of collectivist morality was not a backlash to existing social privileges as historically observed in revolutionary experiences. Here, the plea for the harmonious integration of society was compatible with the continuation of existing social hierarchies.

Second, we should remember that the ethos in question did not constitute a fixed trait in these societies but was, rather, a factor that interacted constantly with political choices and with the economic factors circumscribing such choices. From the perspective of political economy, we may take this ethos as a parameter. But when our focus is on the activation of social solidarity, we ought to consider the interplay between ideological and economic forces.

Whether or not the state could fulfil its promise of continuously broadening integration depended upon the effective amalgamation of political and economic variables within a national development project. For its part, today's solidarity crisis cannot be adequately assessed if we ignore either the ideological consequences of the traditional model of integration or the present vicissitudes of both the state and the economy.

In order to understand why we may be observing some modified sort of amoral familism today and why the possible ways of overcoming this state of affairs are most often construed as altruistic, we must bear in mind that the very form of solidarity which in the past did not recognize private interests as ethically valid today helps fuel restrictive solidarity. As the state authority ceases to be perceived as the natural guardian of the social body, and efforts towards national economic development run into constant roadblocks, there seem to be no universal grounds for solidarity.

Mere physical survival has become the uppermost concern for millions who face a scarcity of private and public goods. The number of destitute in Latin America is alarming, with Brazil holding the lead among the most unequal societies (Reis and Cheibub, 1993). The crisis of the old consent ideology has also made it increasingly more problematic for politics to gain respectability. The current demoralization of politics that one observes in Brazil and Venezuela and the recurring threats to state sovereignty in Colombia and Peru all bear witness to the dilemma.

Some Concluding Observations

The above discussion underlines the paradox of social solidarity throughout most of Latin America: the more that the traditional conceptions of collective identities have been organic and holistic, the more probable become feelings of alienation and motivations for secluding oneself into privatist networks today. The vanishing of a national development compliance ideology paints a bleak picture for the project of integrating the destitute into the larger society and seeing changes in restrictive definitions of the moral unit.

In such contexts, the discourse of the elites often relies on the concept of civil society to play a mystifying role by invoking an illusory communality of interests across different social profiles. This discourse may also be based upon ideals and values that have a philanthropic role but that fail to institutionalize generalized autonomous participation in the political arena.

The national development mystique proclaimed that the fruits of modernization were to be enjoyed by all, and when this ideology fell by the wayside, those worst off were left little alternative but to resort to private defensive networks as a survival strategy. And even the better-off have often reacted to higher criminality rates by reducing the scope of social solidarity.

That the limits of the solidarity unit have shrunk to narrow margins similar to those detected by Banfield in Montegrano can be seen all too often in Brazilians' daily lives. To me, one of the best illustrations is the taxi driver who rants indignantly to his rider about corruption among politicians and bureaucrats, berates the immoral police for accepting bribes, and then cheats this same client by charging more than the legal fare. I could list much other evidence of the reduced scope of solidarity, including the creation of Mafia-type organizations and death squads, violent disputes among drug dealers, etc. The statistics leave no doubt that mutual trust is something that is confined to ever narrower spaces.

The above observations are not incompatible with an inverse trend widely spotlighted in the general press as well as in specialized publications. I refer here to communitarian practices of religious or civic inspiration, such as parish movements, neighborhood associations, and women's movements. As initiatives independent from the state, these have received great attention as alternatives to former corporatist initiatives or as promising expressions of autonomous manifestations meant to benefit society as a whole.

Indeed, many of the aforementioned movements and associations are innovations *vis-à-vis* the traditional model of integration referred to in the previous section. However, there are numerous additional questions to be answered before we can conclude that a strong civil society is emerging within Latin America. First of all, we must question whether a strong civil society in and of itself assures its members equal chances of incorporation into the public arena. Progress towards a universalizing social morality is not automatically assured simply because state corporatism collapses.

A related question of crucial importance concerns the relative costs of association to be borne by different social sectors and groups. Where poverty is rampant and inequality too overwhelming, social solidarity will necessarily be expressed in diverse ways because the shared values and cognitions that tie people together will necessarily display sharp disparities between groups and sectors.

The costs of associating in order to strive for deferred goals will be relatively cheaper if restrictive morality is replaced by a concern for public interests, which could perhaps make the notion of civil society a fruitful concept for Latin Americans and other social exclusionary societies. What are the logical scenarios for the future of collective identities in the area? In other words, what images of civil society can we anticipate? Here I perceive two polar theoretical possibilities.

On the one hand, we might see the picture sketched in the above pages evolving towards further social deterioration, to the point where generalized coordinating problems could eventually lay fertile ground for the implementation of a new social contract. Such evolution would actually imply some sort of a refoundation for civil society. In any case, we cannot tell precisely what might at that point lend feasibility to currently unfeasible agreements and unfeasible general solidarity. In logical terms, this scenario calls for the generalized decay of civil society, followed by the emergence of a successful political project whose terms and conditions we cannot identify in advance.

On the other hand, we might logically foresee the gradual integration of previously excluded groups, while specific interests within the political arena gain ever greater legitimacy. Which social actors would pursue such a solution? In my view, those social sectors that already display some minimal degree of organization around particular interests and yet are not part of the current elites – in short, those political actors who would stand to gain from a broadening of the competitive political arena and from the multiplication of bargains, negotiations, and coalitions, be these based upon material and/or ideal interests.

Most probably, the civil societies that will actually emerge in post-dictatorial Latin America will fall somewhere between these two extremes, depending upon the active interplay of choices and constraints both material and ideological in nature. In any case, what must be kept in mind is that different traditions in collective identity building have greater or lesser affinity with more or less restrictive definitions of civil society.

Latin America's historical experience with social solidarity led to the amalgamation of a nation-state of a particular type: one characterized by a developmental ideology that binds the fate of the national community to state-led economic growth. This model shows elective affinities to organicism, Christian communitarianism, state corporatism, and similar notions that always come to mind when we discuss culture, ethos, or compliance ideology in the region.

Within this picture, private interests have never been seen as legitimate, general interests always taking moral precedence instead. In practice, this attitude fosters particular forms of paternalism, populism, enlightened despotism, etc. Among the destitute, the incentive for joining civic associations is null. Unable to defer gratification, these actors relate to associations merely on a patron–client basis. Thus, while in practice no priority is placed on commitment to public initiatives, in symbolic terms integration is made possible thanks to expectations that state-led national development will bring effective social integration. The non-fulfillment of these developmental prophecies, the ideological, administrative, and economic crisis of the state, and the social anomie of growing numbers all point to the collapse of old conceptions of civil society.

In closing these observations, I would like to draw a few sketchy conclusions suggested by the discussion in the previous pages. The first, and obvious, conclusion is that civic solidarity can decrease or increase as economic and ideological factors change. There is no unilinear path from local to universal, or familistic to civic, social identity.

Second, the Latin American experience also indicates that the decay of state corporatism (or similar forms of organic representations of civil society) may contribute to replicating some sort of amoral familism – or better put, some contraction in social identities – on a macro scale, because this kind of compliance ideology does not engender the consolidation of autonomous social interests.

Third, it may be that extreme forms of social inequality like those observed throughout most of Latin America hamper the generalization of social solidarity because severe disparities in life experiences breed differences in cognitive orientations that are so vast that feelings of belonging simply cannot take root.

Fourth, it is important to bear in mind that problems of social incorporation will never be solved once and for all. The Latin American experience suggests that an integration crisis may be recurring. Moreover, while the magnitude of social exclusion in the Third World may be daunting, we see ever more alarming signs of growing problems of integration in the First World as well. This suggests to me that the concept of civil society will serve us best as an analytical tool if it takes into account the similarities and differences in collective identity detected across different types of society.

Finally, I hold that the notion of amoral familism, developed by Banfield four decades ago, can still be of use to us in reflecting on problems of social subjectivity and social identity building in so far as this concept sheds some light on a kind of contraction of social morality which belies the universalizing notion of solidarity.

References

Adler-Hellman, Judith (1994) 'Mexican Popular Movements, Clientelism, and the Process of Democratization', *Latin American Perspectives*, 21 (2): 124–42.

Alexander, Jeffrey (1990) 'Core Solidarity, Ethnic Out-Groups, and Social Differentiation', in J. Alexander and P. Colomy (eds), *Differentiation Theory and Social Change*. New York: Columbia University Press. pp. 267–93.

Banfield, Edward (1958) *The Moral Basis of a Backward Society*. New York: Free Press.

Boschi, Renato (1987) *A arte da associação, política de base e democracia no Brasil*. Rio de Janeiro: Vértice/Instituto Universitário de Pesquisas do Rio de Janeiro (IUPERJ).

Calderon, Fernando and dos Santos, Mario (1989) 'Movimentos sociais e democracia: os conflitos para a criação de uma nova ordem', in Viola, E., Scherer-Warrer, I. and Krischke, P. (eds), *Crise política, movimentos sociais e cidadania*. Florianópolis: Editora da Universidade Federal de Santa Catarina. pp. 13–37.

Calhoun, Craig (1993) 'Nationalism and Civil Society: Democracy, Diversity and Self-Determination', *International Sociology*, 8 (4): 387–411.

Cardoso, Eliana and Helwege, A. (1992) *Latin America's Economy*. Cambridge, MA: MIT Press.

Cardoso, Ruth (1983) 'Movimentos sociais urbanos: balanço crítico', in B. Sorj and M.H. Almeida (eds), *Sociedade e política no Brasil pós-64*. São Paulo: Editora Brasiliense. pp. 215–39.

Durkheim, Emile (1973) *De la division du travail social*, 9th edn. Paris: Presses Universitaires de France.

Eckstein, Susan (ed.) (1989) *Power and Popular Protest: Latin American Social Movements*. Berkeley, CA: University of California Press.

Hays, Sharon (1994) 'Structure and Agency and the Sticky Problem of Culture', *Sociological Theory*, 12 (1): 57–72.

Huntington, Samuel (1968) *Political Order in Changing Societies*. New Haven: Yale University Press.

Kowarick, Lucio (1987) 'Movimentos urbanos no Brasil contemporâneo: uma análise da literatura', *Revista Brasileira de Ciências Sociais*, 1 (3): 38–50.

Lechner, Norbert (1990) 'A modernidade e a modernização são compatíveis? O desafio da democracia latino-americana', *Lua Nova, Revista de Cultura e Política*, 21: 73–86.

Mainwaring, Scott and Viola, Eduardo (1984) 'New Social Movements, Political Culture and Democracy: Brazil and Argentina in the 1980s', *Telos*, 20 (2): 131–59.

Morse, Richard (1988) *O espelho de Próspero*. São Paulo: Editora Companhia das Letras.

O'Donnell, Guillermo (1994) 'The State, Democratization, and Some Conceptual Problems (a Latin American View with Glances at some Post-Communist Countries)', in W. Smith, C. Acuna and E. Gamarra (eds), *Latin American Political Economy in the Age of Neoliberal Reform*. New Brunswick, NJ: Transaction. pp. 157–80.

Polanyi, Karl (1957) *The Great Transformation*. Boston: Beacon.

Reis, Elisa (1982) 'Elites agrárias, state-building e autoritarismo', *DADOS, Revista de Ciências Sociais*, 25 (3): 275–96.

Reis, Elisa (1992) 'Nationalism and Citizenship: Bringing History Back In', paper presented at the International Conference on Nation, Tribe and Citizenship, Rome: CERFE.

Reis, Elisa and Cheibub, Zairo (1993) 'Mercado, cidadania e consolidação democrática', *DADOS, Revista de Ciências Sociais*, 36 (2): 233–60.

Santos, Wanderley G. dos (1979) *Cidadania e justiça, A política social na ordem brasileira*. Rio de Janeiro: Editora Campus.

Schmitter, Philippe (1971) *Interest Conflict and Political Change in Brazil*. Stanford: Stanford University Press.

Schmitter, Philippe (1974) 'Still the Century of Corporatism?', *The Review of Politics*, 36 (1): 85–131.

Schwartzman, Simon (1982) *Bases do autoritarismo brasileiro*. Rio de Janeiro: Editora Campus.

Simmel, Georg (1908) 'The Poor', in Levine, Donald (ed.), *Georg Simmel, On Individuality and Social Forms, Selected Writings*. Chicago: University of Chicago Press, 1971.

Slater, David (1994) 'Power and Social Movements in the Other Occident: Latin America in the International Context', *Latin American Perspectives*, 21 (2): 11–37.

Stepan, Alfred (1978) *The State and Society, Peru in Comparative Perspective*. Princeton: Princeton University Press.

Vilas, Carlos (1994) 'La hora de la sociedad civil', *Análisis Político*, 21: 5–13.

Viola, E., Scherer-Warrer, I. and Krischke, P. (eds) (1989) *Crise política, movimentos sociais e cidadania*. Florianópolis: Editora da Universidade Federal de Santa Catarina.

Wacquant, Loic (1994) 'O retorno do recalcado: violência urbana, *raça* e dualização em três sociedades avançadas', *Revista Brasileira de Ciências Sociais*, 24: 16–30.

Weffort, Francisco (1990) 'A América errada', *Lua Nova, Revista de Cultura e Política*, 21: 5–40.

Werneck, Luiz J. (1976) *Liberalismo e sindicato no Brasil*. Rio de Janeiro: Paz e Terra.

Wiarda, Howard (1973) 'Toward a Framework for the Study of Political Change in the Iberic-Latin Tradition: The Corporative Model', *World Politics*, XXV (2): 206–35.

Wilson, Richard (1992) *Compliance Ideologies, Rethinking Political Culture*. New York: Cambridge University Press.

3

Between Economic Dissolution and the Return of the Social: The Contest for Civil Society in Australia

Michael Pusey

With the benefit of hindsight most people will agree that the economic policies of Reagan and Thatcher failed. The 'supply-side' economic theories of Milton Friedman and others gave us a bad economics that failed in its own terms. They also produced obviously undesirable social consequences. This much is clear and we sociologists will all say 'We told you so!' But what led to this devastation? Was it the politics or the economics that did the damage? And, how are the two related?

In pondering these questions one is reminded of Weber's rejection of disciplinary boundaries, and of his struggle to distinguish ideal from material interests. These days modern economics is often dismissed, as though it had no real importance, as an increasingly isolated discipline lost in its own games of ideological mathematics. The following discussion will use Australia as a background against which to look anew at some of the driving idealizations of modern economics as they have been applied to yet another English-speaking democracy. I want to use the Australian case to give some stability of reference to what I for convenience call 'economic rationalism' and, most importantly, to its 'attacks' on civil society.

The discussion is set - of course - within a 'normative' framework that sits fairly comfortably under the rubric of 'Western European social democracy'. This may be taken as a 'position' which says that modern nation-societies (and federations like the emerging Europe) have two coordinating structures. On one side they have economies, markets and money, and on the other they have states, bureaucracy and the law. It is with these structures that we collectively coordinate our relations with the rest of the world, our work, our social interactions, and most other areas of our life that we understand as civil society and normatively define, for the most part counter-factually, with notions of citizenship, democracy, and human rights. Even with this much we already have a couple of working definitions of 'economic rationalism'; firstly, as a doctrine which says that 'economies, markets, and money can always, at least *in principle*, deliver better outcomes than states, bureaucracies, and the law'; and secondly (take your pick), as the assumption that 'markets and money are the only *reliable* means of setting a value on anything'.[1]

This also helps define how economic programs of 'structural reform' work in practice. For the economists and reformers economic rationalism involves shifting the burden of coordination from states, bureaucracies and the law to economies, markets and money. The question to which this chapter is addressed can now be phrased in a number of different ways. How does that shift in the burden of coordination appear from the perspective of those social forms that we call 'civil society'? How does economic rationalism attack 'civil society'? To put the question more provocatively, how and in what respects is the process of economic reform 'anti-social'? On what criteria could it be so defined? And how are the criteria set into the economic logic, and into our shifting constructions and defenses of civil society? What are the consequences for civil society when the focus of conflict moves from the relationship between morality and legality to that between morality and efficiency?

By way of introduction the first section applies Touraine's contrast between 'development' and 'modernization' to the Australian case of economic restructuring and 'reform'. The second section addresses the contest between economic reform and civil society in a different way. This is my attempt to specify a semi-'genealogical' pattern in the successive economic idealizations that economic rationalism has used, in the last 50 years or so, to reduce civil society to economic categories. In the last section I argue for the strong position that, in a nation-society like Australia that was 'born modern', civil society itself is the 'raw material' for economic production. The driving pressures of the economic rationalists for economic reform, economic restructuring, and increased productivity are seen here as an attack on civil society and the modalities of time and confidence upon which we depend for mutual self-recognition.

What happened to Australia in the 1980s? The economic context in a nutshell is as follows. Australia is generally supposed to have enjoyed, at different moments in this century, the highest per capita income in the world and, in the 1950s and 1960s, perhaps the most equal distribution of income of any 'developed' nation. These achievements were largely attributable to the successes of a 'nation-building state' which has, for about 70 years:

1 controlled the distribution of *primary* incomes at source through a centralized wage-fixing system

2 protected domestic Australian industry from foreign competition with strong tariffs and import restrictions
3 moderated the price of labor with selective immigration policies.

By 1979 Australia was suffering badly on the so-called 'misery index' of high unemployment and high inflation.[2] Then, from 1983 to the present, and in order to correct deteriorating terms of trade and unsustainable levels of external debt, four successive Labor governments and now one Liberal (Conservative) government have embarked on a program of vigorous economic reform involving: financial deregulation; severe cuts to government spending; and the microeconomic reform of several sectors including transport, communications, and education. These 'reforms' were achieved through a series of semi-corporatist accords with the trade union movement that made way for the management of and substantial reductions in real wage incomes; steep falls in the unit cost of labor; a transfer of the tax burden from the business sector to wage and salary earners; and substantial increases in the profit share of national income. By the early 1990s Australia had one of the most 'flexible' labor markets in the OECD.[3]

Yet, even in the early 1990s these policies had still not attracted commensurate levels of productive investment on a scale that might offset Australia's traditional reliance on (volatile) non-manufactured commodity exports and its very high levels of unemployment: at its peak officially about 12% in 1993; more accurately about 20%. Already by the end of the 1980s the social impact of these policies was more or less beyond dispute. Whatever the beneficial effects of these 'reforms' it is clear that there is no 'trickle-down effect' and that economic rationalism leads, demonstrably, to social inequality (measured by increases in the 'Gini coefficient').[4] In Australia at the end of the 1980s the pattern of inequality in the distribution of income was closest to that of the USA (the most unequal distribution of income of all the developed OECD nations) with matching high levels of both absolute and relative poverty.[5]

Is Economic Rationalism an Endogenous Process?

To some extent this is a familiar question since we are looking at forms of development and modernization that are variable and certainly not externally determined through some 'black box' by an independent dynamic of globalization. Concrete evidence now shows that even the same, or similar, economic prescriptions produce highly variable effects on distributional inequalities in different nations.[6] More generally, Alain Touraine reminds us that cultural and national specificities play a very important role. In the case of each nation the characteristics of the ruling elite(s) are decisive; and so too, second, are relations with more 'developed' nations as well as, third, the characteristics of older social 'forces'.[7] Touraine argues that *development* in the context of 'Third World' and newly industrializing nations should be seen as a *politic* that is typically driven by sometimes very 'traditional' and 'patrimonial' ruling elites (for example the Tunkus in Malaysia, and the elites of some nations in the Middle Eastern Arab world) who may, for all kinds of political reasons, choose to expose their national populations to the pressures of the global economy. He argues in a nearly classical Weberian fashion that *modernization*, on the other hand, should be seen as an *endogenous process*. In the first case we have a 'revolution from above' in which economic rationalist changes – deregulation, marketization, monetization of exchange, forced competition and dependence on market incomes, etc. - are *imposed* upon civil society to break up deeply sedimented social resistances (familial, communal, religious, ethnic, etc.) to the economic disciplines of the 'free market'. In the second case we have a completely different image of endogenously strengthening differentiation of the individual in society and strengthening patterns of formal and strategic rationality that seem variously to shed, dissolve, or residualize pre-existing social norms and cultural values. In this second case the reform programs of a modernizing state will appear more as codifications of an *independently evolving positivization of social relations in civil society*.

This is not solely a matter of theoretical preference and interpretation but also a problem that invites recourse to evidence. Attitude surveys have a certain relevance. By some good chance the National Social Science Survey of Australian 'attitudes' was conducted in 1984–5 just as the programs of economic reform were moving into high gear. Moreover, the survey was made in the wake of two years of intense media 'hype' on the imperatives of economic reform: without all-out free market reform we are doomed to become a 'banana republic'![8] The results of the attitude survey showed that three-quarters of the respondents in a large sample of Australians favored the retention of Australia's centralized wage-fixing system (i.e. a regulated labor market); that less than 16% of them disagreed with a need for tighter control over multinational companies; that about two-thirds favored a mixed economy with the government owning public utilities and even a few key big businesses (e.g. some banks, airlines, telecommunications, and commodity marketing authorities); that less than a third were opposed to increasing taxes on the rich; and so on. The results seem to indicate, along with other comparable research,[9] that Australians favored the *status quo ante*. The survey supports the view that there may have been something like a consensus, at least among so-called 'middle Australians', in favor of Australia's own long-standing structures of social democracy and mixed economy, state intervention, protection, and redistributive justice.[10] At about the same time (1985–6) my own interviews with 215 of the top federal public servants who led the economic reforms present a very different picture. Among the most powerful Canberra central agency economists who captured the Labor government's reform agenda we find that three-quarters of them favored the deregulation of the labor market, and that only about 17% of them thought that market relations between the 'haves' and the 'have nots' were exploitive. Two-thirds or more wanted smaller government, less state involvement, more incentives, and less government control over the economy.[11] Over the next five years they had their way!

In the Australian case economic rationalism (*qua* modernization) is *not* an endogenous process. It is very obviously a 'revolution' that was driven 'from above' and forced on a bemused and even resentful population by a 'reformist' Labor government determined to show that it could do a better job of 'economic management' than the Liberal Party (traditionally the party of business interests). This was a very 'political' process. It was forced with astonishing single-mindedness, and without electorally effective opposition, by federal Labor ministers and their senior economists in the bureaucracy; and it was done with the concerted urging of the 'new right' think-tanks, the financial journalists and 'the quality press', big business, and the finance sector.

What part might older social forces have in explaining the specificities of the modernization process in different nations? Here there is space for one observation only; namely that the success of economic rationalism marked a triumph of the new right at the expense of what remains of Australia's ill-defined and weakly nationalistic 'establishment' of 'old' money, old pastoral interests, old private school 'moral' elites, and the judiciary. Australia is the last of the developed English-speaking 'new nations'.[12] It was 'born modern' with a federal constitution and an original politic that is 'dry', secular, Benthamite and 'anti-metaphysical'. From the very beginning of white invasion and settlement there has been no premodern 'old class'.

Touraine is correct. The Australian case does, indeed, underline the importance of relations between nations in explaining the local specificities of modernization processes. In Australia geographical distance combined with cultural and English language ties to the

United Kingdom and the United States opened the door to 'free' market economic orthodoxies. The record shows, quite clearly, that free market ideologies imbibed in American graduate economics programs, and through secondments to American dominated institutions such as the World Bank, the IMF, GATT, and the OECD, have been decisive in shaping the Canberra reform agenda.[13] The gentler European social democratic variant of the economic reform program was hidden from view by linguistic, cultural, and geographic distances.

This provides the clue to what is, in the Australian case and for Touraine, an inexplicable paradox. Here we have a quintessentially modern nation-society that is in the throes of a forced 'modernization from above' that Touraine would associate with premodern Third World societies. The problem has to do with an old-fashioned and (since I am a Europhile, dare I say it?) a rather Eurocentric notion of colonialism. On that older Weberian view 'development' is a politically inspired escape from traditional authority of a premodern form. It is contrasted, in Touraine's scheme, with a process of modernization represented as its own achievement in two settings: the new Europe and the United States, where, for different historical reasons, there is a radical discounting of the role of the state. Australians do not, and should not, discount the role of the state!

For Australians there are no moderating regional economic treaties, or emerging federations (meta-states) like the new Europe, to shield a nation from global economic forces. Australia is emphatically a nation stuck in an island continent. For Australians the state, especially the Canberra federal state apparatus, is the principal guarantor of 'the achievements of modernity' and thus of forms of civil society that secure identity, universalistic rights, multiculturalism, and the entitlements of citizenship. In Weberian terms legitimate authority of the rational-legal modern kind secures that pattern (always very imperfectly). The Australian situation gives us a 'privileged' experience of the new meaning of *colonialism in a 'postmodern' age.* Except for the heroic case of Aboriginal Australia 'we' are not struggling to preserve eroding forms (religious, local, communal, particularistic, ascriptive) from 'disenchantment' and the modernization of civil society. For Australians economic rationalism is the principal threat to the 'achievements of modernity'. Those achievements can only (?) be secured in and through the state as rights of citizenship, in the face of a postmodernizing economic rationalism that is aimed, in the name of 'free market economic reform', at the destruction of just that relation between state and civil society on which they depend. For Australia the threat in the next century is not secular universalism but the various 'particularisms' and fundamentalisms that erupt after economies, markets, and money have destroyed the effective 'resistances' (including 'legitimacy') on which that secular universalism depends. Colonialism in a postmodern age comes not from the office of the Colonial Secretary but from the International Monetary Fund, the OECD, and the American think-tanks and 'credit rating' houses. It travels by algebra and arrives in 'regression equations' with much abetting from old Cold War warriors who have reinvented themselves as specialists in 'geo-economics'.

Economic Rationalism versus Civil Society?

In the 1990s the focus of economic rationalism in Australia has shifted from macroeconomic policy to microeconomic reform at the industry and enterprise level. For the reformers the opening up of Australia to the new global economy was just a prelude to what they see as the hard work of an *institutional transformation* that will 'make Australia competitive'. The task is defined as a shift in the burden of coordination from states, bureaucracies, and the law on the one side to economies, markets, and money on the other. At the workplace and enterprise level these microeconomic reforms are pressing forward under such rubrics and slogans as 'structural efficiency', 'award restructuring', 'enterprise bargaining', 'increasing competitiveness', 'total quality management', 'gearing up to international best practice', etc.

These reforms are presented as neutral technologies for the redesign of concrete organizations. If the reform process meets with too much of what its advocates tellingly call 'institutional inertia' – often accusingly touted as 'Australia's talent for bureaucracy'[14] – then this will mark, probably only temporarily, a social limit to a process that social theory variously defines as expanding 'commodification', as the expansion of 'productive forces', the expansion of 'technical reason', the expansion of 'strategic rationality', or even the 'colonization of the lifeworld'. From these social theoretical positions what happens at the level of the concrete organization points to what happens – the same process – at the level of institutions and, at the next level of abstraction and generality, to transformations of civil society.

In the Australian case at least these rationalization processes are driven by economists.[15] In what follows I want to relate this expansion of strategic rationality to historical changes in the driving *idealizations of economic reason*. With the help of Figure 3.1 I want to suggest that these idealizations or 'positivities' of economic reason call up different possibilities for 'the return of civil society'.

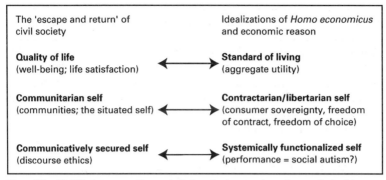

Figure 3.1   *Civil Society versus Economic Rationality (contested templates and criteria)*

In each case there is space only to point (a) to the constructions of 'boundary' between economy and civil society, (b) to implicit templates for institutional design, and (c) to the construction of motivations and expectations. Without wishing to press the notion of a 'genealogy' too far I suggest that there is a pattern in the successive layers of economic idealizations that have been set down one over the other in successive attempts to 'capture' civil society. As one set of idealizations loses 'control over the social' another set is placed over them as a kind of reinforcement of ideas, or 'discourses', that are working synchronically as well. There is no strict causal connection of course, but a generous reader may discern an interesting trend line in this deployment of economic ideas.[16]

Quality of Life versus Standard of Living
At the heart of post-war welfare economics there are two counter-factual ideals: *utility and efficiency.* Economic efficiency is built on a counter-factual notion of price that economists call 'shadow price'. This means the change in aggregate economic well-being brought about by a unit increase in the level of any specific activity. More-over, as Pincus points out,

> If all shadow prices are correct and equal to actual prices, the economy achieves perfect efficiency ... [But] ... The calculation of one shadow price requires the calculation of all shadow prices, as though the economy in reality was fully computable ... They [shadow prices] embody what Hayek showed to be the impossible ideal, the gathering in one central location of all the relevant information inherent in the economy in operation. Although they can be written down in precise if general mathematical formulations, in economic practice brute force is used to simplify the model to arrive at 'reasonable estimates'.[17]

But why does the calculation of one shadow price require the calcu-lation of all shadow prices? Because 'efficiency' means the efficiency of a perfect market idealized as a closed system in which one person's gain shows up, automatically and without 'leakage' in the outcome of a 'zero-sum' game, as someone else's loss. Economists know that actual markets are not perfect markets. But it is their appointed task to make them as perfect as possible. To this end they must strive (with all the counter-factual 'idealism' they can muster) for what they call 'first best' solutions that approximate most closely to the ideal, and avoid settling for 'second best' solutions that accept imperfections in relationships of exchange between social actors. However, in the real world there are still 'market failures' (as with the Great Depression, or when private investment does not produce its own 'merit goods' or infrastructure). And it is here, at the point of market failure, that government intervention and public provision have a 'legitimate' role. Since our concern below will be with what may remain of 'civil society' one should note here at the outset that this is a highly ambivalent notion of 'legitimacy'.

The second idealization treats human welfare as the satisfaction of wants expressed *only* as *utilities*. The consequence is that social welfare can be defined and measured *only* as the utility maximization of individuals, on the assumptions

1 that the individual is the *only* judge of his/her welfare
2 that the welfare of individuals cannot be compared.[18]

There is nothing fanciful or immaterial about these idealizations. They provide the counter-factual standards for measuring the purity, integrity, and rigor of practical reforms that have been applied to just about every sphere of the nation's life. Indeed we are urged to think of them as a kind of DNA code for all economic growth.

Already at this first level (see Figure 3.1) we have some clear specifications for what counts as the *boundary between economy, market, and money, and civil society*. Civil society reappears here as any relationship between social actors, and any social practice that stands between ideal prices and actual prices. Civil society presents itself as a barrier to assimilation into the market of would-be forms of exchange that still elude its reach. For the reformer, civil society appears as a 'stubbornly resisting sludge'[19] that stands between 'first best' and 'second best' economic structures.[20] If we define institutions as 'sets of regulatory norms that give rise to patterns of action, and to concrete social structures of organization'[21] it is clear that few institutions can survive the hot breath of economic reform. Stock exchanges will survive but probably not real firms, and not government departments (except for the economic departments); nor perhaps trade unions, churches, or families! For an institution to be worthy it has to liberate the self from all obligations that inhibit the conversion of intentions, intuitions, purposes, and expectations into calculable utilities.

One testimony to the enormous power of ideology is that utilitarian welfare economics survives still as a coordinating logic for nation-societies. But it 'leaks' for reasons that become apparent as soon as 'standard of living' (which welfare economics defines as aggregate utility measured in dollars by the market) is counterposed with well-being, or 'quality of life'. As Sen demonstrates so eloquently, *valuation does not reduce to utilities* and the same is true of choice and even of desire fulfilment: neither is reducible to utility.[22] Well-being and utility are indeed largely independent one from the other.

That conclusion also constantly emerges from social science surveys of quality of life. In the words of Robert Lane,

> The main issues are not invidiousness of choice, not that the market produces the wrong commodities, not that consumers choose them badly, not that there is 'producer sovereignty'. The issue is that commodities themselves, and the income to purchase them, are only weakly related to the things that make people happy: autonomy, self-esteem, family felicity, tension-free leisure, friendships. This is the major defect of a want satisfying mechanism.[23]

In Australia we find, not surprisingly, that there is almost no *direct* relation at all between money income and the reported life priorities of ordinary Australians. The evidence shows that 'leisure, family life and friends contribute greatly to life satisfaction', and contrary to fundamental nostrums of utilitarian economics, material concerns are not paramount at all.[24] For those of us who may wish to rescue the notion of civil society the implications are clear enough. There is already a case for opposing the economists head-on by defining *civil society as an ensemble of structures that subordinate utility to quality of life*.

For the economic reformers these are serious failures that might allow government intervention on a scale that would give the lie to the basic idealizations of the welfare economics paradigm itself. For the economist there is no problem so long as civil society (the 'sludge' of social obligations, norms, rights, identities, citizenship, and concrete democracy, that fills the space between shadow prices and actual prices) can be defined in terms that require government intervention *purely* as a means of producing greater economic efficiency. The sludge is then still redefined as potential utility and 'government success' can only figure in a single dimension as the corrective for market failure. The success of government can be reckoned only in terms of its own contraction, and of a corresponding expansion of market mechanisms. Still, the problem for our reformers is that this formulation 'leaks'. A majority of Australians seem to agree with principles of redistributive justice premised on the (empirically justified) conviction that markets produce unfair inequalities[25] and, worse, that increases in the standard of living (aggregate utilities) come at the expense of the quality of life. Indeed the leak turns into a flood as ordinary people persist in the view that states, bureaucracies and the law have a primary responsibility for redistributing income fairly, and for providing primary goods and services (e.g. social peace and free health care), that people *require of government per se as the legitimate expectations and entitlements of citizens in a social democracy*. This shows up quite perfectly in the two-tiered 1991 accord mark VI between the government and the trade unions in which a first tier of wage increases was indexed to inflation and awarded by the Industrial Relations Commission across the board to all wage and salary earners (the 'social justice' component): only the 'second tier' of supplementary increases was pegged to productivity agreements that had to be negotiated with employers (the market component).[26]

*The Communitarian Self versus the Contractarian/
Libertarian Self*
At a second level (Figure 3.1) the economic paradigm provides a 'default logic' that promises once again to reassign and to reduce civil society to economies, markets and money. It is here that libertarian and neo-liberal versions of contract are deployed to redefine the normative field between actual prices and shadow prices. Everyone agrees that 'public choice' and 'social choice' theory reaches its limits at the point where the preference ordering of utilities runs up against *pre*-contractual norms.[27] Our space, civil society, is full of 'sludges' that appear to economists, for the most part correctly, as pre-contractual norms! And it is full of practices (e.g. grassroots democracy, political participation, practical cooperation) and 'outdated' structures (trade unions, community organizations, public broadcasting) that go on producing a perpetual surplus of still more normative 'solidarities' that resist translation into priced utilities. The solution comes with what public choice theory sees as its remedial 'amendment' to welfare economics.[28] With the full authority of a Nobel prize the remedy is offered by (among others) James Buchanan in his proclamation of a 'normative individualism' deployed in the service of a new 'contractarian political economy' that will supplant confusing terms such as 'social objectives' and

'national interest' with true 'individual values and interests'. I have followed Buchanan's language very carefully to avoid slippage.[29] The remedy is offered without reticence and with the certainty that 'Economists, almost alone, understand the notion of choice itself ... and that economists who believe in *'Homo economicus'* ... must not be duped or lulled into the neglect of elementary principles ... nor ... fail to recognise that incentives remain relevant in all choice situations.' And he insists on a 'near unanimity' among economists that attempts to impose 'particularised constraints on voluntary exchange [government intervention, tariffs, price floors and ceilings, or prohibitions on entry and exit to the market] destroy generic value'.[30] Again in the words of one of Buchanan's predecessors, 'All motivations are economic motivations.'[31] Such is the arrogance of ideology.

The utilitarian *Homo economicus* of welfare economics finds a new defence. The contractarian amendment projects into the space between shadow/ideal and actual prices an assumption of complete *motivational neutrality of individual choice* that is held to apply in every domain of life without restriction. Pre-contractual norms are invalid *a priori*. The boundary between economy and civil society disappears and institutional design becomes a technical problem of developing 'invisible hand' mechanisms to optimize the choice of a maximizing *Homo economicus* motivated by rational self-interest only. Where utilities will not match up with prices then the solution is to use contracts to capture the otherwise escaping social remainder. This is exactly what the reformers do. All the large consulting houses (Coopers Lybrand, Price Waterhouse, etc.) employ teams of people with double degrees in positivist economics and positivist law to achieve this conversion of civil society into yet-to-be-achieved economic product. As civil society is brought within the boundary of the corporation its normative contents are 'uncoupled' from the public sphere and questions of public legitimacy and consent are transposed into contractual obligations to corporate chiefs and their 'bottom lines'. The contract 'allows' the isolated individual to set notional money values (shadow prices) on all otherwise economically intangible goods such as happy work relations with colleagues, child care, flexibility of time/work, and, in short, the quality of life. Providing that no trade union or government agent is allowed to restrict the employer such contracts will embody a perfect one-to-one equality between the isolated individual and the largest corporations in the land! Freedom of contract joins with freedom of choice in a clear connection with the neo-classical doctrine of consumer sovereignty: and all of this draws, through public choice theory, on libertarian and contractarian, or *modus vivendi*, forms of 'new right' liberalism.

This reinforcement of welfare economics with public choice has been highly successful. And yet still, it leaks! Just as quality of life reappears as the signifier for civil society's escape from totalization as aggregate utility (standard of living), so 'community' reappears as the signifier for its escape from the fatal embrace with the (public choice) contract of *Homo economicus*. 'Community' here is quite likely to mean ascriptive community (*Gemeinschaft*) but it is none-theless powerful in calling up images of a repressed *social* dimension of experience. And it is this which brings us, unexpectedly, back to our judgment that Australia is a society 'born modern'. Australia exemplifies the two inherent limits of community as the site for the spontaneous regeneration of civil society. One such limitation is that it is a vast continent with the most urbanized population in the world and its own, very distinctive, economic history. When we recall that Australia also has a very secular culture the limitation is clear: and so is the contrast with the United States. Australia simply does not have a deep-soil layer of rooted, embedded, ethnic, local, intimate, or religious communities; especially not of the 'unreflec-tive' and essentialist kind. In other nations, however dangerously, civil society can take refuge in 'tribal' solidarities through which 'radically situated' selves may still reach out in a way that is not destructive of mutual self-recognition, civil rights and universalistic norms. The second limitation is one that Australia shares with other smaller and middle-sized non-imperial powers that have only shrinking defenses against the new global economy. In this situation the universalization of the market destroys the capacities of com-munities to reconstitute civil society politically, publicly, or even 'governmentally' in a way that could once again confer rights and publicly legitimate claims on citizens. The problem here is that deregulation, privatization, and international 'best practice' lead straight to private contracts with multinational companies that usually preclude legitimate recourse to government for both social and public goods. Instead the function of government is redefined, in the name of economic restructuring, as the replacement of institutions based on norms with contracts based on interests.

The Communicatively Secured Self versus a Systemically
Functionalized Self
At the third level in the schema in Figure 3.1 there is no leakage save for that which comes from the social movements that are society's only new defense against the economic efficiency of contractarian public choice. Social movements create new norms, identities, and solidarities that transcend the spatial and temporal structures of particular communities. In so doing they depend on the remains of

the public sphere: specifically here on what is left of public broad-casting and of an independent 'quality press'. It is through these remains that social needs achieve mutual recognition of a kind that can translate into legitimate claims on government for legislation to guarantee civil, political, and social rights and the entitlements of citizenship. The rhetoric of the economists and reformers seems to presage a third defense against 'leakage' that is already well articulated in contemporary social theory. The problem with the utilitarian and the contractarian economic reductions is that both posit a choosing self, and therefore a social actor, which still 'prowls like a ghost' in the new 'iron cage' of the neo-classical market. At this third level in our schema the choosing self returns in Rawls's influential prescription as a self that is 'prior to its ends'.[32] For just this reason it escapes full incorporation into the market.

For the economists it is the system that will at last promise success and close off the return of the social. When the market is idealized as a system the space between ideal and actual prices (civil society) will also be idealized in terms of performances that are functionally specified by the requirements of a system. This is exactly what Lyotard means by 'performativity'. The personality, character, integrity, etc. of the social actor has shrunk to yes/no responses made to 'choices' that are redefined now as programmed responses to a cybernetically engineered price system. Here we have a social autism that makes the neo-classical economic model perfect: all choices are *exogenous* choices and all choices appear only as 'revealed preferences' and demonstrations of the economic effici-ency of the *market itself as a mechanism for the substitution and encoding of all values as prices*. Systemically coordinated behavior replaces 'communicatively' coordinated action to 'relieve interpre-tation ... and action from having to take up, formulate, and com-municatively explicate meaning relations'.[33] Responses can be 'spatially and temporally interconnected in increasingly complex webs, without it being necessary for anyone to survey or stand accountable for these communicative networks'.[34] In short, systemi-cally coordinated behavior replaces communicatively coordinated action in every possible value sphere.[35] For civil society to return, the conditions for its own operation must now be reinvented through a 'discourse ethics'.

Economic Rationalism and the Reform of Time and Trust: The 'Creative Destruction' of Civil Society?

Today, in the 'developed' world, explanations of production that rely on what classical economics still calls 'the factors of production' have only a limited usefulness. It is still useful to think of capital, labor, land, and technology as factors of production because this provides the key to the idealized 'first best' solutions for which our economic reformers will always aim. In a low-interest-rate environment capital investments are costly and involve risks. Land and technology also involve various fixed costs. Obviously, the first best solution is always to maximize GDP and profit share with the risk-free and cost-free solution of reducing the input costs of labor and the taxes on which the state depends for its daily operation. That provides the key to what the reformers have been pressing for in Australia for more than a decade. At the surface the logic of reform is simple: destroy the state's role in setting minimum and award wages, and shift the burden of taxation away from business and on to consumers and pay-as-you-earn income taxes, and, by definition, productivity will then increase and this will attract investment premised on the expectation of low and falling wages and taxes. This is the standard 'first best' solution of the IMF, the World Bank, the OECD, GATT, NAFTA, and of American economics everywhere. It has become the standard South American solution for which Washington and the generals in Brazil and Chile have been willing to sacrifice a generation.

But the South American nations are all premodern transplants from the old world. Australians, on the other hand, were 'born modern', believing

> that the state, far from encroaching upon individual rights, would be the
> most likely protector of rights against other agencies of social coercion.
> Australians believed that the major constraints on individual liberty were
> not public but private.[36]

One must therefore argue for the stronger thesis that in a developed, affluent, modern, secular nation like Australia – a nation of middle size situated on the semi-periphery of the world economy – *the input for increased productivity is civil society itself.*

Economic reform is a program that drives at shifting the burden of coordination from states, bureaucracies, and the law on the one side to economies, markets, and money on the other. It is almost by definition a technology for the demolition of a social democratic 'balance' between these two structures – a balance that appears for ordinary citizens in their *normal expectation* of the way things have been, are now, and will continue to be in the future. A recent survey shows for example that Australians are only about half as likely as Swedes to agree that 'the government should provide a job for everyone who wants one' (40% versus 74%): this may be read to mean that Australians accept a small welfare state; that they do not generally construct the state as an employer of last resort; and that they accept that they must take their chances in the marketplace. But, on the other side, Australians cling to the historical expectation that the state will, through the centralized award setting system, regulate the distribution of market incomes to limit social inequalities and to enforce fair remunerations for levels of skill. As one economist has so neatly put it, even under the conservative business-oriented governments of Sir Robert Menzies, income distribution in Australia was governed by the rule that 'the income of no significant group shall fall if that of the others is rising.'[37] So, even in this single example, we see the relations between state and market 'inscribed' into the way in which Australians construct their own life chances and their normative expectations of rights and entitlements. My point will be clearer if I use another personal example. I belong to a state superannuation scheme that is indexed to inflation and will pay me an annuity in retirement that is proofed against the vagaries of the market. The reformers closed that scheme in 1985 and my wife was obliged to join a new and much less generous scheme which functions much more like a conventional bank account. As with my scheme the employer contributes two dollars for the employee's one dollar but there is no indexation of the final package to inflation and so the final benefit depends entirely on how well that fully privatized superannuation fund performs in the marketplace. The reformers closed that second scheme in 1988 and replaced it with a third scheme from which public servants generally receive only the minimum mandatory employer contributions for their retirement. Retirement income depends almost entirely on one's own private savings and investments.[38]

The purpose of these examples will be to show that *economic reform substitutes 'postmodern' time for modern time.* The regulated labor market – and my retirement scheme! – do indeed constitute inflexibilities and imposts for the market. But this is only a side-show. From the business point of view the taxes that pay for my annuity are offset, on the other side, by the pool of savings that is made available for business investment. And since real unit labor costs have been falling steadily to the point where they account in the early 1990s for only about 8% of the input costs of production, they cannot be such a fearsome burden. The real significance of these changing temporal horizons was made clear for me by Raul Pertierra's observation that

> the nation-state is an expression of this collective consciousness of [modern time] whose members are synchronically linked in anticipation of a common future. The nation-state as a synchronic entity enables its

members to experience a common and consciously conventional understanding of sequentiality and alterity.[39]

The problem for the reformer economists starts with the fact that the state allows me to enjoy a mid-term future in a publicly secured time that extends *far beyond what market time can secure.* I am able to project myself into the year 2000 and beyond and to anticipate travel, and bushwalking, and community activism, and other lovely pastimes. This is a concretely anticipated future that is immediately recognizable to others as a 'realistic' possibility: and for just this reason it easily produces mutual recognition, a symbolic affirmation of my social identity (even if my interlocutors think they would like to do something radically different with their retirement), and a projection forward of socially meaningful time that is then filled with all those imaginings that we call culture or signifying practices ... a terrible problem for the market, with worse to come! This socially meaningful anticipation of an achievable future concretizes within temporal projections of a remembered, and always reinvented, cultural past into the present and future. And it therefore projects forward the structure of rights, entitlements, obligations, and citizenship that we recognize as the achievements of modernity. It is just within this horizon that 'practical questions' (and expectations) have, as Habermas would say, 'structure-forming effects'.

In Luhmann's terms these expectations have already done their deadly work of creating meaning and therefore of selecting and suppressing choices that are incommensurate with the 'steering imperatives' of the (market) system. For the system 'the future cannot begin' because the space between ideal and actual prices is again filled with the 'sludge' of civil society made concrete in entitlements and rights and the expectations of citizens for 'social security' and the regulation of the market. *There is an incommensurability between the two modalities of state time and market time.* Market time comes from the opposite 'direction': it comes *at* us, from out of the future, and is experienced not as meaning but, on the contrary, as the blind necessity for surrender and adaptation to the functional requirements of an economic system that is premised *not* on past experience within a nation-state but, instead, on conformity with any and all requirements of a future global economy. The market must have an open future and this means a future in which 'action' is structured 'cleanly' as a response to the price signals that call up projects from out of nowhere. In order to cross this barrier between the two modalities of time we have to give up identity, and mutual recognition, and step out of the sludge of civil society into a modality in which we are each formed 'from the outside in' by the 'incentivations' of the market. Projects and prices call up performances autopoesically, and the unmanageable burden of contingency that we might once have called 'ontological', 'epistemological', or even 'existential' anxiety is safely transposed into what we all now recognize simply as *pressure*. In its most abstract and generic form increased *productivity means the surrender of civil society to pressure*; and, similarly, we also find a resolution here to the famous economic debates between the 'good guys' in Cambridge, UK and the 'bad guys' in Cambridge, Massachusetts over the meaning of capital:[40] in its most abstract and generic form capital is human *dependency*, or more precisely dependency *structured through the medium of market time*. In just the same vein this provides, in Schumpeter's terms, a dynamic definition of capital as the *creative destruction* of civil society. This captures quite precisely how our reformers construe creativity.[41]

The shift in the modality of time from public time to market time is experienced as the shrinking horizon of meaningfully anticipated futures. This is accessible only as a horizon marked by the rise and fall of the Australian dollar, by projections of quarterly shifts in the balance of payments and the level of net foreign debt, by shifts in Australia's credit rating, and especially by ever more stringent assessments of the 'risk' of government intervention in the economy. A couple of years ago I felt my future contracting towards the shorter future of my wife and her colleagues who joined the second and third superannuation schemes. This year, now that the recession has lifted, I fancy I may still have a longer future. But this will not last because the reformers say we must expect more and more of these 'shakeouts'. Every time I visit America I am amazed to find people in the airport concourses 'using time', and money, to read the changes from the futures exchanges that may have occurred since they boarded their flights a few hours before. These various temporal oscillations and 'vibrations' should be read as a ritual hygiene, and further, as a shift from the reflexivity of ordinary reflection to the reflexivity of the market system. They give us a clue as to why time is shorter in America than anywhere else. And they point, finally, to an unburdening of consciousness and a *dematerialization of culture* that reappears here in Australia and on the other side of the civil-society/system relation, as algebraic equations in the Treasury's simulations of the Australian economy.

The shift from public time to market time marks the 'creative destruction' of confidence. Australia must be the only nation in the world in which economists have been publicly charged with the 'rationalization' of the Catholic Church! As part of a shift from the public provision of social services to privately provided services the Canberra reformers have launched an inquiry into the efficiency of all the churches. This is one instance only of comprehensive official 'structural adjustments' that are aimed at extending market mechanisms, and 'competition policy', into statutory marketing schemes (e.g. for wheat and wool); into public utilities; and into professional services including the law; and into *as many areas of the 'non-traded sector' as is feasible.*

In these reforms we see yet another dimension of the 'creative destruction' of civil society that shows up here as the attempt to convert confidence into calculable risks. We are using confidence here in the ordinary garden sense that we use in speaking of 'confidence in our institutions'; confidence in the legal system; confidence in long-standing blue chip business institutions like BHP (Australia's largest corporation); and even confidence that 'cars will not suddenly leave the road and hit me'.[42] Simmel defined this cognitive aspect of confidence as 'weak inductive knowledge'.[43] Clearly confidence has its roots in what we have called 'public time'. It is to be counted as one of the structures of civil society and as an 'achievement of modernity'. Confidence is the 'medium' through which we, as citizens in civil society, project ourselves synchronically into the common anticipation of mutual self-recognition in a modern future governed by universalistic norms (of non-ascriptive, non-particularistic, expectations of rights, and duties, and obligations, and identities, etc.).[44]

It comes then as no surprise that the reformers want to destroy confidence which they understand, from the perspective of their own economic idealizations, as 'inertia' and 'resistance' and as 'economic irrationalism'. Once again they want to increase efficiency by treating civil society as the 'dirty' space between ideal and actual prices that must now be cleansed with a forced conversion of confidence into an (opposite) modality of *risk calculation* that Luhmann calls 'trust'. Luhmann, the most audaciously brilliant of all the systems theorists, has based his whole social systems theory on the idealized 'self-reference', or autopoesis, of markets, money and price. In this vein he defines confidence and risk as two opposite forms of self-reference. Confidence may involve some acceptance of a measure of *external* danger but 'trust', he insists, together with the economists and the market reformers, always involves the *internal* calculation of the risk that the actor takes in making his/her wager or 'investment'. 'Trust,' he says, as always rather waggishly, 'is only required if a bad outcome would make you regret your action.'[45] Trust defined thus is the attitude that the ego of *Homo economicus* takes to the alter in the market exchange: it is the way that 'each deals with the freedom of the others'.[46] Trust is what we expect of citizens redefined as entrepreneurs in a fully, reformed, deregulated, marketized, privatized, 'high-performance society'. But Luhmann is a philosophically intelligent sociologist. He knows what he is proposing and now seems to want to retreat from his own near totalizations of social systems as economic systems. For Luhmann the idealization of the 'free' market paradigm as a theory of society signals its own limits. He observes, with deadly accuracy, that, when seen from this perspective,

> political and economic liberalism attempts to shift expectations from [public] confidence to [economic] trust. Insisting on freedom of choice, liberalism focuses on the individual responsibility for deciding between trust and distrust with respect to politicians, parties, goods, firms, employees, credit, etc. And it neglects the problems of attribution and the large amounts of confidence required for participation in the system.[47]

We stop and take pause. The economic rationalist keeps going at full speed ... why? Because for him [usually a him] it is obvious that 'the social world', whatever that might mean, has been 'reconstructed in terms of *interests*'. For the economic rationalist it is 'natural' (the empiricist residue) for us to assume that your interaction with me is governed by your reading of my interests. I, for my part, read you in just the same way with the expectation that your interests will be contingent on the uncertainties of your situation and so different from mine. 'The interests of others are reliable precisely because they are interests.'[48] The reforms are designed to make them more so. The over-reach is getting clearer: to expand opportunities, and to make more space for just this kind of 'rational' behavior, we must – let's use the reformist euphemism – 'loosen up' our institutions. Institutions like the courts, or the Industrial Relations Commission, or even those highly established business institutions like BHP, inspire confidence. But unfortunately they limit strategic action based, as it must be for the economic rationalist, on the unfettered reciprocal calculation of interest, risk, and 'trust'. Institutions so defined inhibit initiative by constraining the field of action with a deadening conformity to norms. As polluting norms re-enter the space between ideal and actual prices they again put a straitjacket on choice and opportunity and limit efficiency. We must bravely choose choice and self-reliance with the 'creative destruction' of confidence. This will release new energies by breaking down traditions, solidarities, identities, norms and institutions into fully 'incentivated' individual action that can then be automatically coordinated with price signals. As John Hewson, a one-time IMF economist and former leader of the opposition, proclaimed publicly, 'You cannot have too much change and you cannot do it quickly enough.'[49] Although they may deny it the reformers do favor 'change for change's sake' because this destroys (public) 'confidence' and so, *faute de mieux*, forces us instead into (private) risk-calculating relations of (economic) 'trust'.

'Confidence,' as Jack Barbalet explains so elegantly, does indeed provide the 'affective basis of action and agency'.[50] The cognitive support for confident action depends on an inductive 'next step' that goes beyond what is strictly given, to assume that generalization beyond existing situations is possible and, indeed in some measure, a reliable but not certain basis for expectation. Inductive logic gives us the confidence to assume, in Hume's words, a 'constant conjunction betwixt cause and effect'.[51] Moreover, if we are to take Keynes's word for it, 'weak inductive knowledge' is the *sine qua non* even for investment confidence as well. If action cannot be based on calculation, what then is its source? Keynes's answer is that 'a large proportion of our positive activities depend on spontaneous optimism rather than on a mathematical expectation.' As Keynes goes on to explain, 'most ... of our decisions to do something positive ... can only be taken as a result of animal spirits – of a spontaneous urge to action rather than inaction, and not as the outcome of a weighted average of quantitative benefits multiplied by quantitative probabilities.'[52]

Keynes did not take a prejudicial attitude to existing institutions. On the contrary, he saw social institutions as the enabling context for economic action. Institutions provide the taken-for-granted referents, the givens, that give us the measure of confidence we require in order to step forth into the unknown with that kind of wager that we call an investment. Without that 'weak inductive knowledge' that we call 'confidence' we could never arrange priorities and risks into just the hierarchical order of probability that establishes the essential conditions, according to the economists and rational choice theorists, for the very kind of rational economic behavior they want to construct. Again Luhmann understands the limits of these technologies of reform and, indeed, the limits of his own positions:

A lack of confidence may mean, without further reflection, a lack of trust, and lack of trust means that behaviours which presuppose trust will be ruled out. So wealthy Brazilians invest in superfluous apartment buildings for wealthy Brazilians, but not in industry. Whole categories of behaviour may effectively be precluded, and this further reinforces a situation in which one cannot have confidence in the system ... The lack of confidence will lead to feelings of alienation and eventually to retreat to smaller worlds of purely local importance, to new forms of 'ethnogenesis' ... to fundamentalist attitudes [and so on].[53]

Once more we find implicit in all of this the problem of time and temporal horizon. 'Confidence, trust and loyalty are emotions which function not merely in time but are about time': again Barbalet notes Keynes's observation that 'agents feel most secure about present facts', and these therefore (in Keynes's words) 'enter into the formation of our long term expectations'.[54] As Hume said a couple of hundred years before him: 'We are determined by custom alone to suppose the future comfortable to the past.'[55] So, we have an answer as to why it is that the economic reformers succeed in producing the opposite of what they want: namely a preference on the part of Australian business for low-quality, low-risk, short-term investments that will recoup invested capital in no more than three or four years. In other ways the creative destruction of confidence shows up in increasing crime rates and the spate of white collar fraud that has led to enormous increases in the real cost of insurance. The same explanations account for the chronically low levels of domestic savings in Australia. For want of confidence in the future I might as well consume now!

As we have seen the economic rationalists see exposure to the market as a way of 'shaking out' those restraints that civil society sets on the market and thus of forcing individuals into relationships of more open strategic calculation one with another. For the reformers the resulting expansion of uncertainty appears as 'opportunity' (they are so stupid that they even equate contingency with opportunity!). It is assumed that this creates new energy and dynamism and in this we see more than a dash of postmodernist cum Nietzschean 'will' and prejudice. They have no understanding that the pressure to act or be damned under increasingly uncertain circumstances destroys mutual self-recognition, increases 'transaction costs' and, most importantly here, creates a sense of alarm and urgency that shortens time horizons. Barbalet uses Kurt Lewin's studies of hope and morale to show where this leads: 'the more constrained the time perspective the lower the range of activity and initiative, and the more expansive the time perspective the higher the inclination to action.'[56] So the quest for full 'incentivation' is a recipe not for increasing energy but instead for running the system into an entropy of senseless immediacy.

Conclusion

In a careful conclusion (that would take too long) I would need to affirm that economists are correct in asserting that exchange is fundamental, and even that it can always be improved with what they call 'invisible hand mechanisms'. Modern developed societies need efficient economies and markets and are unimaginable without them. We may agree that any such complex society 'will require a high degree of system differentiation' and will 'have to rely in part on mechanisms of coordination other than building consensus in language, which is in many situations a luxury'.[57]

In Australia 'we' have already entered what Lasch rightly calls an 'impending age of limits'[58] and the problem is that our 'reformers' are still bent on a war against all social forms that elude their economic reductions and totalizations. For those of us who want to do more than simply say 'no', the intellectual challenge is to find the criteria for drawing the 'limits' that must emerge in a three-way relation between civil society on the one hand, and the two co-ordinating structures of economies, markets and money *and* states, bureaucracies and the law on the other. Seen from this perspective it looks very much as though civil society itself has become the fuel for economic development and, indeed, that it is burning up at an enormous rate. No one wants to treat civil society as some kind of fixed quantity that cannnot regenerate itself; that is an old-fashioned dogma. We know that our ordinary social interactions are constantly creating new possibilities for mutual self-recognition, association, and mutual obligation that may settle into institutional forms (and even into institutional forms that could more firmly secure our modern rights, solidarities, and identities). The greater and present danger comes from the opposite dogma of the economists and reformers: namely that economies, markets and money offer the only reliable way of setting values on anything; that the coordination of economies and markets should as far as possible always replace coordination through states and regulative law; and that forms of association among individuals in civil society are in any case infinitely adaptive.[59]

Notes

This is a slightly altered version of a paper of the same title given in the theory section of the XIIIth World Conference of Sociology at Bielefeld, Germany, July 1994.

1 See M. Pusey, 'Australia's Economic Emperor Has No Clothes', *Sydney Morning Herald*, 17 October 1991, where these two definitions first appeared in the national media debate that ensued from my *Economic Rationalism in Canberra: A Nation-Building State Changes its Mind*, Cambridge, 1991. To my surprise most of my opponents accepted these definitions of their own positions and the term 'economic rationalism' stuck as Australia's name for *laissez-faire*, 'free' market, economic liberalism of the kind that Americans and Britons associate with 'supply-side' Reaganomics and Thatcherism of the 1980s.

2 P. Brain, A. Jolley and I. Manning, 'Labour Market Reforms for Australia',

Restructuring Australia, no. 8, March 1988, National Institute of Economic and Industry Research, pp. 34–55.

3 OECD Economic Surveys, *Australia*, 1987/88, OECD, Paris, p. 70.

4 P. Saunders, 'Deregulation and Inequality', Working Paper 10, July 1993, Centre for Applied Economic Research, University of New South Wales, Sydney.

5 P. Saunders, 'Economic Adjustment and Distributional Change: Income Inequality in Australia in the Eighties', Discussion Paper 47, Social Policy Research Centre, University of NSW, November 1993.

6 A.B. Atkinson, 'What Is Happening to the Distribution of Income in the UK?', Working Paper WSP/87, 1993, Welfare State Program, London School of Economics, quoted in Saunders, 'Deregulation and Inequality'. Also 'Growth, Competitiveness, Employment: The Challenges and Ways Forward into the 21st Century', Commission of the European Communities, Brussels, 1993.

7 Alain Touraine, 'Qu'est-ce que le développement?', *L'Année sociologique*, 1992, 42, pp. 47–85.

8 This phrase stuck in the Australian public imagination from the moment it was first used in May 1986, by the then Treasurer, Paul Keating (Prime Minister from 1994).

9 S. Svalfors, 'Labourism vs Social Democracy? Attitudes to Inequality in Australia and Sweden', Social Policy Research Centre, University of New South Wales, 1993.

10 J. Braithwaite, 'Economic Policy: What the Electorate Thinks', in J. Kelly and G. Bean (eds), *Australian Attitudes*, Allen and Unwin, Sydney, 1988, Chapter 2.

11 For the early findings see M. Pusey, 'Our Top Public Servants under Hawke', *Australian Quarterly*, Autumn 1988, vol. 60, no. 1, pp. 109–23; 'From Canberra the Outlook is Dry', *Australian Society*, July 1988, pp. 20–7; and 'The Impact of Economic Ideas on Public Policy in Canberra', *Economic Papers*, December 1990, vol. 9, no. 4, pp. 80–91.

12 For a comparative study see Seymour Martin Lipset, *The First New Nation*, Basic Books, New York, 1963, Chapter 7, and Louis Hartz (ed.), *The Founding of New Societies*, Harcourt Brace, New York, 1964.

13 See M. Pusey, *Economic Rationalism in Canberra*, Chapter 3.

14 This tag originates from Alan Davies, *Australian Democracy*, 2nd edn, Longman Cheshire, Melbourne, 1964, p. 1.

15 Including public choice theorists, management consultants, and accountants.

16 I make no claim here for any corresponding 'evolution' in our ideas of the social.

17 Jonathon Pincus, 'Market Failure and Government Failure', in Stephen King and Peter Lloyd (eds), *Economic Rationalism: Dead End or Way Forward*, Allen & Unwin, Australia, 1993. I rely on Pincus heavily in this paragraph and have reconstructed his concepts to suit my purpose here.

18 Daniel Bell, 'Models and Reality in Economic Discourse', in Daniel Bell and Irving Kristol (eds), *The Crisis in Economic Theory*, Basic Books, New York, 1981, p. 56.

19 See my *Economic Rationalism in Canberra*.

20 One could even provide a useful operational definition of civil society as anything that appears to the most intelligent pure economist as frustration!

21 This very helpful definition is the one used by 'The Reshaping Australian Institutions: Towards and Beyond 2001' project of the Research School of Social Sciences at the Australian National University.

22 Amartya Sen, *The Standard of Living*, Cambridge University Press, Cambridge, 1987.

23 Robert Lane, 'Markets and the Satisfaction of Human Wants', *Journal of Economic Issues*, vol. xii, no.4, December 1979, pp. 799–827.

24 These are the results of the National Social Science Survey reported by Bruce Headey, 'The Life Satisfactions and Priorities of Australians', in Kelly and Bean, *Australian Attitudes*, Chapter 11.

25 The more moderate economists have always held this to be true and will, under pressure, say it publicly.

26 OECD Economic Surveys, *Australia* 1989/90, OECD, Paris, Chapter 3.

27 Jon Elster (ed.), *Rational Choice*, New York University Press, New York, 1986, introduction.

28 The public choice 'amendment' to welfare economics is explained clearly, by two long-time associates of James Buchanan, Geoffrey Brennan and Loren Lomasky, in their excellent *Democracy and Decision: The Pure Theory of Electoral Preference*, Cambridge University Press, Cambridge, 1993.

29 J. Buchanan, 'Contractarian Political Economy and Constitutional Interpretation', *AAE Papers and Proceedings*, vol. 78, no. 2, May 1988.

30 J. Buchanan, 'Economics in the Post-Socialist Century', *Economic Journal*, January 1991, vol. 101, no. 404, pp. 15–21.

31 Ludvig von Mises, *Epistemological Problems*, p. 61 as quoted by Robert Lane, 'Markets'.

32 John Rawls, *A Theory of Justice*, Belknap Press of Harvard University, Cambridge, MA, 1971.

33 Niklas Luhmann, as quoted here by J. Habermas, *The Theory of Communicative Action*, vol. 2, Beacon Press, Boston, p. 63.

34 Luhmann, as quoted by Habermas in *The Theory of Communicative Action*, vol. 2, p. 263.

35 See Pusey, *Economic Rationalism in Canberrra*, Chapters 5 and 6.

36 R. Rosecrance, 'The Radical Culture of Australia', in Hartz, *The Founding of New Societies*, p. 310.

37 Max Corden as quoted in Frances Castles 'Australia and Sweden: The Politics of Economic Vulnerability', *Thesis Eleven*, no. 16, 1987, pp. 112–22. The Liberal governments of Sir Robert Menzies held office from 1949 to 1966.

38 This is all in a state of flux and the government is moving to redress Australia's low levels of savings with new mandatory but privately organized superannuation schemes with compulsory employer contributions that most closely resemble those of Western Europe.

39 R. Pertierra, 'Trust and the Temporal Structure of Expectations in a Philippine Village', *The Australian Journal of Anthropology*, 1992, 3 (3), pp. 201–17.

40 G. Harcourt, 'Capital Theory: Much Ado About Something', in his *The Social Science Imperialists*, Routledge, London, 1982.

41 By the same token investment, in its most abstract and generic form, must translate, in some yet to be codified 'Star Wars' language of economic idealizations, as an autopoesic evacuation and proofing of 'free' and 'empty' market time against 'occupied' public time (or, even as the availability of whatever structural force is necessary to guarantee the conversion of civil society, and all use values, into exchange values).

42 N. Luhmann, 'Familiarity, Confidence, Trust: Problems and Alternatives', in

Diego Gambetta (ed.), *Trust: Making and Breaking Cooperative Relations*, Basil Blackwell, Oxford, 1988.

43 Actually Simmel says trust (not confidence) is a form of 'weak inductive knowledge'. However, since he uses trust to mean exactly what here in this context both Luhmann and I mean by 'confidence', I have allowed myself this license. A discussion appears in Anthony Giddens, *The Consequences of Modernity*, Polity Press, Cambridge, 1990, pp. 29–36.

44 With Habermas and Jean Cohen I want to define these universalistic norms as counter-factual norms in a universal discourse ethics: see especially Jean Cohen, 'Discourse Ethics and Civil Society', in David Ramussen (ed.), *Universalism vs Communitarianism: Contemporary Debates in Ethics*, MIT Press, 1990.

45 Luhmann, 'Familiarity'.

46 John Dunn, 'Trust and Political Agency', in Gambetta, *Trust*.

47 Luhmann, 'Familiarity', p. 99. The square bracket insertions are mine: and may not be acceptable to Luhmann.

48 Luhmann, 'Familiarity', p. 101.

49 As quoted by Alan Woods in *The Australian*, 13 October 1992.

50 Jack Barbalet, 'Confidence, Time and Emotion in the Sociology of Action', *Journal of the Theory of Social Behaviour*, vol. 23, no. 3, Sept. 1993, pp. 229–49.

51 David Hume, 'An Abstract of a Treatise of Human Nature', in Anthony Flew (ed.), *David Hume: On Human Nature and the Understanding*, Collier Macmillan, New York, 1962, p. 292

52 I am paraphrasing Barbalet's point here.

53 Luhmann, 'Familiarity', pp. 103–4.

54 J.M. Keynes, *General Economic Theory*, p.148, as quoted by Barbalet, 'Confidence'.

55 Hume, 'An Abstract', pp. 294–6.

56 Barbalet, 'Confidence'.

57 Thomas McCarthy, *Ideals and Illusions: On Reconstruction and Deconstruction in Contemporary Social Theory*, MIT Press, Cambridge, MA, 1991, pp. 168–9.

58 Christopher Lasch, *The True and Only Heaven*, Norton, New York, 1991.

59 Michael Pusey, 'Economic Rationalism', in Jay Shafritz (ed.), *International Encyclopedia of Public Policy and Administration*, Henry Holt and Co, New York, 1997, pp. 734–6.

4

Civil Society, Patronage, and Democracy

Luis Roniger

The wave of democratization that inundated Latin America, Southern Europe and Eastern Europe in the last decades made it impossible to ignore civil society. The process of transformation was in more than one way the result of internal contradictions, struggles, and the unraveling of ruling coalitions, followed by the redrawing of international boundaries and agreements. But as it was paralleled by the decentralization of power structures and the empowerment of civil society, this wave of political change in the late 1970s and 1980s generated expectations of a radical break with the past and anticipation that the more hierarchical aspects of the reconstituted societies would soon become remnants of history. A radical change in the character of the public sphere was anticipated.

Expectation had it that social movements, voluntary associations and intermediate institutions of civil society would not only effect an overall reconstruction of the political centers, but also reformulate community along democratic lines, through (a) a strong emphasis on participation and (b) the endorsement of an egalitarian vision of rights and entitlements. Eventually, the initial burgeoning of civil society and the participatory flavor of the new social movements effected far-reaching changes in political regimes, especially in formerly authoritarian settings. Both in the countries which had just completed the transition to democracy, and in the more established democracies, distrust increased toward traditional forms of party politics and politicians, reflecting a world-wide trend of dissolution of controls, fragmentation, and a search for more 'genuine' forms of democracy.[1]

In light of the subsequent dislocation of established patterns of interaction, and in many societies the abrupt explosion of civil, ethnic and nationalist conflicts which border on a Hobbesian 'state of nature', a more cautious appraisal, especially concerning the variable forces and pragmatic realities of the new regimes, is in order. This chapter aims to provide some of the necessary tools for an appraisal of some of the dimensions involved in the trend towards democratization and decentralization which can also grapple with the disruptive after-effects. This will be done through an exploration of the relationship between the discussions on the development of civil society and research on the transformative capacity and impact of patronage and clientelism. In addition to analytical elaboration, we suggest approaching sociopolitical developments from the perspective of the pragmatic dimensions of public life and politics. This agenda will incorporate research on patronage and civil society into the analysis of the prospects of social change beyond contemporary political revamping.

Civil Society and the Transformation of the Public Sphere

Beginning in the late eighteenth century, a process of struggle and change led, first in the West and then in non-Western contexts, to a widening of political participation and a crystallization of citizenship ideals, civil freedoms, and legal frameworks aimed at subjecting traditional authority to the scrutiny of representative forms of government (Habermas, 1989; Hirschman, 1982; Calhoun, 1992). This transformation was connected to long-term socioeconomic change which was precipitated by the consolidation of self-conscious (e.g. bourgeois) sectors willing to promote such processes as marketization, monetarization, and rationalization and to generate a reconstruction of state–society relations. Sociocultural change was also involved in the development of urban culture, modern science, educational systems, public spatial environments, and new forms of social communication. A new link between the public and private domains emerged in tandem with the consolidation of the modern state, which has been expressed with shifting connotations in the idea of civil society (Cohen and Arato, 1992; Seligman, 1992).

The concept of civil society alludes to the existence of organized public life and free associations beyond the tutelage of the state, yet oriented toward the public sphere and toward influencing public policies.[2] The range of arenas and social sectors involved varies contextually, involving in most cases voluntary associations, social movements, the market, and intermediary institutions such as councils and local frameworks. Their impact has been increasingly mediated by the press, as the result of alphabetization, and by the electronic media, as the result of technological innovations. Whatever the concrete nature of the organizational and structural web, from an analytical perspective civil society refers to the interlinking arena where private interests meet public concerns and both are mutually structured in a public sphere with its own rules. Under certain conditions but not necessarily in all situations, these relationships may be institutionalized, e.g. in the form of rights and entitlements.

Civil society can be nurtured through involvement in participatory activities and grassroots organizations, through the establishment of centers of sociability like clubs and voluntary associations; through increased public interaction in a framework of open lectures, recreational locales, and museums; by means of communication – written and electronic – that empower and substantiate the citizens' sense of autonomy from the logic of regulation by the state and the sense of autonomy to participate and promote their interests within the organizational mechanisms of regulation.

Beyond the variability of civil society across historical and cultural settings (even within the West), the concept in modern times reflects a basic configuration in which society stands apart from the state, develops autonomously – 'as the site of alternative hegemonies' in Gramscian terms – and becomes increasingly conscious of such autonomy at both the individual and the collective levels (Taylor, 1989; Adamson, 1987). The concept of civil society envisages the existence of public space that not only is structured politically 'from above', but also becomes increasingly visible and 'open' to public debate and public opinion (Nedelsky, 1989; Keane, 1988a; Taylor, 1990; Cohen and Arato, 1992; Seligman, 1992; Fraser, 1992). It thus requires agents 'involved both in private dealings and in debating and acting out different versions of the public interest' (Pérez-Díaz, 1993: 57).

The strengthening of civil society has deeply affected the development of modern public spheres in general and constitutional democracies in particular. Associational life became a major medium for debates about the public interest, for the definition of connections between private interests and public commitments, for the elaboration of ideas about civil freedoms and entitlements, and for the search for legal constraints on the exercise of public authority. 'These . . . formed the context in which older hierarchical principles of deference and ascribed social status gave way to public principles of rational discourse, and emergent professional and business groups could nourish and assert their claims to a more general social and political leadership' (Boyte, 1992: 343; and see Habermas, 1989: 25–6; Ezrahi. 1990).

Whereas the concept was phrased originally in connection with the nature of modernity,[3] in the last decade the revival of interest in civil society has been connected with the process of democratization. This has created a widespread conceptual identification between civil society, democracy, and equality. Late-twentieth-century societies, governments, and parties have embraced the rhetoric of civil society and have claimed they stand for genuine, popular democracy. Yet, in both historical and contemporary terms, this identification is more conceptual than factual.

Historically, the bourgeoisie struggled to achieve a change in the aristocratic institutional setup but at the same time it opposed popular participation and plebeian pressures to democratization. Indeed, until the mid nineteenth century and in many cases even later, the demand for democracy was expressed in the radical cry of the disenfranchised, including women, while the powerful continued to deny the legitimacy of that demand – paradoxically in the name of reason, rationality, and civility (Keane, 1988b; Eley, 1992; Ryan, 1992; Borón, 1995). By the end of the nineteenth century, with the monopolization of the economy and the increasing role of the state as the social regulator of conflicts, the public sphere began to atrophy and to break up into a mass of contesting interests. Cultural and structural developments in the twentieth century have further eroded interactive associational life and public commitments, and have re-created 'the public' as a mass of passive, atomized producers/consumers, many of them sunk in civil apathy (Keane, 1988a; Lipovetsky, 1983; Boyte, 1992).

Throughout contemporary processes of sociopolitical transformation, the complexity of civil society (or, as some would put it, its ambiguity) has again come to the fore. True enough, changes have occurred in the definition of what is political, in the range of private activities considered of some public and political significance, in the access of social sectors to the centers of power, in linkages among sectors of civil society and between them and the state, and most important from the point of view of patronage, in the types of entitlements extended. Yet after the initial enthusiastic endorsement of the demolition of overwhelming state controls – especially but not exclusively in Eastern Europe – a growing awareness developed that, in the words of John Keane, civil society may under certain circumstances 'haemorrhage to death', degenerate into civil war and looting; in short, lead to the destruction of normative daily life. Or, in turn, result in the reinstatement of authoritarian expectations in societies with erstwhile centralized polities.

In that sense, what is at stake is a configuration of the public sphere, in which civil society does not necessarily stand in a zero-sum game *vis-à-vis* the state. A strong civil society does not necessarily necessitate the demolition of the state but rather its legal constraint and subjection to public accountability. Civil society can be strengthened through the existence of effective and accountable state structures (Held, 1987: 267–99; Roniger, 1991; Fraser, 1992).

In a parallel manner, a realization occurred that civil society is not

coterminous with democracy. It has been observed that in Eastern
Europe the idea of civil society was instrumental in reflecting
dissidence and the shaping of new solidarities, i.e. in disengaging
from state regulation and demolishing the latter's controls; yet, that
it may be less useful in accounting for the consolidation of democracy in the post-communist period (see, for example, Sztompka,
1992). Similarly, in Iran, the strength of the civil society did indeed
reshape the state, but it did little to generate democracy (Savory, in
Bosworth et al., 1993: 821–44). In contrast, civil society in Japan is
weak and yet democracy functions, albeit with recurring scandals
and corruption (Hoston, 1992; Duss, 1993). In India both civil society
and democracy may be working effectively, albeit again not in
mutually reinforcing directions (Price, 1993). Finally, in Russia, the
weakness of civil society is a serious hindrance to the establishment
of democratic institutions (Vorozheikina, 1994). Historically, both
the idea and the reality of civil society have preceded the development of democracy. While there are points of convergence around
pluralism and the dispersion of interests and social forces, the
pluralistic character of society neither ensures democracy nor
implies a strengthening of the open domain of public life.

Under special circumstances, a vital civil society may sustain and
be reinforced by a viable constitutional democracy, through institutionalized forms of interaction and exchange that can prevent the
monopolization of power and resources. Democracy can be
strengthened when citizens engage in joint action while sharing a
broad commitment to the public sphere and the fostering of public
judgment, civil responsibility and problem-solving capabilities. For
instance, in countries such as Argentina, Chile and Uruguay, the
groups and non-governmental organizations that opposed the military governments in the 1970s and 1980s over human rights violations became core organizations of civil society as they embodied the
moral opposition to authoritarian rule. These groups and NGOs (for
example, the *Madres de Plaza de Mayo*, the *Servicio de Paz y
Justicia*, the *Vicaría de la Solidaridad*, *AFDD*, *CELS* and many
others) carried out this role in a forceful manner as the public
spheres reopened in the transition to democracy. These self-
managed organizations, autonomous from the state and linked to
institutional networks, played a central role in forwarding human
rights issues and demands. Moreover, they provided through their
mobilization 'from below', a model of organization and participation
that was relatively novel in the context of the Southern Cone.
Despite their marginalization in recent years, their example has
provided a long-term counter-legacy favoring the creation of a
democratic culture rooted in society and the establishment of

mechanisms of pluralistic control of the state (Lehmann, 1990; Lowden, 1996; Roniger and Sznajder, 1997). However, sometimes civil societies defy the logic of constitutional democratic regimes and a gap opens between the formal aspects of public life and the pragmatic (so-called 'real') workings of the sociopolitical arena, as reflected in analyses of Mediterranean cultures and societies conducted since the 1960s and 1970s (Boissevain, 1966; Galt, 1974; Blok, 1974; PittRivers, 1977). In either case, the 'construction of reality' hinges on social interaction and exchange as a contextual, pragmatic phenomenon. At this level of interplay between the logic of modern constitutional democracy and the praxis and pragmatics of everyday life and social action, moral obligations and commitments are enmeshed and reformulated in recurrent patterns of action and exchange through a web of movements, communities, associations and relationships. Within them the hierarchical logic of patronage may be projected as a mechanism influencing and sometimes even conditioning the timing, mechanics, and variable outcomes of the current processes of democratization.

Modern Constitutional Democracy, Civil Society, and Patronage

In the wake of the great revolutions and the Enlightenment, constitutional regimes emerged within which an increasing number of groups and sectors of society gained access to the public sphere, often through turbulent struggles, leading to the configuration of modern constitutional democracies. Emerging first in the United States, under the idea of popular sovereignty, constitutional democracy spread to various European and Latin American countries and, later on, to Asian and African societies. As the epitome of universalistic standards of public behavior and supposedly open 'rules of the game', constitutional democracy became a dominant and yet fragile institutional framework of modernity. Its rules focus on elected representative institutions assumed to ensure the accountability of rulers through the recurrent replacement of those in positions of authority and the distribution of power in society. Yet, again, the procedural principle of electoral representation – that both rulers and contenders are subject to the law and to clearly defined rules according to which they compete for the support of the public – can be sustained when there is commitment to the system that will ensure the accountability of rulers.

Political pluralism does not ensure that the rules of the constitutional game would be defined in terms of civility – i.e. the acceptance of norms and attitudes allowing for a neutral political language that binds various groups together, in their engagement in the realm of public goods and the building of a 'moral community' as well as in their disengagement through the tolerant recognition of multiculturalism and difference. Here the interplay between modern constitutional democracy and civil society turns again into a critical factor in shaping a committed pluralism or just pluralism of a disengaging type (Shils, 1991; Melucci, 1989; Kopelowitz, 1996; Alexander and Smith, 1993).

There are at least two different dimensions or levels of analysis. At the level of principles, the logic of civil society and democracy runs counter to the logic of patronage and clientelism. As is well known, clientelistic arrangements are built upon asymmetric, but mutually beneficial, open-ended transactions that are based on the differential control by social actors over the access and flow of resources in stratified societies (Lemieux, 1977; Graziano, 1975; 1983; Gellner and Waterbury, 1977; Eisenstadt and Lemarchand, 1981; Clapham, 1982). Basically, clientelism creates an inherently contradictory situation. Asymmetrical power and inequalities are structured together with interpersonal commitments, and potential or actual coercion coexists with an ideological emphasis on the voluntary nature of the attachment (Eisenstadt and Roniger, 1984). The structure of limiting payoffs can be maintained only by making payoffs; the covered, informal, and extra-legal character of such bonds is used to assert public claims over goods and services and to bolster and propagate public images of power and reputation. Such arrangements are maintained through perpetual contest, resource manipulation, and instability. Whereas in antiquity patronage formed part of the normative framework of society and could hardly be thought of as conflicting with legal institutions (Wallace-Hadrill, 1989: 5–6), in modern societies it is in fact built around such a conflict. While in principle and by law the patronized partners (the so-called 'clients') have access to power centers and the ability to convert resources autonomously, they do not actualize this potential because it is neutralized by the patrons' or brokers' control of the avenues to resource conversion and access to political centers. Yet, as in antiquity, mediation is projected into the institutional arena. Such mediation is contingent on the clients entering into a relationship of exchange that necessarily limits the scope and convertibility of resources freely exchanged.

In addition, the individual not only is expected to provide his patron or broker with specific resources but must also accept the latter's control over his access – and that of other clients – to markets and public goods, and over his ability to convert resources fully. In Javier Auyero's terms (1997), clientelism can be enacted at the micro-level as 'problem holders' meet 'problem solvers' in situations of structural inequality and imbalance. In a parallel manner, the patron's position is not as solid as it may seem, nor is it guaranteed, for instance by kinship or other ascriptive criteria. On the contrary, although patrons and brokers invest much time and energy in gaining and retaining control over clients, their control is never fully legitimized; it is vulnerable to attack by social forces committed to formal, universalistic principles of social organization and exchange, by the competition of other patrons and brokers, potential and actual, and by social forces excluded from clientelistic relations. Owing to these constant threats, patrons and brokers are compelled to rely on their followers to solidify their position. The patron and broker must also relinquish some of the short-term material gains that might accrue from a position of pre-eminence in order to earn the right to determine the basic rules of the social relationships. In return the client is protected from social or material insecurity, and is provided with goods, services and social advancement.

Thus complementary exchange strategies are built, which signal what political scientist Vincent Lemieux (1987) defines as a 'double transformation': an abdication of autonomy on the client's part and a relaxation of hierarchical controls on the patron's or broker's part, through which the former's lack of power becomes dominated power and the latter's lack of domination becomes dominating authority. These exchange strategies are not only affected by immediate, mostly technical considerations of power, access to resources and instrumentality, but often encompass mutual, relatively long-term, compromises based on commitments and personal goodwill as the prerequisite for the maintenance of ongoing social relationships.

Jürgen Habermas in particular emphasizes the contradiction between the logic of civil society and the logic of hierarchical models. In his pioneer work, *The Structural Transformation of the Public Sphere*, he endorses the modernity program of Western liberal thought, by characterizing civil society as

> the possibility of an objective agreement among competing interests in accord with universal and binding criteria. Otherwise the power relation between pressure and counter pressure, however publicly exercised, creates at best an unstable equilibrium of interests, supported by temporary power constellations, that in principle is devoid of rationality according to the standard of a universal interest. (1989: 234)

Following a perspective of ideal typification, in the Weberian sense, many conceive the nature and functions of representation as radically different from the nature and roles of clientelism in the historical settings in which both have been institutionalized.

Whereas representation belongs to the legal order, patronage defies it by addressing the appropiation and manipulation of resources. At this level of analysis, clientelism is seen as going against the modern notion of representation, which assumes these elements: a system of public rights; a public debate on what should be conceived of in principle as rights and enjoyed in practice as entitlements; safeguards protecting the latter from infringement; and a competitive system for establishing rights and priorities and for controlling their implementation according to public rules (Adamson, 1987: 335–6; Rosen, 1992). From this perspective, patronage is shown to neutralize the system of representation, of assignment of rights, by placing 'friends' in the strategic positions of power and control. This mode is often inimical to the institutionalization of public accountability and therefore stands in contradistinction to a politics open to generalization and participation, and to a discourse aimed at the protection of individual and collective liberties and rights.

The second perspective moves analysis to the level of interplay between the logic of modern constitutional democracy and the praxis and pragmatics of social action. From this perspective, which attempts to understand how principles and commitments are enmeshed and reformulated in recurrent patterns of action and exchange through a web of relationships, movements and coalitions, the crucial focus of analysis becomes the institutionalization of specific patterns of representation and participation in the public sphere. From this perspective, it is possible to think of patronage in terms of representation by applying a definition of the latter that incorporates manipulation, symbolic ambiguity, and power accumulation as well as expressive dimensions of reciprocity, goodwill and ritualization. Truly enough, by acting as patrons and clients, individuals are not interested in the generality of equality and legal rules; they are interested in persons and resources. They do not seek to promote a rule for citizens as such; they are on the lookout for situations that are to their advantage, on the basis of favoritism. As such, patron–client networks are used to divert public resources. Yet research also indicates that patronage is an important mechanism for obtaining transactional benefits, both within backgrounds of peripherality/dependency and within backgrounds of access to public goods and the public distribution of private goods. Patronage has been instrumental in providing local–regional–national mechanisms of interrelation and integration by institutionalizing mechanisms of resource allocation. While these mechanisms run counter to universalistic standards, they are sensitive to local sentiment and personal sensitivities and provide ways of incorporating new sectors of the population such as immigrants; and, in advancing political actors with an entrepreneurial ability (see, for example, Hermitte and Bartolomé, 1977; Clapham, 1982: 14–15; Korovkin, 1988). From this perspective, it is often claimed that as long as patron–client exchanges maintain some balance of reciprocity and mutual benefit, the participation in broader political and economic markets by the 'capi-clientele' (to borrow Gaetano Mosca's expression) – be he or she a broker, a patron or a patron-broker – constitutes a means for individuals in their entourage to influence decisions in the arena that connects public and private life. In this sense, sometimes patronage can be seen to reconcile public and private authority and formal and informal rules of the game.

This duality reflects a major tension of modern democratic polities. As part of the Western political tradition, modern democracies are built on citizenship – which implies political equality but leaves the economic domain open to inequalities. Thus equality and freedom may move in separate and even opposite directions, as noted long ago by Alexis de Tocqueville in his classic *Democracy in America*. Sectors benefiting from patronage may see it as a pragmatic avenue of controlled freedom, useful for advancing in social, economic, and political domains that are regulated by competition for access to power, resources, and services. At the same time, patronage may be resented, criticized, and opposed by social forces and coalitions wishing to curtail its presence alongside bureaucratic universalism and market rationality.

The Dynamics, Transformation, and Demise of Patronage

The contradictory role of patronage is highlighted by research on its fragility, volatility, and continuity or demise in contemporary societies.

The contradictions and instability inherent in patronage and clientelism are symptomatic of the macrosocial context in which they arise. Unlike societies in which hereditary ascriptive principles predominate, patronage and clientelism flourish where markets are no longer controlled through primordial units and allow for an open flow of resources and opportunities for mobility. This trend, however, goes hand in hand with a strong tendency toward unequal access to markets and sociopolitical spheres. As they affect distribution and redistribution, clientelism and patronage remain subject to the dynamics of the political economy. Accordingly, a decrease in people's vulnerability, the patrons' or brokers' loss of control, a decline in the supply of resources, a lack of demand for the patrons' (or the clients') resources and services – or changes in the opposite direction – all these may in the short term contribute to the fragility of clientelistic commitments and over the long term may shatter the salience of various forms of patronage. The marketization of economies, accelerated urbanization, and the expansion of the regulatory, extractive, or even sporadic mobilizing activities of central administrations may affect them as well. Research has shown that the spread of market forces and/or the establishment of forceful administrations eroded patrimomial patterns of social exchange in rural Third World settings, making the terms of trade increasingly oppressive for rural clienteles (Scott and Kerkvliet, 1973; Scott, 1976). Similarly, the impact of world economic trends, fluctuations in the international price of commodities, the complexity of international trade, banking, and aid – all these affected the pool of patronage resources available to states and other agencies, and influenced patterns of control, distribution, and redistribution (Lemarchand, 1990; Eddie, 1991). Moreover, as these arrangements are not fully legitimized, they remain vulnerable to the challenge of countervailing social forces.

From the perspective of the political matrix, patronage can be analyzed in terms of its functions, its operational enactment, and the political strategies enacted by both the social forces involved in clientelistic arrangements and the forces working against patronage. These dimensions should be analyzed contextually, as they develop differently in different societies and situations. Here I would like merely to reflect on the general trends of patronage in representative democracies. Two lines of analysis can be suggested, each calling for further research.

One line emphasizes the interplay of historical timing and the crystallization of specific institutional patterns (which may become institutional traditions with the passing of time). Martin Shefter (1977) has suggested that the timing of the formation of a political party, together with its prior access (or lack of access) to state resources, is crucial in deciding the party's subsequent attitude to patronage – both before and after it accedes to formal power. Similarly, René Lemarchand has reflected on the higher presence of patron–client relations in the Third World in terms of historical timing:

> Where the historical experience of Third World societies differs fundamentally from that of Europe is that among the former the demands and frustrations of the rural sectors found an outlet in electoral channels long before their social identities were allowed to crystallize along class lines. The result has been a process of fragmented restructuration which offered ample scope for the reemergence of patron–client ties in the guise of nominally modern institutions ... It is primarily where social change has lagged substantially behind political

modernization that clientelistic forms of dependency have been more resilient. (1981: 19)

Reg Whitaker (1987) too has suggested timing as the crucial variable in patronage taking on a different shape in Anglo-Saxon countries. In the United States, for example, he found that the democratization of patronage preceded the emergence of a modern bureaucratic state, thus producing a pattern with a markedly decentralized and party bias. In Canada, in contrast, the early consolidation of the bureaucratic state produced a pattern of patronage in which elites maintained strong control and patronage assumed a more organizationally based character. Similarly, in China, there has been a steady expansion of the public sphere and yet the primacy of the state in the shaping of the public sphere has been maintained; no effective assertion has developed of civic power *vis-à-vis* the state; and most Chinese citizens have continued to conceive social existence mainly in terms of obligations and interdependence rather than in terms of rights and responsibilities (Wakeman, 1993).

This leads to the second line of analysis, also largely unmapped, which stems from the realm of cultural and political traditions shaped historically, at critical 'junctures'. These traditions are constitutive of collective identities, the shaping of which involves always a process of struggle, both social-political and discursive-symbolic. Such a struggle concerns the never-ending process of definition of criteria of inclusion and exclusion, determining access to resources, entitlements and positions and their allocation among different sectors, individuals and strata. In addition, this process may also involve a struggle over the definition of concepts of authority, concepts of accountability and patterns of legitimation; in short, over the visions embodied by the political order and over its functioning.

Representative democracies, for instance, put emphasis on the competition for power and distrust concentrations of power. Institutionally, they predicate a separation of powers, the development of mutual checks and balances in government, accountability and institutionalized arrangements for the regular and continuous replacement of rulers. Ultimately such a matrix implies the existence of a pluralistic distribution of centers of power, a civil society, and social space independent of state power. As such, it is concerned with representation or, in the classic terminology of Verba and Almond, with processes of aggregation and articulation of interests according to certain rules of the game.

Patronage concerns the patterns of participation; accordingly, it can accommodate to such tenets of modern constitutional regimes as the legitimation of multiple interests, at both the individual and the group level, and the recognized autonomy of civil society *vis-à-vis* formal political institutions. Competition for positions of formal power becomes connected with the public projection in its various forms (appearance, reputation, credibility, etc.) and with symbolic struggles over the definition and enactment of evaluative criteria. Moreover, during periods of political setback to welfare state policies and social democratic programs, neo-liberalism and market ethics gain influence. Promotion of liberalization, reduction of state intervention in favor of market mechanisms, privatization of state-owned and state-supported services, curtailment of union power, among other processes, further fragment society and heighten the need for support networks. Patronage, when available, remained throughout political revamping in Poland, Russia, Hungary, Turkey, Brazil or Argentina as important as ever, as observers of these settings indicate (Tarkowski, 1992; Sik, 1993; Vorozheikina, 1994; Güneş-Ayata, 1994; Gay, 1994; Auyero, 1997).

In addition, it seems that in representative democracies, even more than in other political regimes, patronage can be highly effective in encouraging and rewarding party activists and in molding incumbency to public offices in accordance with politically sensitive stances. Within such a framework, patronage can be translated into political influence and can become entrenched in the actual workings of democratic polities. It continues to be useful in the competition for power and, once power is achieved, for effectively formulating and implementing policies. Accordingly, it is to be expected that positions of high trust (at least in the political realm) continue to be filled in accordance with patronage considerations, albeit with due attention to capabilities and efficiency (Simpson, 1988; Clark, 1994).

The altered environment of post-industrial societies can therefore explain a paradox remarked on by sociologist Robin Theobald (1992) in discussing the survival of patronage in developed societies. There, patronage becomes more 'classified' – that is, it tends to be restricted to those with professional or business qualifications in the upper strata of the society, rather than being a phenomenon typical of the lower classes. In addition, patronage cannot be confined to politics in the narrow sense; it proliferates as well in the arts, the academy, the church, the media, and even in business – whenever we are dealing with the power of appointment and the granting of access to benefits, goods, services, influence, and honors.

Accordingly, there are grounds for the claim that even though it may run against the public, visible face of modern democracies, patronage has continued to be instrumental. It is compatible with non-clientelistic practices and leads under certain circumstances to the strengthening of organizations – once it is recognized and not concealed – adding commitment and loyalty to occupational qualifications needed to access office incumbency. Moreover, in many modern societies, as in antiquity, the polity can hardly be envisaged as running smoothly without the operation of patronage, nowadays in areas as varied as party activism, procedural administration, and access to governmental contracts and economic ventures. Doubtless, patronage is controversial, and not only for its secluded and alegal character; often, owing to an indiscriminate identification of patronage with corruption, we ignore patronage as long as possible or disguise it as friendship, which is more acceptable in terms of the proclaimed ethos of modern equality (Roniger and Güneş-Ayata, 1994).

In view of the persistence of mediation in modern democratic polities, it might be in the public interest to recognize patronage, demanding that it be exercised with visibility and as such subject to public evaluation and accountability. To publicize the private domain, I suggest, is probably the best way to avoid the privatization of the public domain.

In many contemporary democracies, patronage has remained legally unstructured, ambiguous from a conventional point of view, and open to conflicting interpretations and instrumental manipulations. With Canadian political patronage in mind, Jeffrey Simpson has emphasized this aspect of the phenomenon:

> Patronage usually breaks no laws and merely raises questions about proper moral and ethical conduct in government, the acceptability of which often has [as] much to do with the eye of the beholders, that is the political culture of the country or province, as it does with the political acts in question. (1988: 387)

As modern capitalistic and democratic settings endorse the openness of the system in universalistic or quasi-universalistic terms, patronage is opposed by countervailing forces: political organizations within civil society, social forces willing to support autonomous channels of communication with the center, and constituencies for bureaucratic autonomy. These social and political forces may attempt to represent the general interest or persuasively construct a particular interest in terms of its translation into a concern basic to society at large (Alexander, 1995). But usually, this involves a routine process of discursive-symbolic debate and social-political struggle, worked out within the parameters that are part of legitimacy systems historically encoded in the institutional format of a society. In times of crisis, the specific debates may be connected more explicitly to pressures leading to changes in the setting of norms, political ground rules, and the redefinition of the public sphere.

Changes in the perception of patronage, if they occur under such circumstances (they may not), are of consequence for patronage if they result in the institutionalization of mechanisms through which citizens can press for their rights and entitlements. Such changes include civil service reforms, non-partisan public systems, recognized charters of rights, controls over party fundraising, and non-partisan comptrollers as a prestigious and trustworthy branch of government. The functioning of these institutional mechanisms, it is worth emphasizing, hinges on public support for a configuration of the public sphere structured around public accountability and responsiveness to turn more and more discrete issues into publicly negotiable and politically consequential programs.

But even as public accountability and a discourse aimed at the protection of individual and collective rights are institutionalized, the change may affect the character of mediating mechanisms that structure specific ways of access to loci of power, of distribution of resources and of regulation of saliency of claims in the cultural agenda of a society; it does not lead to a demise of mediation itself as part of public life. Mediation, whether of a more open and generalizable nature or of a more closed and hierarchical character, should be expected to continue to play a major role in the workings of contemporary institutions, as the latter continue to work through the tensions between their formal logic and the pragmatics of everyday life and social action.

Notes

This chapter elaborates arguments first presented in an article published in the *International Journal of Comparative Sociology*, volume XXXV, 1994. Thanks are due to Mario Sznajder for his comments and suggestions.

1 In other areas, developments have differed radically. In some of the Muslim countries, the world-wide disenchantment with modern rationality and secularism has become culturally linked with fundamentalist fervor and religious revivalism. In Asia, various types of authoritarian regimes have retained their image as guarantors of accelerated economic development, although they face pressures toward democratization. In sub-Saharan Africa, the Balkans, and Central and Eastern Europe, the appeal of democracy has been tempered by ethnic tensions, xenophobia, and civil war.

2 In this sense, civil society can influence the public sphere also from within, e.g. through representative institutions and autonomous courts, thus bringing the executive power to reckon its broader social accountability. When this is the case we can refer, following Nancy Fraser (1992), to the development of a 'strong public sphere'.

3 Basically, in relation to structural differentiation and the distinction between state and society.

References

Adamson, W. (1987) 'Gramsci and the Politics of Civil Society', *Praxis International*, 7 (3/4): 320–39.

Alexander, J.C. (1995) 'Collective Action and Democratic Discourse: Social Movements as "Translations" of Civil Society', paper presented at the SCASS Seminar on Revolutions, Uppsala, June 1995.

Alexander, J.C. and Smith, P. (1993) 'The Discourse of American Civil Society: A New Proposal for Cultural Studies', *Theory and Society*, 22 (2): 151–208.

Auyero, J. (1997). 'Evita como performance. Medicación y resolución de problemas entre los pobres urbanos del Gran Buenos Aires', in idem ed. *Favores por votos? Estudios sobre clientelismo político contemporáneo*. Buenos Aires: Losada.

Blok, A. (1974) *The Mafia of a Sicilian Village*. Oxford: Basil Blackwell.

Boissevain, J. (1966) 'Patronage in Sicily', *Man (N.S.)*, 1: 18–33.

Borón, A. (1995). *Estado, Capitalismo y Democracia en América Latina*. Buenos Aires: Ediciones Imago Mundi.

Boyte, H.C. (1992) 'The Pragmatic Ends of Popular Politics', in C. Calhoun (ed.), *Habermas and the Public Sphere*. Cambridge, MA: MIT Press. pp. 340–57.

Calhoun, C. (1992) *Habermas and the Public Sphere*. Cambridge, MA: MIT Press.

Clapham, C. (ed.) (1982) *Private Patronage and Public Power*. New York: St Martin's Press.

Clark, T.N. (1994) 'Clientelism USA: The Dynamics of Change', in L. Roniger and A. Güneş-Ayata (eds), *Democracy, Clientelism and Civil Society*. Boulder, CO: Lynne Rienner. pp. 121–44.

Cohen, J.L. and Arato, A. (1992) *Civil Society and Political Theory*. Cambridge, MA: MIT Press.

Duss, P. (1993) 'Bounded Democracy: Tradition and Politics in Modern Japan'. Stanford University, manuscript.

Eddie, C.J. (1991) *Democracy by Default: Dependency and Clientelism in Jamaica*. Boulder, CO: Lynne Rienner.

Eisenstadt, S.N. and Lemarchand, R. (eds) (1981) *Political Clientelism, Patronage, and Development*. London: Sage.

Eisenstadt, S.N. and Roniger, L. (1984) *Patrons, Clients, and Friends*. Cambridge: Cambridge University Press.

Eley, G. (1992) 'Nations, Publics, and Political Cultures', in C. Calhoun (ed.), *Habermas and the Public Sphere*. Cambridge, MA: MIT Press. pp. 289–339.

Ezrahi, I. (1990) *The Descent of Icarus*. Cambridge, MA: Harvard University Press.

Fraser, N. (1992) 'Rethinking the Public Sphere', in C. Calhoun (ed.), *Habermas and the Public Sphere*. Cambridge, MA: MIT Press. pp. 109–42.

Galt, A.H. (1974) 'Rethinking Patron–Client Relationships: The Real System and the Official System in Southern Italy', *Anthropological Quarterly*, 47 (2): 182–202.

Gay, R. (1994). *Popular Organization and Democracy in Rio de Janeiro: A Tale of Two Favelas*. Philadelphia: Temple University Press.

Gellner, E. and Waterbury, J. (eds) (1977) *Patrons and Clients in Mediterranean Societies*. London: Duckworth.

Graziano, L. (1975) *A Conceptual Framework for the Study of Clientelism*. Cornell University Western Societies Program Occasional Papers 4, New York.

Graziano, L. (1983) 'Introduction. Issue on Political Clientelism', *International Political Science Review*, 4 (4): 425–34.

Güneş-Ayata, A. (1994) 'Patronage in Turkey', in L. Roniger and A. Güneş-Ayata (eds), *Democracy, Clientelism and Civil Society*. Boulder, CO: Lynne Rienner. pp. 19–28.

Habermas, J. (1989) *The Structural Transformation of the Public Sphere*. London: Polity.

Held, D. (1987) *Models of Democracy*. Stanford: Stanford University Press.

Hermitte, A. and Bartolomé, J. (eds) (1977) *Procesos de articulacion social*. Flacso and Amorrortu.

Hirschman, A.O. (1982) *Shifting Involvements*. Princeton: Princeton University Press.

Hoston, G.A. (1992) 'The State, Modernity and the Fate of Liberalism in Pre-War Japan', *Journal of Asian Studies*, 51 (2): 287–316.

Keane, J. (1988a) 'Despotism and Democracy', in J. Keane (ed.), *Democracy and Civil Society*. London: Verso. pp. 35–71.

Keane, J. (ed.) (1988b) *Democracy and Civil Society*. London: Verso.

Kopelowitz, E. (1996). 'Equality, Multiculturalism and the Dilemmas of Civility in Israel'. *International Journal of Politics, Culture and Society*, 9 (3): 373–400.

Korovkin, M.A. (1988) 'Exploitation, Cooperation, Collusion: An Enquiry into Patronage', *Archives Europeennes de Socilogie*, 29: 105–26.

Lehmann, D. (1990) *Democracy and Development in Latin America*. Cambridge: Polity Press.

Lemarchand, R. (1981) 'Comparative Political Clientelism: Structure, Process and Optic', in S.N. Eisenstadt and R. Lemarchand (eds), *Political Clientelism, Patronage and Development*. Beverly Hills: Sage. pp. 7–32.

Lemarchand, R. (1990) 'The State, the Parallel Economy, and the Changing Structure of Patronage Systems', in D. Rothchild and N. Chazan (eds), *The Precarious Balance: State and Society in Africa*. Boulder, CO: Westview. pp. 149–70.

Lemieux, V. (1977) *Le Patronage politique: une etude comparative*. Quebec: Les Presses de l'Université Laval.

Lemieux, V. (1987) 'Le Sens du patronage politique', *Journal of Canadian Studies*, 22 (2): 5–18.

Lipovetsky, G. (1983) *L'Ere du vide: essais sur l'individualisme contemporain*. Paris: Gallimard.

Lowden, P. (1996) *Moral Opposition to Authoritarian Rule in Chile, 1973–1990*. New York: St Martin's Press.

Melucci, A. (1989) *Nomads of the Present*. Philadelphia: Temple University Press.

Nedelsky, J. (1989) 'Reconceiving Autonomy: Sources, Thoughts and Possibilities', *Yale Journal of Law and Feminism*, 1 (1): 7–36.

Pérez-Díaz, V. M. (1993) *The Return of Civil Society*. Cambridge, MA: Harvard University Press.

Pitt-Rivers, J. (1977) *The Fate of Schechem, or the Politics of Sex*. Cambridge: Cambridge University Press.

Price, P. (1993) 'Democracy and Ethnic Conflict in India', *Asian Survey*, 33 (5): 493–506.

Roniger, L. (1991) 'Public Trust and the Consolidation of Latin American Democracies', in A.R.M. Ritter, M.A. Cameron and D.H. Pollock (eds), *Latin America to the Year 2000*. New York: Praeger. pp. 147–60.

Roniger, L. and A. Güneş-Ayata (eds) (1994) *Democracy, Clientelism and Civil Society*. Boulder: Lynne Rienner.

Roniger, L. and M. Sznajder (1997) 'The Legacy of Human Rights Violations and the Collective Identity of Redemocratized Uruguay', *Human Rights Quarterly*, 19 (1): 55–77.

Rosen, P. (1992) 'The Constitutional Conundrum of Hate Legislation', in A.G. Gagnon and A.B. Tanguay (eds), *Democracy with Justice*. Ottawa: Carleton University Press. pp. 35–51.

Ryan, M.P. (1992) 'Gender and Public Access: Women's Politics in Nineteenth-Century America', in C. Calhoun (ed.) *Habermas and the Public Sphere*. Cambridge, MA: MIT Press. pp. 259–85.

Savory, R.M. (1993) 'Islam and Democracy: The Case of the Islamic Republic of Iran', in C.E. Bosworth et al. (eds), *The Islamic World: Essays in Honour of Bernard Lewis*. Princeton: Darwin Press.

Scott, J. (1976) *The Moral Economy of the Peasant*. New Haven, CT: Yale University Press.

Scott, J. and Kerkvliet, B. (1973) 'How Traditional Rural Patrons Lose Legitimacy: A Theory with Special Reference to Southeast Asia', *Cultures et developpement*, 5 (3): 501–40.

Seligman, A. (1992) *The Idea of Civil Society*. New York: Free Press.

Shefter, M. (1977) 'Patronage and its Opponents'. Cornell University Western Societies Program Occasional Papers 8, Ithaca, NY.

Shils, E. (1991) 'The Virtue of Civil Society', *Government and Opposition*, 26 (1): 3–20.

Sik, A. (1993) 'Networking in Capitalist, Communist and Post-Communist Societies'. Wissenschaftzentrum Berlim für Sozialforschung.

Simpson, J. (1988) *Spoils of Power*. Toronto: Collins.

Sztompka, P. (1992) 'Dilemmas of the Great Transition', *Sisyphus*, 2 (8): 9–28.

Tarkowski, J. (1992) 'Transition to Democracy or Transition to Ochlocracy?', *Sysiphus*, 8 (1): 139–49.

Taylor, C. (1989) *Sources of the Self*. Cambridge: Cambridge University Press.

Taylor, C. (1990) 'Modes of Civil Society', *Public Culture*, 3 (1): 95–118.

Theobald, R. (1992) 'On the Survival of Patronage in Developed Societies', *Archives Europeennes de Sociologie*, 33: 183–91.

Vorozheikina, T. (1994) 'Clientelism and the Process of Political Democratization in Russia', in L. Roniger and A. Güneş-Ayata (eds), *Democracy, Clientelism and Civil Society*. Boulder, CO: Lynne Rienner. pp. 105–20.

Wakeman, F. Jr (1993) 'The Civil Society and Public Sphere Debate', *Modern China*, 19 (2): 108–38.

Wallace-Hadrill, A. (ed.) (1989) *Patronage in Ancient Society*. London: Routledge and Kegan Paul.

Whitaker, R. (1987) 'Between Democracy and Bureaucracy: Democratic Politics in Transition', *Journal of Canadian Studies*, 22 (2): 55–71.

5

Civil Society and Uncivil Organizations

Göran Ahrne

Who can be against civility? The idea of civil society is an idea about improved qualities in interaction between people and in relations between individuals and society. It is a discussion about forms of interaction to allow people to be individuals at the same time as they are parts of a society.

The creation of civil society presupposes and implies a precarious balance between individual participation and social obligations. It is a coincidence of private interests with those of society. In civil society people are supposed to act voluntarily and with a moral conviction. Civility should not rest on coercion, manipulation, or monetary rewards. Civil society has been described as 'the place where people pause to reflect on the moral dilemmas they face' (Wolfe, 1989:233).

The way to get things done in civil society is to convince people or to create a spirit of community that also includes strangers. In this respect the notion of civil society transcends the narrow boundaries of communities. Civil society is also connected with the idea of democracy, but not any kind of democracy. And civil society is not necessarily an arena for politics. Too much politics may be destructive for the delicate social relations of civil society and may threaten 'a genuinely pluralistic and actively self-organizing civil society' (Keane, 1988a: 28).

Much of the thinking about civil society has a normative character. It is an imagination and a social construction that 'cannot be seen "out there" in a self-evident, natural or transparent way' (Tester, 1992: 14). Yet, in political or ideological discussions the idea of civil society is often used as a figure that is compared with really existing organizations or institutions (see, for instance, Etzioni, 1993). It is often presented as a social alternative in contrast to the despotism of both the state and the market. But many of the proponents of civil society warn against associating this alternative with any concrete social arrangements. 'The normative dimensions of the civil society–state distinction need to be elaborated sufficiently to show their relevance for thinking about concrete institutional procedures and struggles without, however, becoming too closely identified with specific institutions and thereby sharing their contingency' (Keane, 1988a: 28).

Even if the qualities of civil society cannot be molded into particular institutions, the questions concerning the organizational forms of civil society are not uninteresting and they cannot be avoided. How can we recognize civil society if we do not know what it looks like? How can we create a civil society if we do not have any blueprints?

Many of the concepts around civil society resemble ideas about how to create excellent organizations. Questions about relations between participation and authority, democracy and efficiency, hierarchy and influence, bureaucracy and creativity revolve around the same problems as the discussions around civil society, and they encounter the same problems. I will argue that one cannot think about civil society without framing the discussion in terms of organizational forms, and both the discussion of organizational forms and the discussion about civil society involve ideas about how to arrange human interaction. That is why it is fruitful to compare the discussion about civil society with a discussion of organizational form.

An analysis of civil society is inescapably caught up in a framework of institutions and organizations. If there is one thing that the discussants agree upon it is a sharp distinction between the state and civil society. Even though it is hard to know what civil society is, one thing seems to be clear: it is distinct and, as a social phenomenon, different from the state. Thus, at least negatively, civil society is defined in terms of organizational and institutional forms.

The notion of civil society has to be understood in a historical perspective. John Keane (1988b) traces the emergence of the distinction between state and civil society to the late eighteenth century and writers such as Adam Ferguson and Thomas Paine. For them civil society was a precondition and an arena for the creation of a free and natural interaction among free individuals (Keane, 1988b: 49; Tester, 1992: 47–51).

Except for the distinction between civil society and the state there does not seem to be a good deal of agreement on what constitutes civil society. Several other institutional boundaries have been suggested. One is the distinction between the family or the household and civil society. According to Hegel civil society is outside the household, but it includes the market economy. It is not a harmonious sphere, and it is often characterized by conflict (Keane, 1988b). But most proponents of civil society as a normative concept hesitate to include the market, capitalism or large corporations into civil society. The early writers on civil society 'were not blind apologists of capitalism' (1988b: 64). They were generally against both state power and corporate practices, and their aim was to establish a new public sphere.

Recent thinkers such as Alan Wolfe and Pierre Rosanvallon put civil society in a strong opposition to both the market and the state (Calhoun, 1993: 392). In Wolfe's version there are obvious similarities between the state and the market. Both markets and states are destructive. People are treated not as people but as citizens or opportunities, and they are tied together not because they want to be, but because of an immediate self-interest or on some external authority. In the market or in the state people are not treated as capable of 'participating in the making of their own moral rules' (Wolfe, 1989: 12). For Rosanvallon (1988: 199) civil society is important because it offers an alternative between state control and a liberal scenario resting on market solutions and privatization.

Following this discussion it becomes clear that the definition of civil society is negative: it is more about what it is not than what it is. For most writers, though, civil society involves relationships that go beyond the family but are not within the realm of the state. 'Civil society is about our basic societal relationships and experiences; it is about what happens to us when we leave our family and go about our own lives' (Tester, 1992: 8).

But what does civil society consist of? Which are its positive organizational forms? The most natural organizational form to be associated with civil society is probably voluntary associations. Keane (1988a: 20) mentions 'non-market non-state organizations' such as churches, professional organizations, and political parties as components of modern civil societies. But he also says that modern civil societies are mixtures of elements without a common denominator or a generative first principle. All voluntary associations, however, do not automatically seem to qualify as civil organizations. If such organizations have grown too large or become too hierarchical they are excluded from civil society (1988a: 12).

Apart from voluntary associations, forms of interaction that are seen as natural elements of civil societies include 'communities, friendship networks, solidaristic workplace ties, spontaneous groups and movements' (Wolfe, 1989: 20). Rosanvallon (1988: 205) also mentions neighborhood groups, and Alberto Melucci (1988: 248) talks about new social movements as 'networks submerged in everyday life'.

What kinds of social phenomena are these forms of interaction? What can they achieve? How permanent and accessible are they? Can they be consciously created? Can they survive? What security do they give? Is power extinct from civil society?

Organized Interaction

The idea of civil society has been developed in contrast to other institutional arrangements: the state, the household, the economy, or the market. Civil society does not denote a new kind of society; it is not a new social system, but it is presented as an alternative social sphere. The problem is, however, that we do not really know much about this sphere other than some of its possible qualities. What are we supposed to do there except be nice to each other? Even though it is supposed to be self-organizing we need to know a little more about its organizing principles in order to be able to 'think about concrete institutional procedures' of civil society. Which are these principles? What is such stuff as dreams are made on?

To investigate the proposed forms of interaction in civil society I will follow up the supposed contrast between civil society and other forms of institutional arrangements and try to estimate differences and similarities. In doing this I will concentrate upon some of the main features of all organized interaction to see if and how they characterize interaction in civil society.

In an article about 'new organizational forms' Wolf Heydebrand (1989) has suggested six dimensions to delineate variations in forms of work organizations: size of labor force, object of labor, means of labor, division of labor, control of labor, and ownership. I will argue that these six categories can be reduced to four dimensions that are the key features of all kinds of organization. The size of the labor force is a matter of people affiliated with an organization. Ownership and employment denote different forms of affiliation. Other forms of affiliation are membership, citizenship, and also kinship. The form of affiliation determines the rights towards the organization (Keeley, 1988). Are there any forms of affiliation in civil society?

Both object of labor and means of labor are related to the collective resources of an organization. All organizations seem to be founded around a set of collective resources, and access to these resources motivates people to join organizations and to stay with them (Hechter, 1987). It is access to resources that calls for a regulation of affiliation. Affiliation implies both obligations and rights in relation to the collective resources. Resources give power. How are collective resources kept and distributed in civil society?

Division of labor implies a system of rules and a coordination of activities within any organization. In much organization theory this phenomenon is seen as hierarchy or bureacracy. All organizations, however, do not have a hierarchy or a bureaucratic structure. But all organizations have a set of rules. Are there any rules in civil society?

Finally, organization also implies control. In all organizations the performance of each affiliate is controlled by other affiliates. This is required to try to make people contribute to the collective resources in the long run. Forms and extent of control vary, but there is no organization that does not have some form of control as an important part of its activities. Is there control in civil society? As soon as human interaction involves the collection and distribution of collective resources it needs some form of organization, i.e. it will comprise the regulation of affiliation, it will need mechanisms of coordination such as rules and it will involve some form of control (Ahrne, 1994). What kind of affiliation is there in civil society, or is it open to anybody? Who is eligible, who has access, what are the requirements to get access? Can you get excluded? One type of criticism that has been formulated against the notion of civil society is that it excludes women (Pateman, 1988). Are there any rules in civil society, and who controls collective resources and resources of power? These are all questions that are reasonable to ask about civil society.

Uncivil Organizations?

Like much organization theory, theories about civil society are normative. The theory is about how things should be to achieve certain qualities or values. In much organization theory it is easy to recognize the main themes characterizing the thinking about civil society. There are many ideas around, and many concepts have been invented to describe the dream of the zipless organization, the organization as a creation where individual affiliates are coordinated into a 'fused group' (Sartre, 1976) without ever losing their individual autonomy and creativity. To reach such a state of affairs one cannot force people to participate and it is not enough to offer monetary rewards. Chester Barnard (1968: 148) has described this state as 'the condition of communion' involving a feeling of personal comfort in social relations, solidarity and providing opportunity for comradeship. 'The need for communion is a basis of informal organization that is essential to the operation of every formal organization' (1968: 148). The dilemma of seeking to achieve spontaneous involvement in organizational activities has also been analyzed as the need for irrational organizations (Brunsson, 1985).

The message is similar in arguments in favor of industrial democracy. Participative democracy can be seen as an outstanding method to achieve mobilization of resources, loyalty and support towards decisions (see Gustavsen, 1992: 120). Gustavsen (1992: 3) also talks about the importance of a democratic dialogue within work organizations as an exchange of ideas and arguments.

Adhocracy is a term to denote a new kind of business organization that seems to keep a delicate balance between individual affiliates and the collective effort of all through an organic structure and decentralization without a single concentration of power (see Mintzberg, 1979: 459). An adhocracy seems to fit well with ideas pertaining to civil society. Among the preconditions for the emergence of adhocracies are dynamic and complex environments that make the organization dependent on the information from each individual employee. Adhocracies often have a large share of employees with expert knowledge. Civil relations within an adhocracy are contingent on the special environment and the tasks of such an organization. This form of organization, however, is often not very stable. According to Mintzberg (1979: 455) it is 'difficult to keep any structure in that state for long periods of time'. There is a tendency in such an organization to 'bureaucratize itself as it ages' or to become dissolved. Adhocracies are short-lived either because they fail or because they succeed (1979: 456).

Ideas of informal or irrational organization and participative democracy are thoughts that pertain to relations and interactions inside business organizations that formulate the same questions as the discourse about civil society, i.e. the relation between private interests and external authority (Tester, 1992: 4). How to make people participate with a moral enthusiasm and at the same time follow orders and rules is in fact a common problem in much organization theory. The lesson from organization theory is that such states of affairs are very delicate indeed and difficult to achieve. Although they are not incompatible with organizational rules and control or with various forms of affiliation, instances of positive informal or irrational organization are short-lived. Is the establishment of civil society a way to make such processes survive?

Voluntary Associations and Social Movements

Voluntary associations have been designated to be the most typical organizational form of civil society. To what extent can voluntary associations be expected to constitute the cornerstones of civil society? First of all, the quality of voluntariness is definitely in accordance with the notions of civil society. In voluntary associations people cannot be forced to do things, since they always have the option to exit. Membership in voluntary associations also implies a notion of democracy and equality. All members have in principle equal rights to take part in decisions. In this sense voluntary associations combine freedom with equality, and they give preconditions for a democratic dialogue.

Yet, there are limits to the freedom and equality in voluntary associations. One such limit is the issue of affiliation. One cannot decide on one's own to become a member of a voluntary association. One has to apply and it is up to the other members to make decisions about affiliation. You need to embrace certain values, ideologies or ideas otherwise you will not be accepted as a member or you may be excluded. All voluntary associations are exclusive in this sense to a lesser or greater degree (Ahrne, 1994). There is also a certain amount of control in all voluntary associations. In many parties or churches the requirements on ideological consistency are strong, and many voluntary associations have sophisticated methods of monitoring through the requirements to attend meetings and ceremonies, for instance (Hechter, 1987).

One or two voluntary associations do not make a civil society. It takes a multitude of voluntary associations to make a civil society. But many voluntary associations also depend on the state for their activities and their aims are often directed at involving the state in their sphere of activities. Women's organizations put demands on the state to take measures in areas such as abortion, daycare or equal pay. Ecology organizations turn to the state for rigorous pollution standards or international agreements to protect the environment (Weir, 1993: 86–7). Thus, even if voluntary associations belong to civil society they cannot be understood without considering their relations with and dependence on the state.

It seems, however, that all voluntary associations do not necessarily fit into civil society. If they are too large or too hierarchical the civil standards may not be fulfilled. And this dilemma exists in nearly all voluntary associations. The contradictions within voluntary associations between the democratic decision process and the need for quick strategic decisions in a hostile environment that Robert Michels analyzed early this century are still there: all voluntary associations are ridden by a 'tendency to oligarchy' (1962: 70).

This may be one of the reasons why many proponents of civil society, instead of talking about voluntary associations, mention movements or new social movements as one of the main forms of civil society (see, for instance, Wolfe, 1989: 20). In contrast to voluntary associations, movements or new social movements are regarded as fluid and lacking boundaries and criteria of affiliation (see Dalton et al., 1990: 13). Movements are supposed to be less hierarchical and rigid. They are more flexible and are often described as spontaneous. Movements seem to fit in well with a notion of civil society.

Alberto Melucci (1988: 248–9) associates new movements with alternative cultures or lifestyles. Their activities are mainly symbolic challenges to existing relations of power, and they are not political in a traditional sense. Their arenas are 'public spaces independent of the institutions of government, the party system and state structures' (1988: 258). Such activities enable movements not to become institutionalized. At the same time movements emerge 'only in limited areas, for limited phases' (1988: 248).

In the reported research on new social movements it has been emphasized that in the long run when it comes to strategic decisions on the use of collective resources new social movements 'are faced with an insoluble predicament' (Kuechler and Dalton, 1990: 228). To be able to make such decisions, all types of movements have to set limits on who is allowed to participate. They are forced to abandon their openness and to construct criteria for affiliation. In this respect new social movements are no different from traditional voluntary associations. It may be argued that the character of movement is associated with the newness of the organization just as in the case of adhocracies. In the long run such movements or organizations will either be dissolved or turn into traditional voluntary associations. Many existing voluntary associations started as movements propagating and practicing an alternative lifestyle, for instance the Temperance Movement (Weir, 1993: 84). The emergence and development of movements is a cyclical phenomenon (1993: 90). Alain Touraine talks about the life and death of movements and about the natural history of social movements: 'Once relations become institutionalized, social movements degenerate into political pressure' (1981: 100). This is obvious if, for instance, we reflect on the history of the Solidarity movement in Poland, which was one of the foremost examples of movements in civil society during the 1980s (see Keane, 1988a: 5).

The organizational forms of civil society seem to be fragile. Voluntary associations are no guarantees for civil society, and new social movements are not very persistent. They necessarily grow old or perish. Moreover, voluntary associations are often intolerant, and members who do not have the right opinions or do not behave well will be excluded. Some of the fastest growing movements in the world today are religious fundamentalist movements of various creeds or ethnic movements with strong demands on their members in terms of ideological commitment and correct behavior.

Networks

Networks are another form of interaction that has been suggested as typical of and favorable for the establishment of civil society. Alan Wolfe mentions families and friendship networks as exemplary institutions of civil society, since 'it can only be within the intimate realm, surrounded by those we know and for whom we care, that we learn the art of understanding the moral positions of others' (1989: 233). And Pierre Rosanvallon (1988: 205) mentions mutual aid networks as alternatives to the state and the market for the provision of welfare. He acknowledges the rediscovery of 'underground networks of family solidarity' (1988: 208) as sources of economic support.

There are other types of network. Charles Perrow discusses small firm networks as a possible alternative for the return of civil society. According to Perrow, civil society has been weakened through the 'absorption of society by large organizations' (1993: 111). He describes civil society as 'that precious area outside the big organizations, public and private, an area with a minimum either of market-driven behavior or of hierarchy'. And he argues that small firm networks are 'linked together with a sense of community of fate' (1993: 132).

The appeal of networks seems to be great. In a network, relations between people are based not on calculation but on reciprocity. Relationships are more personal. Networks are supposed to be more flexible. 'Networks are "lighter on their feet" than hierarchies' (Powell, 1991: 271).

But what are the obstacles for establishing networks? If a network is such a nice form of interaction, why are there still so many other types of organization around? I will argue that there are clear limits to what networks can achieve. It is often said that networks are particularly useful when it comes to the efficient transaction of reliable information (1991: 272). But for the collection or distribution of other types of resources networks may be much less reliable.

Access to information may be restricted to people who are already within a network, since the specific information may give advantanges that would disappear if too many people had the same information. Yet, in principle, it is possible to give away and split information to a greater extent than in the case of resources such as food or money. That is one reason why the collection and distribution of the latter type of collective resources require another form of organization with stronger obligations and control.

Entries into networks are generally more selective and exclusive than entries into voluntary associations. Networks often imply particularism (1991: 273). If one needs to know the people, be their friends or be related to them to be able to enjoy the intriguing interaction of civil society, it will be an exclusive social establishment indeed. Maybe practices of civil society presuppose exclusivity. At least it is necessary to discuss the issue of affiliation in an assessment of the preconditions for civil society, i.e. 'the problem of identifying "the people" who may be members of a discursive public or a civil society' (Calhoun, 1993: 393).

Conclusions: The Fragility of Civil Society

How to establish conditions that will enable people to participate voluntarily, without being forced to or without thinking only about the money they will get, and still obey orders and follow rules they do not like themselves, is a salient dilemma for organization theories and proponents of civil society alike. In organization theory the notion of civility in interaction has been described as, for instance, a condition of communion, or as participative democracy. Adhocracies have been regarded as particularly civil organizations in this sense, as well as some voluntary associations, above all of the new social movement type. But adhocracies do not seem to last very long. They have a tendency to bureaucratize or dissolve. Social movements face the same problems, at least in hostile environments, through the contradiction between democratic participation and the need for quick decisions.

It seems to be as difficult to establish and reproduce a civil society as it is to establish and reproduce excellent organizations. In the notion of civil society there are inherent contradictions between reflexivity and order and between heterogeneity and equality (Tester, 1992: 130, 173). Activities in civil society cannot be comprehended without relating them to their necessary organizational forms. And none of the forms that have been mentioned in connection with civil society have proved to be without restrictions that are inherent in all organizations. Organizations tend to be rather uncivil. Equality presupposes some form of exclusivity. Networks are exclusive, as well as kinship relations and voluntary associations including social movements. The need to regulate affiliation to organizations is a threat towards the heterogeneity of civil society. The quality of civil society cannot exceed the qualities of its organizational forms.

A correspondence between reflexivity and order is only possible for short periods. The contradictory qualities of civil society can only emerge through the coincidence of parallel processes where heterogeneity and equality or reflexivity and order emanate from different sources. Once they have become dependent upon the same source, the same organizational structure, they will counteract each other and the result will be either dissolution or petrification of the interaction. A condition of communion needs to be reinforced from sources motivating participants outside the organization. It requires a precarious balance between centripetal and centrifugal forces that cannot be upheld through an inner logic (Ahrne, 1994). If a state of order is reached, people's motives and involvement will inevitably change.

Civil society as well as organizations need to be analyzed in a context of various forms of organizational and institutional arrangements. A civil participation is contingent on the flow of people and organizations in the environment, and it cannot be created, still less established. It happens through the coincidence of several processes in the interaction between people and organizations on certain occasions.

Probably every organization that collects and distributes collective resources in one form or another has to be exclusive. Thus, if we want civil society to be open we cannot expect activities involving the distribution of collective resources to be part of its agenda. For such purposes more resolute structures are required. Perhaps there are only certain types of activity that may take place in truly civil forms. It has been suggested that 'the heart of contemporary civil society is public discourse' (Alexander, 1992).

The original argument about civil society makes assertions about institutional arrangements in that it places civil society in contrast to the state. Yet, the analysis of organizational forms of civil society demonstrates that there are no single forms to assure a permanent establishment of a civil society. It has to be understood in the interplay between different organizational alternatives and processes. On the other hand, we can also conclude that there are no organizational forms as such that are completely incompatible with the notion of civil society. An occasional correspondence between reflexivity and order may happen in all kinds of organizational forms, including states and business enterprises, depending upon the organizational constellation and the timing of events. The motives and the morale of participants emerge in their encounter with all kinds of institutions and organizations. The notion of civil society cannot be grasped inside any special type of organization – only in the interaction between a multitude of organizational forms.

References

Ahrne, Göran (1994) *Social Organizations: Interaction Inside, Outside and Between Organizations*. London: Sage.

Alexander, Jeffrey (1992) 'Comment'. American Sociological Association, unpublished manuscript.

Barnard, Chester (1968) *The Functions of the Executive*. Cambridge, MA: Harvard University Press.

Brunsson, Nils (1985) *The Irrational Organization: Irrationality as a Basis for Organizational Action and Change*. Chichester: Wiley.

Calhoun, Craig (1993) 'Nationalism and Civil Society: Democracy, Diversity and Self-Determination', *International Sociology*, 8 (4): 387–412.

Dalton, Russel J., Kuechler, Manfred and Burklin, Wilhelm (1990) 'The Challenge of New Movements', in Russel J. Dalton and Manfred Kuechler (eds), *Challenging the Political Order: New Social and Political Movements in Western Democracies*. Cambridge: Polity.

Etzioni, Amitai (1993) *The Spirit of Community: Rights, Responsibilities, and the Communitarian Agenda*. New York: Crown.

Gustavsen, Björn (1992) *Dialogue and Development: Theory of Communication, Action Research and the Restructuring of Working Life*. Assen: Van Gorcum.

Hechter, Michael (1987) *Principles of Group Solidarity*. Berkeley, CA: University of California Press.

Heydebrand, Wolf (1989) 'New Organizational Forms', *Work and Occupations*, 16 (3): 323–57.

Keane, John (1988a) 'Introduction', in John Keane (ed.), *Civil Society and the State: New European Perspectives*. London: Verso.

Keane, John (1988b) 'Despotism and Democracy', in John Keane (ed.), *Civil Society and the State: New European Perspectives*. London: Verso.

Keeley, Michael (1988) *A Social-Contract Theory of Organizations*. Notre Dame, IN: University of Notre Dame Press.

Kuechler, Manfred and Dalton, Russel, J. (1990) 'New Social Movements and the Political Order: Inducing Change for Long-Term Stability?', in Russel J. Dalton and Manfred Kuechler (eds), *Challenging the Political Order: New Social and Political Movements in Western Democracies*. Cambridge: Polity.

Melucci, Alberto (1988) 'Social Movements and the Democratization of Everyday Life', in John Keane (ed.), *Civil Society and the State: New European Perspectives*. London: Verso.

Michels, Robert (1962) *Political Parties*. New York: Free Press.

Mintzberg, Henry (1979) *The Structuring of Organizations*. Englewood Cliffs, NJ: Prentice-Hall.

Pateman, Carole (1988) 'The Fraternal Social Contract', in John Keane (ed.), *Civil Society and the State: New European Perspectives*. London: Verso.

Perrow, Charles (1993) 'Small Firm Networks', in Sven-Erik Sjöstrand (ed.), *Institutional Change: Theory and Empirical Findings*. Armonk, NY: Sharpe.

Powell, Walter W. (1991) 'Neither Market nor Hierarchy: Network Forms of Organization', in Grahame Thompson, Jennifer Frances, Rosalind Levacic and Jeremy Mitchell (eds), *Markets, Hierarchies and Networks: The Coordination of Social Life*. London: Sage.

Rosanvallon, Pierre (1988) 'The Decline of Social Visibility', in John Keane (ed.), *Civil Society and the State: New European Perspectives*. London: Verso.

Sartre, Jean-Paul (1976) *Critique of Dialectical Reason 1: Theory of Practical Ensembles*. London: New Left Books.

Tester, Keith (1992) *Civil Society*. London: Routledge.

Touraine, Alain (1981) *The Voice and the Eye: An Analysis of Social Movements*. Cambridge: Cambridge University Press.

Weir, Lorna (1993) 'Limitations of New Social Movement Analysis', *Studies in Political Economy*, 40 (Spring): 73–102.

Wolfe, Alan (1989) *Whose Keeper? Social Science and Moral Obligation*. Berkeley, CA: University of California Press.

PART II

BIFURCATING DISCOURSES

6

Citizen and Enemy as Symbolic Classification: On the Polarizing Discourse of Civil Society

Jeffrey C. Alexander

Sociologists have written much about the social forces that create conflict and polarize society, about interests and structures of political, economic, racial, ethnic, religious, and gender groups. But they have said very little about the construction, destruction, and deconstruction of civic solidarity itself. They are generally silent about the sphere of fellow feeling that makes society into society and about the processes that fragment it.[1]

I would like to approach this sphere of fellow feeling from the concept of 'civil society'. Civil society, of course, has been a topic of enormous discussion and dispute throughout the history of social thought. Marx and critical theory have employed the concept to theorize the very lack of community, the world of egoistic, self-regulating individuals produced by capitalist production. I am relying for my understanding of the term on a different tradition, on the line of democratic, liberal thought that extended from the seventeenth century to the early nineteenth, an age of democratic theorizing that was supplanted by industrial capitalism and the concern with 'the social question' (cf. Keane, 1988a; 1988b; Cohen, 1982).

I will define *civil society* as a sphere or subsytem of society that is analytically and, to various degrees, empirically separated from the spheres of political, economic, and religious life (see Alexander, 1995, 1997). Civil society is a sphere of solidarity in which abstract universalism and particularistic versions of community are tensely intertwined. It is both a normative and a real concept. It allows the relation between universal individual rights and particularistic restrictions on these rights to be studied empirically, as the conditions that determine the status of civil society itself.

Civil society depends on resources, or inputs, from these other spheres, from political life, from economic institutions, from broad cultural discussion, from territorial organization, and from primordiality. In a causal sense, civil society is dependent on these spheres, but only by what Parsons called a 'combinatorial logic'. Civil society – and the groups, individuals, and actors who represent their interests in this system's terms – pulls together these inputs according to the logic and demands of its particular situation. This is to say that the solidary sphere that we call civil society has relative autonomy and can be studied in its own right (cf. Durkheim, [1893] 1933; Parsons, 1967; 1977).

Against the new utilitarianism (for example, Coleman, 1990; cf. Alexander, 1992) and critical theory (Habermas, 1988) alike, therefore, I wish to defend the position that there is, indeed, a *society* that can be defined in moral terms. The stipulations of this moral community articulate with (not determine) organizations and the exercise of power via institutions like constitutions and legal codes on the one hand, and 'office' on the other. Civil society also has organizations of its own: the courts, institutions of mass communication, and public opinion polls are all significant examples. Civil society is constituted by its own distinctive structure of elites, not only by functional oligarchies that control the legal and communications systems, but by those that exercise power and identity through voluntary organizations ('dignitaries' or 'public servants') and social movements ('movement intellectuals': Eyerman and Jamison, 1991).

But civil society is not merely an institutional realm. It is also a realm of structured, socially established consciousness, a network of understandings that operates beneath and above explicit institutions and the self-conscious interests of elites. To study this subjective dimension of civil society we must recognize and focus on the distinctive symbolic codes that are critically important in constituting the very sense of society for those who are within and without it. These codes are so sociologically important, I would argue, that every study of social/sectional/subsystem conflict must be complemented by reference to this civil symbolic sphere.

The codes supply the structured categories of pure and impure into which every member, or potential member, of civil society is made to fit. It is in terms of symbolic purity and impurity that centrality is defined, that marginal demographic status is made meaningful and high position understood as deserved or illegitimate. Pollution is a threat to any allocative system; its sources must either be kept at bay or transformed by communicative actions, like rituals and social movements, into a pure form.

Despite their enormous behavioral impact, however, pure and impure categories do not develop merely as generalizations or inductions from structural position or individual behavior. They are imputations that are induced, via analogy and metaphor, from the internal logic of the symbolic code. For this reason, the internal structure of the civil code must become an object of study in itself. Just as there is no developed religion that does not divide the world into the saved and the damned, there is no civil discourse that does not conceptualize the world into those who deserve inclusion and those who do not.[2] Members of national communities firmly believe that 'the world', and this notably includes their own nation, is filled with people who either do not deserve freedom and communal support or are not capable of sustaining them (in part because they are immoral egoists). Members of national communities do not want to 'save' such persons. They do not wish to include them, protect them, or offer them rights because they conceive them as being unworthy and amoral, as in some sense 'uncivilized'.[3]

This distinction is not 'real'. Actors are not intrinsically either worthy or moral: they are determined to be so by being placed in certain positions on the grid of civil culture. When citizens make judgments about who should be included in civil society and who should not, about who is a friend and who is an enemy, they draw on a systematic, highly elaborated symbolic code. This symbolic structure was already clearly implied in the very first philosophical thinking about democratic societies that emerged in ancient Greece. Since the Renaissance it has permeated popular thinking and behavior, even while its centrality in philosophical thinking has continued to be sustained. The symbolic structure takes different forms in different nations, and it is the historical residue of diverse movements in social, intellectual, and religious life – of classical ideas, republicanism and Protestantism, Enlightenment and liberal thought, of the revolutionary and common law traditions. The cultural implications of these variegated movements, however, have been drawn into a highly generalized symbolic system that divides civic virtue from civic vice in a remarkably stable and consistent way. It is for this reason that, despite divergent historical roots and variations in national elaborations, the language that forms the cultural core of civil society can be isolated as a general structure and studied as a relatively autonomous symbolic form.[4]

The basic elements of this structure can be understood semiotically: they are sets of homologies, which create likenesses between various terms of social description and prescription; and antipathies, which establish antagonisms between these terms and other sets of symbols. Those who consider themselves worthy members of a national community (as most persons do, of course) define themselves in terms of the positive side of this symbolic set; they define those who are not deemed worthy in terms of the bad. It is fair to say, indeed, that members of a community 'believe in' both the positive and the negative sides, that they employ both as viable normative evaluations of political communities. For the members of every democratic society, both the positive and the negative symbolic sets are thought to be realistic descriptions of individual and social life.[5]

The binary discourse occurs at three levels: motives, relations, and insititutions. The motives of political actors are clearly conceptualized (What kind of people are they?) along with the social relations and institutions they are capable of sustaining. [6]

Let us first discuss motives. Code and counter-code posit human nature in diametrically opposed ways. Because democracy depends on self-control and individual initiatives, the people who compose it are described as being capable of activism and autonomy rather than as being passive and dependent. They are seen as rational and reasonable rather than as irrational and hysterical, as calm rather than excited, as controlled rather than passionate, as sane and realistic, not as given to fantasy or as mad. Democratic discourse, then, posits the following qualities as axiomatic: activism, autonomy, rationality, reasonableness, calm, control, realism, and sanity. The nature of the counter-code, the discourse that justifies the restriction of civil society, is already clearly implied. If actors are passive and dependent, irrational and hysterical, excitable, passionate, unrealistic, or mad, they cannot be allowed the freedom that democracy allows. On the contrary, these persons deserve to be repressed, not only for the sake of civil society, but for their own sakes as well. These qualities are schematized in Table 6.1.

On the basis of such contradictory codes about human motives, distinctive representations of social relationships can be built. Democratically motivated persons – persons who are active, autonomous, rational, reasonable, calm, and realistic – will be capable of forming open social relationships rather than secretive ones; they will be trusting rather than suspicious, straightforward rather than calculating, truthful rather than deceitful. Their decisions will be based on open deliberation rather than conspiracy, and their attitude

Table 6.1   *The discursive structure of social motives*

Democratic code	Counter-democratic code
Activism	Passivity
Autonomy	Dependence
Rationality	Irrationality
Reasonableness	Hysteria
Calm	Excitable
Self-control	Passionate
Realistic	Unrealistic
Sane	Mad

toward authority will be critical rather than deferential. In their behavior toward other community members they will be bound by conscience and honor rather than by greed and self-interest, and they will treat their fellows as friends rather than enemies.

If actors are irrational, dependent, passive, passionate, and unrealistic, on the other hand, the social relationships they form will be characterized by the second side of these fateful dichotomies. Rather than open and trusting relationships, they will form secret societies that are premised on their suspicion of other human beings. To the authority within these secret societies they will be deferential, but to those outside their tiny group they will behave in a greedy and self-interested way. They will be conspiratorial, deceitful toward others, and calculating in their behavior, conceiving of those outside their group as enemies. If the positive side of this second discourse set describes the symbolic qualities necessary to sustain civil society, the negative side describes a solidary structure in which mutual respect and expansive social integration has been broken down (see Table 6.2).

Table 6.2   *The discursive structure of social relationships*

Democratic code	Counter-democratic code
Open	Secret
Trusting	Suspicious
Critical	Deferential
Honorable	Self-interested
Conscience	Greed
Truthful	Deceitful
Straightforward	Calculating
Deliberative	Conspiratorial
Friend	Enemy

Given the discursive structure of motives and civic relationships, it should not be surprising that this set of homologies and antipathies extends to the social understanding of political and legal insitutions themselves. If members of a national community are irrational in motive and distrusting in social relationships, they will naturally create institutions that are aribitrary rather than rule regulated, that emphasize brute power rather than law and hierarchy rather than equality, that are exclusive rather than inclusive and promote personal loyalty over impersonal and contractual obligation, that are regulated by personalities rather than by office obligations, and that are organized by faction rather than by groups that are responsible to the needs of the community as a whole (see Table 6.3).

These three sets of discursive structures are tied together. Indeed, every element in any one of the sets can be linked via analogical relations – homologous relations of likeness – to any element in another set on the same side. 'Rule regulated', for example, a key element in the symbolic understanding of democratic social institutions, is considered homologous – synonymous or mutually reinforcing in a cultural sense – with 'truthful' and 'open', terms that define social relationships, and with 'reasonable' and 'autonomous', elements from the symbolic set that stipulates democratic motives. In the same manner, any element from any set on one side is taken to be antithetical to any element from any set on the other. According to the rules of this broader cultural formation, for example, 'hierarchy' is thought to be inimical to 'critical' and 'open' and also to 'activistic' and 'self-controlled'.

When they are presented in their simple binary forms, these cultural codes appear merely schematic. In fact, however, they reveal the skeletal structures on which social communities build the familiar stories, the rich narrative forms, that guide their everyday, taken-for-granted political life.[7] The positive side of these structured sets provides the elements for the comforting and inspiring story of a

Table 6.3   *The discursive structure of social institutions*

Democratic code	Counter-democratic code
Rule regulated	Arbitrary
Law	Power
Equality	Hierarchy
Inclusive	Exclusive
Impersonal	Personal
Contractual	Ascriptive loyalty
Social groups	Factions
Office	Personality

democratic, free, and spontaneously integrated social order, a civil society in an ideal-typical sense. People are rational, can process information intelligently and independently, know the truth when they see it, do not need strong leaders, can engage in criticism, and easily coordinate their own society. Law is not an external mechanism that coerces people but an expression of their innate rationality, mediating between truth and mundane events. Office is an institutional mechanism that mediates between law and action. It is a calling, a vocation to which persons adhere because of their trust and reason. Those who know the truth do not defer to authorities, nor are they loyal to particular persons. They obey their conscience rather than follow their vulgar interest; they speak plainly rather than conceal their ideas; they are open, idealistic, and friendly toward their fellow human beings.

The structure and narrative of political virtue form the discourse of liberty. This discourse is embodied in the founding documents of democratic societies. In America, for example, the Bill of Rights postulates 'the right of people to be secure against unreasonable searches' and guarantees that 'no person shall be deprived of liberty without due process of law.' In so doing it ties rights to reasons and liberty to law. The discourse is also embodied in the great and the little stories that democratic nations tell about themselves, for example, in the American story about George Washington and the cherry tree, which highlights honesty and virtue, or in English accounts of the Battle of Britain, which reveal the courage, self-sufficiency, and spontaneous cooperation of the British in contrast to the villainous forces of Hitlerian Germany.

Whatever institutional or narrative form it assumes, the discourse of liberty centers on the capacity for voluntarism. Action is voluntary if it is intended by rational actors who are in full control of body and mind. If action is not voluntary, it is deemed to be worthless. If laws do not facilitate the achievement of freely intended action, they are discriminatory. If confessions of guilt are coerced rather than freely given, they are polluted.[8] If a social group is constituted under the discourse of liberty, it must be given social rights because the members of this group are conceived of as possessing the capacity for voluntary action. Political struggles over the status of lower-class groups, racial and ethnic minorities, women, children, criminals, and the mentally, emotionally, and physically handicapped have always involved discursive struggles over whether the discourse of liberty can be extended and applied. In so far as the founding constitutional documents of democratic societies are universalistic, they implicitly stipulate that the discourse can and must be.

The elements on the negative side of these symbolic sets are also tightly intertwined. They provide the elements for the plethora of taken-for-granted stories that permeate democratic understanding of the negative and repugnant sides of community life. Taken together, these negative structures and narratives form the 'discourse of repression'. If people do not have the capacity for reason, if they cannot rationally process information and cannot tell truth from falseness, then they will be loyal to leaders for purely personal reasons and will be easily manipulated by them in turn. Because such persons are ruled by calculation rather than by conscience, they are without the honor that is critical in democratic affairs. Since they have no honor, they do not have the capacity to regulate their own affairs. It is because of this situation that such persons subject themselves to hierarchical authority. These anti-civil qualities make it necessary to deny such persons access to rights and the protection of law.[9] Indeed, because they lack the capacity for both voluntary and responsible behavior, these marginal members of the national community – those who are unfortunate enough to be constructed under the counter-democratic code – must ultimately be repressed. They cannot be regulated by law, nor will they accept the discipline of office. Their loyalties can be only familial and particularistic. The institutional and legal boundaries of civil society, it is widely believed, can provide no bulwark against their lust for personal power.

The positive side of this discursive formation is viewed by the members of democratic communities as a source not only of purity but also of purification. The discourse of liberty is taken to sum up 'the best' in a civil community, and its tenets are considered to be sacred. The objects that the discourse creates seem to possess an awesome power that places them at the 'center' of society, a location – sometimes geographic, often stratificational, always symbolic – that compels their defense at almost any cost. The negative side of this symbolic formation is viewed as profane. Representing the 'worst' in the national community, it embodies evil. The objects it identifies threaten the core community from somewhere outside it. From this marginal position, they present a powerful source of pollution.[10] To be close to these polluted objects – the actors, structures, and processes that are constituted by this repressive discourse – is dangerous. Not only can one's reputation be sullied and one's status endangered, but one's very security can be threatened as well. To have one's self or movement be identified in terms of these objects causes anguish, disgust, and alarm. This code is taken to be a threat to the very center of civil society itself.

Public figures and events must be categorized in terms of one side of this discursive formation or the other, although, when politics functions routinely, such classifications are neither explicit nor subject to extended public debate.[11] Even in routine periods, however, it is their specification within the codes of this underlying discourse that gives political things meaning and allows them to assume the role they seem 'naturally' to have.[12] Even when they are aware that they are struggling over these classifications, moreover, most political actors do not recognize that it is they who are creating them. Such knowledge would relativize reality, creating an uncertainty that could undermine not only the cultural core but also the institutional boundaries and solidarity of civil society itself. Social events and actors seem to 'be' these qualities, not to be labeled by them.

The discourse of civil society, in other words, is concrete, not abstract. It is elaborated by narrative accounts that are believed to describe not only the present but also the past faithfully. Every nation has a myth of origin, for example, that anchors this discourse in an account of the historical events involved in its early formation.[13] Like their English compatriots, early Americans believed their rights to have emerged from the ancient constitution of eleventh-century Anglo-Saxons.[14] The specifically American discourse of liberty was first elaborated in accounts of Puritan saints and later in stories about revolutionary heroes. It was woven into the myth of the yeoman farmer and then into tales about cowboys and still later into pulp stories about detectives and the malcontents they hoped to ferret out. The discourse of repression was made palpable through early religious accounts of miscreants and stories about loyalists and aristocrats in the Revolutionary War. Later it was elaborated in accounts of wild Indians and 'popist' immigrants and then in regional myths about treason during the Civil War.[15]

For contemporary Americans, the categories of the pure and the polluted discourses seem to exist in just as natural and fully historical a way. Democratic law and procedures are seen as having been won by the voluntary struggles of the founding fathers and guaranteed by historical documents like the Bill of Rights and the Constitution. The qualities of the repressive code are embodied in the dark visions of tyranny and lawlessness, whether those of eighteenth-century British monarchs or Soviet communists. Pulp fiction and highbrow drama seek to counterpose these dangers with compelling images of the good.[16] When works of the imagination represent the discursive formation in a paradigmatic way, they become contemporary classics. For the generation that matured during World War II, for example, George Orwell's *Nineteen Eighty-Four* made the discourse of repression emblematic of the struggles of their time.

Within the confines of a particular national community, the binary codes and concrete representations that make up the discourse of civil society are not usually divided up between different social groups. To the contrary, even in societies that are rent by intensive social conflict, the constructions of both civic virtue and civic vice are in most cases widely accepted.[17] What is contested in the course of civic life, what is not at all consensual, is how the antithetical sides of this discourse, its two symbolic sets, will be applied to particular actors and groups. If most of the members of democratic society accepted the 'validity' and 'reality' of *Nineteen Eighty-Four*, they disagreed fundamentally over its relevant social application. Radicals and liberals were inclined to see the book as describing the already repressive or at least imminent tendencies of their own capitalist societies; conservatives understood the work as referring to communism alone.

Of course, some events are so gross or so sublime that they generate almost immediate consensus about how the symbolic sets should be applied. For most members of a national community, great national wars clearly demarcate the good and the bad. The nation's soldiers are taken to be courageous embodiments of the discourse of liberty; the foreign nations and soldiers who oppose them are deemed to represent some potent combination of the counter-democratic code.[18] In the course of American history, this negative code has, in fact, been extended to a vast and variegated group, to the British, native peoples, pirates, the South and the North, Africans, old European nations, fascists, communists, Germans, and Japanese. Identification in terms of the discourse of repression is essential if vengeful combat is to be pursued. Once this polluting discourse is applied, it becomes impossible for good people to treat and reason with those on the other side. If one's opponents are beyond reason, deceived by leaders who operate in secret, the only option is to read them out of the human race. When great wars are successful, they provide powerful narratives that dominate the nation's post-war life. Hitler and Nazism formed the backbone of a huge array of Western myth and stories, providing master metaphors for everything from profound discussions about the 'final solution' to the good-guy/bad-guy plots of television dramas and situation comedies.

For most events, however, discursive identity is contested. Political fights are, in part, about how to distribute actors across the structure of discourse, for there is no determined relation between any event or group and either side of the cultural scheme. Actors struggle to taint one another with the brush of repression and to wrap themselves in the rhetoric of liberty. In periods of tension and crisis, political struggle becomes a matter of how far and to whom the discourses of liberty and repression apply. The effective cause of victory and defeat, imprisonment and freedom, sometimes even of life and death, is often discursive domination, which depends on just how popular narratives about good and evil are extended. Is it protesting students who are like Nazis or the conservatives who are pursuing them? Are members of the Communist Party to be understood as fascistic or the members of the House Un-American Activities Committee who interrogate them? When Watergate began, only the actual burglars were called conspirators and polluted by the discourse of repression. George McGovern and his fellow Democrats were unsuccessful in their efforts to apply this discourse to the White House, executive staff, and Republican Party, elements of civil society that succeeded in maintaining their identity in liberal terms. At a later point in the crisis, such a reassuring relation to the culture structure no longer held.

The general discursive structure, in other words, is used to legitimate friends and delegitimate opponents in the course of real historical time. If an independent civil society were to be fully maintained, of course, the discourse of repression would be applied only in highly circumscribed ways, to groups like children and criminals who are not usually taken to be in sufficient possession of their rational or moral faculties. It is often the case, indeed, that individuals and groups within civil society will be able to sustain the discourse of liberty over a significant period. They will be able to understand their opponents as other rational individuals without indulging in moral annihilation.

Over an extended historical period, however, it is impossible for the discourse of repression not to be brought into significant play and for opponents to be understood as enemies of the most threatened kind. It may be the case, of course, that the opponents are, in fact, ruthless enemies of the public good. The Nazis were moral idiots, and it was wrong to deal with them as potential civic participants, as Chamberlain and the other appeasers did. The discourse of repression is applied, however, whether its objects are really evil or not, eventually creating an objective reality where none had existed before. The symbolism of evil that had been applied by the Allies in an overzealous way to the German nation in World War I was extended indiscriminately to the German people and governments of the post-war period. It produced the debilitating reparations policy that helped establish the economic and social receptiveness to Nazism.

This points to the fact that the social application of polarizing symbolic identifications must also be understood in terms of the internal structure of the discourse itself. Rational, individualistic, and self-critical societies are vulnerable because these very qualities make them open and trusting, and if the other side is devoid of redeeming social qualities, then trust will be abused in the most merciless terms. The potential for dependent and irrational behavior, moreover, can be found even in good citizens themselves, for deceptive information can be provided that might lead them, on what would seem to be rational grounds, to turn away from the structures or processes of democratic society itself. In other words, the very qualities that allow civil societies to be internally democratic – qualities that include the symbolic oppositions that allow liberty to be defined in any meaningful way – mean that the members of civil society do not feel confident that they can deal effectively with their opponents, from either within or without. The discourse of repression is inherent in the discourse of liberty. This is the irony at the heart of the discourse of civil society.

Notes

Published in M. Lamont and M. Fournier (eds), *Cultivating Differences* (University of Chicago Press, 1992). Sections have earlier appeared in Italian (Alexander, 1990b).

1 For a general discussion of the poverty of recent social scientific treatments of politics and democracy in particular, from a perspective that emphasizes the importance of the civil sphere, see Alexander (1990a).

2 In this sense (cf. Barthes, 1977), there is a 'structure' and a 'narrative' to the discourse of civil society. The first, the binary discourse that describes those who are in and those who are out, should be theorized in terms of the legacy of the Durkheimian tradition. As I have argued elsewhere (Alexander, 1982; 1988a), Durkheim's ambition was to create a theory of 'religious society', not a social theory of religion, and his major contribution in this regard was his conceptualization of the sacred and the profane as the primitive elements of social classification. The narrative element of contemporary discourse can be taken from Weber's historical investigations into what Eisenstadt (1986) has called the religions of the Axial Age. Weber's principal insight in this regard (cf. Alexander, 1989b) was that these religions introduced a fateful tension between this world and the next that could be resolved only through salvation and that, henceforth, a focus on eschatology and theodicy dominated the religious consciousness of the age. It is a relatively simple thing to see how Durkheim's structural categories provide the reference points for the journey of salvation that Weber describes. (For the prominence in historical religions of the devil imagery, see Russell, 1988).

The central challenge for developing a useful symbolic approach to politics is to translate the understanding and relevance of this classical sociological work on the centrality of religion in traditional society into a framework that is relevant for contemporary secular societies. This means going beyond the overly cognitive emphasis of semiotic and poststructuralist analysis – from Lévi-Strauss to Michel Foucault – that typically highlights 'discourse' in a manner that removes it from ethical and moral concerns and from affectivity as well. This removal is one problem with the recent 'linguistics turn' in history, which in so many other respects is vital and important.

3 Rogin's (1987) is the only body of social scientific work of which I am aware that seeks to place this concern with the projection of unworthiness at the center of the political process. He describes his work as the study of 'demonology'. From my perspective, there remain several problems with this serious investigation. (1) Because Rogin's conception of motive is psychological – he does look at social structure – he provides no independent analysis of symbolic patterns. (2) Because he focuses exclusively on overt practices of violent domination – particularly of American whites over Native Americans – he fails to tie demonology to either the theory or the practice of civil society, which can and does allow the inclusion as well as the exclusion of social groups. (3) Because Rogin studies exclusively oppressed groups, he locates his terminology in terms of the aberrant behavior of conservatives, whereas it is just as common among left-wing and centralist forces.

4 This broad argument, of course, cannot even begin to be supported in the present essay. The focus on particular strands of culture that actually have caused or underlain the specific democratic traditions and structures of particular nations has generated a vast field of scholarship for most of this century, singling out specific religious, social, and intellectual movements, influential thinkers, and great books. In American political historiography, for example, one can trace the debate between those who emphasize Locke, like Louis Hart, those who emphasize Puritanism, like Perry Miller, and those who emphasize republicanism, like Bernard Bailyn and J.G.A. Pocock.

When one surveys even a small part of this enormous historiographic field, the dangers of examining only particular causal studies at the expense of broader hermeneutic constructions soon become apparent. It seems clear that many different historical movements contributed to the emergence of democratic discourse and practice and that, indeed, each is responsible for the particular emphasis, constructions, and metaphors that make every national and even regional configuration of democracy unique. At the same time, it is also clear that there is an overarching 'structure' of democratic discourse that is more general and inclusive than any of these particular parts. In one sense, this structure actually preceded these early modern and modern movements because it was already formed in its broad outlines in ancient Greece. More important, this structure is more general because its broader range is implied by the 'silences', the 'what is not said', of each particular positive formulation of freedom and civility. This is the advantage of the dualistic approach recommended here.

5 It is precisely this dualistic, or, in Hegel's sense, dialectical quality of symbolic systems that discussions of culture in modern society have generally overlooked. Whether framed as 'values', 'orientations', or 'ideologies', culture has been treated in a one-sided and often highly idealized way. Not only has such an approach made culture less relevant to the study of social conflict, but it has also produced an atomistic and ultimately fragmented understanding of culture itself. Whether in the writings of Parsons, Bellah, and Kluckhohn on the one hand, or Marx, Althusser, and Gramsci on the other, culture is identified in terms of discrete normative ideals about the right and the good. Certainly, political culture is normative and evaluative. What is vital to recognize, however, is that this quality does not mean that it is either one-sided or idealized. To the contrary, as structuralists from Saussure to Barthes and Lévi-Strauss would insist, political culture has a binary structure, a structure that I view as establishing the categories of sacred and profane of civic life. Indeed, it is only within

the contradictory pull of these oppositional forces that the cultural dynamics of the political world emerge. From the perspective offered here, it is precisely this dualistic or 'dialectical' quality of symbolic systems that discussions of culture in modern society have generally overlooked.

From the perspective offered here, all cultural systems involve an inherent strain, or tension, as each side of the duality that is culture gives rise – indeed, necessitates – its moral, cognitive, and affective antithesis. Because this internal dynamism is overlooked, cultural analysis is too often taken to imply a static approach to society, in contrast to social structural analysis, which typically focuses on conflicts between institutions and groups. When those who acknowledge the importance of culture do focus on dynamics, they typically do so by analyzing the tension between internally integrated cultural patterns and a society that fails to supply the resources necessary to fulfill (institutionalize) them. This leads to discussions about the failure of socialization and the breakdown of social control, which focus primarily on the social rather than cultural sources of conflict and strain and give an unrealistically utopian, or reformist, picture of the opportunities for creating an integrated and non-conflictual society. Of course, there have been a number of students of culture who have recognized internal strains, but they have done so in a manner that portrays these divisions as historically contingent and reflecting social conflict and, therefore, as associated only with particular cultural systems of passing phases of development (e.g. the work of Raymond, Gramsci, and Bourdieu).

6 The following discussion can only appear schematic. It summarizes an ongoing exploration into the elementary structures that inform the complex and messy mixture of meaning and motives that form the basis for civic cultural life. I want to stress that, despite their schematic form, these models of structure have not been deduced from some overarching theory of action, culture, or democratic societies. Rather, they have been induced from three different sources: (1) American popular magazines, newspapers, and television news reports during the period 1960–80 (see, for example, Alexander, 1989a); (2) an examination of popular discourse, as recorded in secondary and primary material, during crisis periods of American history from the Revolution through Contragate (Alexander and Smith, 1992); and (3) an examination of some of the principal themes and symbolic structures of Western political philosophy.

One qualification that must be registered at this point concerns the boundary at which these codes cease to compel and the codes that inform other kinds of (presumably non-civil) societies begin. For example, many modernizing but non-democratic theories and movements employ much the same set of binary oppositions while placing their emphasis on a different side. Fascist and Nazi societies and capitalist and communist dictatorships employ related types of codes, although they differ in strategic ways (Lefort, 1988). What all these societies have in common with democratic societies is some degree of what must very awkwardly be called 'modernity', a social-cum-cultural complex that emphasizes rationality and self-control, two elements of what I will describe as the discourse of liberty. Communist and fascist dictatorships combine these elements with a collectivist, or corporeal, emphasis that belies the individualistic emphasis of the civil society code; both, in their revolutionary emphases, also exalt a vitalistic, and irrational, approach to action.

7 To translate fully into an understanding of the discursive nature of everyday life, in other words, semiotic or structural analysis must give way to narrative analysis. Narrative transforms the static dualities of structure into patterns that can account for the chronological ordering of lived experience that has always been an essential element in human history (see Ricoeur, 1984; Entrikin, 1990).

8 Until the twentieth century, confession was apparently a uniquely Western phenomenon, one that emerged in tandem with the gradual social recognition of the centrality of individual rights and self-control for the organization of political and religious societies. At least from the Middle Ages on, criminal punishment was not considered to be fully successful until the accused had confessed his or her crimes since only this confession demonstrated that rationality had been achieved and individual responsibility assumed. The discourse of civil society is, therefore, inextricably tied to public confession of crimes against the individuals that compose the collectivity and, indeed, of crimes against the collectivity itself. This is demonstrated by the great effort that is expended on extorting fraudulent confessions in those situations where coercive force has obliterated civility, as in instances of political brutality in democratic societies and show trials in dictatorships (see Hepworth and Turner, 1982).

9 In discussing this process, Aristotle (1962: 109) combined different references from different levels of civil discourse: 'The name of citizen is particularly applicable to those who share in the offices and honors of the state. Homer accordingly speaks in the *Iliad* of a man being treated "like an alien man, *without honor*", and it is true that those who do not share in the offices and honors of the state are just like resident aliens. To deny men a share [may sometimes be justified, but] when it is done by subterfuge its only object is merely that of hoodwinking others.' Aristotle's translator, Ernest Barker, footnotes this discussion with a comment that illustrates the rule of homology I am suggesting here, according to which concepts like honor, citizenship, and office are effectively interchangeable: 'The Greek word *time* which is here used means, like the Latin *honos*, both "office" and "honor". The passage in the *Iliad* refers to honor in the latter sense: Aristotle himself is using it in the former; but it is natural to slide from one into the other.'

10 The role of the sacred and profane in structuring primitive consciousness, action, and cosmology is widely understood. See, for example, the classic exposition by Durkheim ([1912] 1963) in *The Elementary Forms* and its important reformulation in Caillois (1959), the provocative treatment of archaic religion by Eliade (1959), and the powerful overview provided by Franz Steiner (1956). The challenge, again, is to find a way to translate these understandings of religious processes into a secular frame of reference.

11 'In an existing ethical order in which a complete system of ethical relations has been developed and actualized, virtue in the strict sense of the word is in place and actually appears only in exceptional circumstances when one obligation clashes with another' (Hegel, 1952: 108).

12 The omnipresence of cultural frames within even the most mundane political process is powerfully argued by Bennett (1979). The 'naturalness' of cultural codes is argued here from the macroscopic perspective. From the perspective of individual interaction, the argument can be made in terms of phenomenology.

Certainly, Bourdieu's (1984) work represents an important contribution to the 'secularization' of the Durkheimian tradition and its instantiation in a social structural and micro-sociological frame. Bourdieu's concentration on vertical rather than horizontal social divisions, however, and his insistence that symbolic boundaries are modeled on and derive from social, primarily economic, distinctions detract from the cultural interest of his writing. Bourdieu conceives of the social codes not as a differentiated, representational system of society but as a hegemonic code tied directly to the interest of the powerful. How liberating conflict and democracy are possible in this model is not at all clear.

13 For a discussion of the role of the myth of origin in archaic societies, which has

clear implications for the organization of mythical thought in secular societies, see Eliade (1959). For a contemporary discussion of secular society that employs the notion of origin myth to great advantage, see Apter (1987).

14 For this belief in the existence of an ancient constitution and the role it played in the ideological discourse of the American Revolution, see Bailyn (1963). For background, see Pocock (1974).

15 For Puritans and revolutionaries as figures in the discourse of liberty, see, for example, Middlekauff (1972) and, more systematically, Bailyn (1963). Bailyn, and the many who have followed him, have argued that the ideology that inspired Americans during the revolutionary period was mainly a negative and conspiratorial one, that it was the fear of being overtaken and of being manipulated by the revengeful and evil British, with their royalty and their empire, that primarily inspired the American nation. In fact, however, even on the basis of the material that Bailyn himself provides, it is clear that the American Revolution rested on the bifurcation and interconnection of two discourses and that each could be defined only in terms of order.

For the myth of the yeoman farmers and its intrinsic connection to the discourse of liberty, see the brilliant and still compelling work by Henry Nash Smith (1950: especially Part 3). For the relation between this mythical discourse and narratives about cowboys, mountain men, and detectives, see Smith (1950: Part 2, especially 90–122). In his work on the manner in which Hollywood's stories about 'G-men' fit into these archetypes, Powers emphasizes the manner in which these central characters embodied the contrasts of the overarching discourse. The 'mystery' that provides the focus of the detective story rests on the circumstances that allow 'a startlingly intelligent hero' to finally pick 'a devious murderer out of a crowd of equally likely suspects' (Powers, 1983: 74). See also Curti's (1937: 765) argument that the mystical exploits of these early dime-store heros 'confirmed Americans in the traditional belief that obstacles were to be overcome by the courageous, virile, and determined stand of the individual as an individual'.

For mythical constructions of religious miscreants in terms of the discourse of repression, see early Puritan discussions of antinomianism, particularly Anne Hutchinson's (Erikson, 1965). For stories about the evils of the loyalists and aristocrats in the Revolution, see Bailyn (1974). For the mythical reconstruction of the Native American in terms of the discourse of repression, see Slotkin (1973). Higham's work (1965: e.g. 55, 138, 200) is filled with examples of how earlier core groups in American society constructed Southern and Central European immigrants under this repressive discourse. These immigrants were often involved in the radical labor politics of the day. Higham displays the antinomian character of the discourse that was used to understand these struggles, and their immigrant participants, in a particularly sharp way.

16 The counterpositioning of heroic enactors of liberty with criminals who act out of uncontrolled passion seems to have been the major point of the 'action detective' genre that emerged in pulp fiction in the late nineteenth century, whose popularity has continued unabated in the present day (see Cawelti, 1976; Noel, 1954). This genre provided the symbolic framework for J. Edgar Hoover's highly successful manipulation of the popular image of the FBI, as Powers (1983) demonstrates. Thus, when Americans looked at Hoover, Powers writes, they 'saw ... not a spokesman for a partisan political philosophy, but a suprapolitical national hero' (1983: xii) modeled on the action genre. Powers emphasizes the binary nature of the discourse that hallowed Hoover's actions, arguing that, 'for the mythological process to produce a Hoover-style hero, there had to be a universally understood formula within the culture for

dealing with the sort of villain who had come to represent the public's fears' (1983: xiv). In the popular-culture/political-culture hybrid of the twentieth century, the criminals pursued by 'officials' were persistently portrayed as subject to 'gang rule', which posed the danger that this form of repressive social organization would spread to 'still wider areas of life' (1983: 7). For their part, the G-men pursuing these criminals were portrayed both as 'rebelliously individualistic' (1983: 94) and as the upholders of rational law, as involved in 'an epochal struggle between lawful society and an organized underworld'.

17 This suggests a modification of my earlier, more traditionally functionalist model of the relations between codes and conflict groups (Alexander, 1988b). Rather than neatly separating refracted value conflicts from columnized ones, I would note the possibility that there may be a more general discourse from which even columnized, fundamentally conflictual cultural groupings derive their ideologies. The issue is one of level of generality.

18 Philip Smith (1991) has documented the bifurcated discourse of war in his insightful investigation of the cultural underpinnings of the British war with Argentina over the Falkland Islands. For a more impressionistic but still fascinating account of the powerful role that semiotic codes play in producing and enabling war, see Fussell (1975).

Note

This chapter was first published in *Cultivating Differences* (1992), edited by Lamont and Fournier. It is reproduced here with kind permission of the University of Chicago Press.

References

Alexander, Jeffrey C. (1982) *The Antinomies of Classical Thought: Marx and Durkheim*. Vol. 2 of *Theoretical Logic in Sociology*. Berkeley and Los Angeles: University of California Press.

Alexander, Jeffrey C. (ed.) (1988a) *Durkheimian Sociology: Cultural Studies*. New York: Cambridge University Press.

Alexander, Jeffrey C. (ed.) (1988b) 'Three Models of Culture/Society Relations: Toward an Analysis of Watergate', in Jeffrey C. Alexander (ed.), *Action and Its Environments*. Berkeley and Los Angeles: University of California Press.

Alexander, Jeffrey C. (1989a) 'Culture and Political Crisis', in Jeffrey C. Alexander (ed.), *Structure and Meaning: Relinking Classical Sociology*. New York: Columbia University Press.

Alexander, Jeffrey C. (1989b) 'The Dialectic of Individuation and Domination: Weber's Rationalization Theory and Beyond', in Jeffrey C. Alexander (ed.), *Structure and Meaning: Relinking Classical Sociology*. New York: Columbia University Press.

Alexander, Jeffrey C. (1990a) 'Bringing Democracy Back In: Universalistic Solidarity and the Civil Sphere', in Charles Lamert (ed.), *Intellectuals and Politics: Social Theory Beyond the Academy*. Newbury Park, CA: Sage.

Alexander, Jeffrey C. (1990b) 'Morale e Repressione', *MondOperaio* (Rome), no. 12 (December): 127–30.

Alexander, Jeffrey C. (1992) 'Shaky Foundations: The Presuppositions and Internal

Contradictions of James Coleman's *Foundations of Social Theory', Theory and Society*, 21: 203–17.

Alexander, Jeffrey C. (1995) 'Collective Action, Culture, and Civil Society: Secularizing, Updating, Inverting, Revising, and Displacing the Classical Model of Social Movements', in M. Diani and J. Clarke (eds), *Alain Touraine*. London: Falmer Press. pp. 205–34.

Alexander, Jeffrey C. (1997) 'The Paradoxes of Civil Society', *International Sociology*, 12 (2): 115–33.

Alexander, Jeffrey C. and Smith, Philip (1992) The ' Discourse of American Civil Society: A New Proposal for Culture Society', typescript.

Apter, David (1987) 'Mao's Republic', *Social Research*, 54: 691–729.

Aristotle (1962) *The Politics of Aristotle*, trans. Ernest Barker. New York: Oxford University Press.

Bailyn, Bernard (1963) *The Ideological Origins of the American Revolution*. Cambridge, MA: Harvard University Press.

Bailyn, Bernard (1974) *The Ordeal of Thomas Hutchinson*. Cambridge, MA: Harvard University Press.

Barthes, Roland (1977) 'Introduction to the Structural Analysis of Narratives', in *Image, Music, Text*. New York: Hill & Wang.

Bennett, W. Lance (1979) 'Imitation, Ambiguity, and Drama in Political Life: Civil Religion and the Dilemmas of Public Morality', *Journal of Politics*, 41: 106–33.

Bourdieu, Pierre (1984) *Distinction*. Cambridge, MA: Harvard University Press.

Caillois, Roger (1959) *Man and the Sacred*. New York: Free Press.

Cawelti, John (1976) *Adventure, Mystery and Romance: Formula Stories as Art and Popular Culture*. Chicago: University of Chicago Press.

Cohen, Jean (1982) *Class and Civil Society: The Limits of Marxian Critical Theory*. Amherst, MA: University of Massachusetts Press.

Coleman, James (1990) *Foundations of Social Theory*. Cambridge, MA: Belknap.

Curti, Merle (1937) 'Dime Store Novels and the American Tradition', *Yale Review*, 26: 765.

Durkheim, Emile (1933) *The Division of Labor in Society* (1893). New York: Free Press.

Durkheim, Emile (1963) *The Elementary Forms of Religious Life* (1912). New York: Free Press.

Eisenstadt, S.N. (ed.) (1986) *The Origins and Diversity of Axial Age Civilizations*. Albany, NY: State University of New York Press.

Eliade, Mircea (1959) *The Sacred and the Profane*. New York: Harcourt.

Entrikin, Nicholas (1990) *The Betweenness of Place*. Baltimore: Johns Hopkins University Press.

Erikson, Kai (1965) *Wayward Puritans*. New Haven, CT: Yale University Press.

Eyerman, Ron and Jamison, Andrew (1991) *Social Movements: A Cognitive Approach*. Cambridge: Polity.

Fussell, Paul (1975) *The Great War in Modern Memory*. New York: Oxford University Press.

Habermas, Jurgen (1988) *Critique of Functionalist Reason*. Vol. 2 of *Theory of Communicative Action*. Boston: Beacon.

Hegel, G.H.W. (1952) *Philosophy of Right*. New York: Oxford.

Hepworth, Mike and Turner, Bryan S. (1982) *Confession: Studies in Deviance and Religion*. London: Routledge & Kegan Paul.

Higham, John (1965) *Strangers in a Strange Land*. New York: Atheneum.

Keane, John (ed.) (1988a) 'Despotism and Democracy: The Origins and Development of the Distinction between Civil Society and the State, 1750–1850', in *Civil Society and the State*. London: Verso.

Keane, John (1988b) 'Remembering the Dead: Civil Society and the State from Hobbes to Marx and Beyond', in *Democracy and Civil Society*. London: Verso.

Lefort, Claude (1988) *Democracy and Political Theory*. Cambridge: Polity.

Middlekauff, Robert (1972) 'The Ritualization of the American Revolution', in Lawrence Levine and Robert Middlekauff (eds), *The National Temper* 2nd edn. New York: Harcourt Brace.

Noel, Mary (1954) *Villains Galore*. New York: Macmillan.

Parsons, Talcott (1967) 'Durkheim's Contribution to the Theory of Integration of Social Systems' (1960). Reprinted in *Sociological Theory and Modern Society*. New York: Free Press.

Parsons, Talcott (1977) *The Evolution of Societies*, ed. Jackson Toby. Englewood Cliffs, NJ: Prentice Hall.

Pocock, J.G.A. (1974) *The Ancient Constitution and the Feudal Law*. Bath: Chivers.

Powers, Richard (1983) *G-Men: Hoover's FBI in American Popular Culture*. Carbondale, IL: Southern Illinois University Press.

Ricoeur, Paul (1984) *Time and Narrative*, vol. 1. Chicago: University of Chicago Press.

Rogin, Michael (1987) *Ronald Reagan: The Movie, and Other Essays in American Demonology*. Berkeley and Los Angeles: University of California Press.

Russell, Jeffrey Burton (1988) *The Prince of Darkness*. Ithaca, NY: Cornell University Press.

Slotkin, Richard (1973) *Regeneration through Violence: The Mythology of the American Frontier, 1600–1860*. Middletown, CT: Wesleyan University Press.

Smith, Henry Nash (1950) *Virgin Land: The American Western as Symbol and Myth*. Cambridge, MA: Harvard University Press.

Smith, Philip (1991) 'Codes and Conflict: Toward a Theory of War as Ritual', *Theory and Society*, 20: 103–38.

Steiner, Franz (1956) *Taboo*. London: Cohen & West.

7

Barbarism and Civility in the Discourses of Fascism, Communism, and Democracy: Variations on a Set of Themes

Philip Smith

Ambiguity and Utopianism in Sociological Discourse on Civil Society

The only good thing about debates is the ideas one has afterwards.
(Arno Schmidt, *Aus dem Leben eines Fauns*)

While tending towards hyperbole, Arno Schmidt's dictum is one that has a certain applicability to recent debates about civil society. Sociological interest in 'civil society' had simmered through the 1980s, mostly fueled by the empirical work of Alain Touraine (e.g. 1983) and the theoretical projects of thinkers like Jean Cohen (e.g. 1982), Andrew Arato (e.g. 1981) and John Keane (e.g. 1988). In late 1989 and 1990 the gently bubbling pot of inquiry suddenly boiled over. The more or less peaceful overthrow of communist rule in Eastern Europe and the Soviet Union had to be explained somehow – and for many the concept of civil society provided a ready-made if massively under-theorized solution.[1] In universities throughout the world seminar series and conferences were hastily thrown together. Speakers were flown in from Eastern Europe as scholars reached for their top shelves and blew the dust from copies of works by Hegel, Marx, Rousseau and Ferguson.

In this initial period much was said about civil society even if, one suspects, few were quite certain what it exactly was. As a reborn tool of sociological discourse, the vague concept of 'civil society' initially signified only by virtue of a morally loaded negative dialectic: all that one could be really certain of was that civil society was 'not the state' and that it was somehow 'good'. The meta-narrative underpinning this initial theoretical movement saw civil society as a moral conscience, a social-systemic superego that sometimes heroically, sometimes stoically resisted the invasions of the rapacious, totalitarian and amoral state.

Over the past five or so years there has been undoubted progress in adding content to form. The ambiguities, ellipses and abstractions of the quasi-Hegelian theorizing of earlier debates have given way to far greater conceptual clarity and detailed, empirically driven research. We have begun to unpack the nebulous concept of civil society that initially caused so much excitement – and confusion. The negative definitions which identified civil society in contrast to the state have been replaced by more positive, empirically grounded conceptions of the cultural and social structural features of a civil society. As a signifier within sociological discourse 'civil society' has become multi-vocal (Turner, 1970), pointing attention simultaneously in a number of directions. In particular empirical progress has been made in investigating civil society in terms of four areas, even though the linkages between these areas remain to be more fully specified:

1 the private sphere of sexuality, reproduction, leisure and the family
2 the sphere of market-oriented economic relationships
3 the 'public sphere' of discourse and the mass media
4 the grassroots activity of social movements and voluntary associations.

In addition to these more empirically driven domains, theoretical progress has been made at the grandest levels. We now understand more clearly than before the differing – sometimes contradictory – visions of 'civil society' in the work of Hegel, Marx and their enlightenment predecessors (cf. Kumar, 1993).[2]

Since 1989, then, research on civil society has slowly realized the potential of an initially vague and unsatisfactory concept. Yet, if one important legacy of those early days – namely the indeterminacy of the object of study – has been confronted, another remains to be addressed. This is the problem of the moral status of 'civil society' in sociological theory.

Although the Central European revolutions of 1989 were invaluable in providing a moral and intellectual impetus for research on civil society, they also introduced distorting normative premises. In a *Weltanschauung* of utopian theorizing, where a 'good' civil society was conceptually juxtaposed to an 'evil' totalitarianism, there could be little room for a more analytic and relativistic but less Manichean approach. Such an approach might point to the existence of distinctive forms of public sphere that actually supported state power in totalitarian contexts (Bruckner et al., 1977; Benz, 1990). It might also explore similarities in institutional arrangements between civil and incivil societies, or acknowledge the existence of a mass basis of support for authoritarianism (see Radel, 1975: 4; Benz, 1990). Or, turning from institutions to culture, such an approach could explore continuities between democratic and counter-democratic political codes rather than assuming them to be fundamentally antithetical. This chapter takes up this last issue and undertakes a three-way comparison of the discourses of fascism and communism with those of liberal-democratic civil society. Its intention is not only to illuminate the structure and workings of each discursive code, but also to explore their relationships and commonalities in an analytically rather than politically reflexive fashion.

Democracy, Fascism and Communism as a System of Transformations

The comparative understanding of any empirical phenomena requires a theoretical framework. We can understand fascist, democratic and communist discourses using a 'culture area' approach (Kuper, 1982; Radcliffe-Brown, 1913; 1930). Most elaborately developed in the field of anthropology, the culture area approach attacks the idea of 'isolated, bounded and timeless tribal cultures' (Kuper, 1982: 4) and instead examines patterns of concomitant variation and structural transformation of cultural practices amongst neighboring peoples or amongst peoples who are otherwise linked by geographical, political, historical and social ties. Culture area analysis can consider the social structural processes through which ideas and institutions are exchanged within a culture area (e.g. networks, migration, trade, the mass media, organizations). Understanding these aspects of the emergence and transmission of ideologies requires a kind of culture area analysis which looks more at material, political and organizational factors and the role of concrete historical agents, both individual and collective. In this chapter, however, my aim is limited to a formal analysis of a system of *cultural* transformations.

We can understand the various forms of political discourse produced by occidental society as a system of cultural transformations (Lévi-Strauss, 1964; 1966; 1977) in which a central group of concepts is shifted through various permutations like the elements within a kaleidoscope. This approach allows not only the identification of family resemblances between related political/civil discourses, but also their systematic theorization.[3] Cultural innovation and the creation of new cultural discourses should be understood as a process in which interested parties respond to social, cultural and psychological problems through acts of *bricolage* (Lévi-Strauss, 1966).

The creation of fascist, communist and liberal-democratic

ideologies involved powerful existing discourses and symbols being taken up and worked in new ways. These new ideologies provided moral and mythical solutions to the existential and practical dilemmas of modernity – alienation and anomie, class and ethnic conflict, industrialization and the dislocation of traditional sources of social and moral support (cf. Parsons, 1954b). What Lévi-Strauss has termed the logic of transformation provided cultural innovators with limited, structured options. The irruption of new ideologies involved the paradigmatic recombination of the signifiers of the *langue* of the existing discourses of liberalism, republicanism and the Judeo-Christian tradition. For this reason, at the level of deep structure the voices of fascism and communism are inextricably linked to the liberal-democratic culture they fervently oppose.

Civil/political discourses can be understood as sign systems which arrange concepts in patterns of binary opposition. These concepts mark off the sacred from the profane, the desired from the damned, the civilized from the barbaric. But if the tendency towards binarism is a universal of political and civil discourses, the empirical specification of the civil and the barbaric is contingent. Within a given culture area transformations may take place which redefine the morally and politically desirable. Given the binary structure of civil/political codes, discourses can be transformed in two ways. Firstly, metonymic changes can take place in which particular dyads gain or lose relative levels of power within a discourse. In this way particular concepts and binary dyads can take on master or auxiliary (cf. Becker, 1963) status in the organization of civil discourse, becoming more or less influential in shaping policy or mobilizing popular sentiment.[4] Both communism and democracy, for example, argue for the importance of 'equality', but it has far more power in organizing social life under communism than democracy. Inversions (metaphoric changes) are more fundamental in that they exchange concepts between central organizing categories in a discourse, breaking down and reworking its entire fabric. Because inversions radically restructure the categorical status of signifiers within a discourse they offer stronger possibilities for the reconstitution of political and moral life. What is considered civil in one political code might, through the process of inversion, become barbaric and polluted in another. As we shall see, these shifts in the moral weight of signifiers provide the basis for the mutual critique of fascism, communism and democracy by each other.

It is through these two transformative processes that fascist and communist discourses emerged in opposition to democratic discourse, becoming consolidated in the earlier part of the twentieth century.[5] They offered a 'concrete and stable system of symbols' around which the sentiments of individuals could crystallize (Parsons, 1954b: 126). The simple logic of the binary sign system and the 'retrievability' (Schudson, 1989) for members of its established resonant concepts provided for the solidity and popularity of these new discourses. As templates with which actors could pattern their experiences of the world, fascism, communism and democracy offered equally compelling and consistent treatments of familiar themes to those living in the first part of the twentieth century and the possibility for their 'creative and productive' conversion into a 'new vision of society' (Falasca-Zamponi, 1992: 81).

The remainder of this chapter provides an empirical illustration of these themes. It demonstrates how a dialectic of civility and barbarism lies beneath all three political systems and how they can be understood relationally as a series of transformations of a common underlying set of orienting concepts. The empirical section begins with a discussion of democratic civil discourse, in part because such a discourse is probably most familiar to the reader, but also because this discourse was the historically dominant form against which the counter-democratic alternatives were formulated.

The Civil Discourse of Democracy

The understanding of the semiotic foundations of democratic civil discourse presented here draws upon recent neo-Durkheimian work which argues that binary codes organize core concepts within civil discourse in terms of the sacred and the profane (Alexander, 1991; Alexander and Smith, 1993; Smith, 1991; 1994). The code of democratic civil discourse classifies human motivations and forms of association according to sacred and profane criteria. From a semiotic perspective, the agenda of liberal democracy – and indeed any other political system – can be understood as the institutionalization of sacred concepts, and the exclusion or marginalization of that deemed profane. Civil discourses under democracy play a role in regulating and shaping social processes by typifying policies, actors and institutions in terms of the binary codes. Indeed, the state itself can be assured of legitimacy only if it is able to make its actions accountable in terms of this code (Table 7.1).

Democratic discourses argue for the primacy of reason and law, rather than power and emotion, in the regulation of civil life (Locke, 1946), As Marcuse argued, the 'vital' element of liberal-democratic discourses was 'an optimistic faith in the ultimate victory of reason, which will realize itself above all conflicts of interests and opinion in the harmony of the whole' (Marcuse, quoted in Vajda, 1971: 45). According to the liberal-democratic model the ideal collectivity

Table 7.1   *Codes of liberal democracy*

Sacred	Profane
Order	Disorder
Individual	Group
Reason	Emotion
Active	Passive
Law	Power
Equality	Hierarchy
Inclusive	Exclusive
Autonomy	Dependence

consists of active and autonomous individuals as opposed to groups (Adam Smith, 1801; 1880; Locke, 1946). Equality is important for democratic discourses, but individuals have only a formal equality and it is legitimate for them to be substantively unequal in terms of access to scarce resources. Democratic civil discourses usually argue for inclusion and assert that the gradual expansion of civil status will bring fulfillment to all. Although democratic discourses agree that there should be order, this is not a particularly salient concept except in periods of backlash politics inspired by Puritan or civic republican ideals.[6]

The Discourse of Fascism

Fascism remains the only distinctive major political tradition to emerge in the twentieth century. Fascism should be considered as a radically anti-modern movement (Benjamin, 1973) that arose as a response to the dislocations and anxieties produced by societal rationalization (Parsons, 1954a; 1954b; Lipset, 1983). Fascist movements did not argue, however, for the rolling back of societal evolution and the return to feudal, agricultural ways of life. Indeed, the fascist obsession with technology, foreshadowed by Italian futurism, demonstrates if anything a heightened interest in the facilities produced by the modern social system (cf. Oestereicher, 1974). Rather than rejecting modernity *tout court*, fascism aimed at reincorporation of *gemeinschaftlicht* elements into a modern differentiated and industrial social system (cf. Dandeker, 1985: 356; Falasca-Zamponi, 1992: 80). A defining feature of fascist ideology is that whilst undertaking a critique of modernity, it was able to achieve a successful accommodation with modernity's institutional and technical developments. In this respect fascism was more adaptive than earlier communitarian movements of the right which had proposed various utopian solutions premised upon the assumption of a fundamental isomorphism between primordial, moral sentiments and pre-industrial modes of economic production. The failure of organizations fueled by such philosophies to gain lasting power underwrites the lack of realism inherent in their outlook. In essence their views were simply poorly adapted to the exigencies of a complex world. In contrast fascism achieved considerable political success through its recognition of modernity. The stress placed upon the seizure of the state apparatus and the organization of disciplined, hierarchical party units are but two fruits of this ideological moment which were translated into successful political strategies.

This is not to deny that fascist movements often had a romantic vision of the past as a golden age of community and organic unity, and at the same time interpreted the present in profane terms. The writings of Hitler and Mussolini, for example, are replete with the analysis of the failings of modern society: rampant individualism, chaos and disorder, the alienating properties of reason, the impersonality and rootlessness of contractual interpersonal ties. In contrast to this profane world in the present, they depicted the nostalgic world of the past and the new golden age that fascism was to bring in the future. In this sense fascism should be considered a revolutionary movement in that it envisaged a fundamental change was necessary to the moral ties binding society together and also to the institutional arrangements that grew from these ties. To understand the origins of this highly successful political culture, it is useful to examine how its discourses transformed existing democratic discourse.

The desire for order is common to all known societies, and can perhaps be considered a universal feature of human culture and psychology (Douglas, 1969; Freud, 1989). To a certain extent the desire for order in fascist movements can be understood as a response to the objective disorder and anomie created by societal modernization (cf. Parsons, 1954b). However, the fascist drive for order was also motivated by an abiding symbolic concern which elevated the question of order from a concern to an obsession. As one fascist apologist put it: 'Fascism means, in fact, the return to order' (Palmieri, 1962: 344). We need only note here the manifestation of a concern for order in various forms of fascist *parole* like militaristic parades, marches and uniforms, and the high levels of legitimacy given to state intervention in the economy such as corporatist industrial relations. Mussolini's proud boast to have made the trains in Italy run on time should be considered primarily as a reflection of this abiding cultural imperative. By way of contrast liberal-democratic society was typically diagnosed in profane terms:

it lacked order; it was decadent; it had no strong authority; it was ruled by the weak and permissive (cf. Eatwell, 1992: 175, 182). Arising from this emphasis on order was a strong tendency to maintain symbolic order through enforcing rigid boundaries around the national or racial community (cf. Durkheim, 1964; Vajda, 1971: 55). In consequence exclusion rather than inclusion was the norm, with racial and residential (national) criteria controlling access to the societal community. For this reason, fascist parties when they came to power tended to implement a politics of radical exclusion which aimed to destroy groups symbolically classified as polluted or liminal, including Jews, Gypsies, foreigners, communists and homosexuals (cf. Parsons, 1954a: 119).

In contrast to liberal democracy, fascist movements elevated the group over and above the individual, seeking to 'integrate all particularities into the "whole"', i.e., the "natural organic" whole or the "nation"' (Vajda, 1971: 45). It is for this reason that fascism emphasizes the primacy of organic unity and the moral solidarity of society – as embodied in the *Volk* or the corporatist state – over and above the rights of the individual (Berezin, 1991: 643; Cohen, 1962: 256-7; cf. O'Sullivan, 1983: 131ff; Weber, 1964: 42). In the last instance the duty of the individual was to accommodate group needs and even to sacrifice themselves for the sake of the collectivity:

> The activities of the individual may not clash with the interests of the whole, but must proceed within the frame of the community and be for the general good. (*First Program of the Nazi Party*, cited in Weber, 1964: 154)

> The individual exists only in so far as he is subordinated to the interests of the state, and as civilization becomes more complex, so the liberty of the individual must be increasingly restricted. (Mussolini, quoted in Mack Smith, 1983: 140)

This emphasis on the solidaristic group made the autonomy of individuals or societal institutions far less salient than in liberal democracy. Because the true interests of the individual were identified with those of the collectivity, fascist collectivism argued that autonomy was important only at the level of the primordial or national group. True freedom was a collective freedom to pursue a racial or national destiny, not an illusory and decadent individual freedom. Actions born of this collective freedom were to be driven by non-rational, rather than rational motives. As one commentator has put it: 'For fascist ideology, both liberalism and Marxism were, as particularistic rationalism, the antipodes of fascism' (Vajda, 1971: 45).

For this reason the fascist critique of liberal democracy held that reason had perverted the thought and unity of the people, in turn leading to passivity and sterile contemplation rather than vigorous and virile action. Fascist discourses went beyond those of democracy in asserting that progressive accumulation and moral progress must be replaced by 'youthful dynamism' (Dandeker, 1985: 355) and a 'radical activism' that was akin to 'permanent revolution' (Eatwell, 1992: 186). When Mussolini argued that fascism was 'action rather than theory', or Gentile (1962: 341) that 'fascism prefers not to waste time constructing abstract theories about itself', the implicit equation was between reason and passivity. Hitler's sneering critique of the intellectual as a 'walking encyclopedia' or as a 'walking dictionary' taps much the same vein as does the general fascist disdain for intellectuals and the universities (cf. Mack Smith, 1983: 180). Even science was treated with suspicion. Mussolini, for example, argued that 'free science could, by definition, produce only contradictory solutions' and that it needed central direction under fascism (1983: 134). Only in the guise of technology were the products of reason accepted, and then only when harnessed to appropriate nationalistic and militaristic ends as an expression of an action-oriented, dynamic culture.

What could replace reason in guiding action and society? Drawing upon romanticism (Parsons, 1954a: 123) and folk traditions as well as Darwinian theory and aspects of irrationalist philosophy (e.g. Cohen, 1962: 257; Eatwell, 1992: 177; Nietzsche, 1966; Sorel, 1915; cf. Vajda, 1971: 47), fascist discourses argued that racial or national instinct, passion and (particularly in Southern and Eastern Europe) a deep inner faith provided more secure grounds for action, order and solidarity than a fickle reason. Mussolini, for example, 'took pride in acting by instinct and intuition, unlike ordinary mortals who needed to calculate pros and cons with care' (Mack Smith, 1983: 113). The extraordinary vitality and masculine vigor of fascism – its 'strength through joy' dynamism – was built, it was argued, upon these irrational grounds.[7] It is for this reason that Mussolini's leading biographer has been able to argue that Italian fascism was an 'essentially spiritual movement' (1983: 138; cf. Parsons, 1954b: 125). This was an opinion clearly shared by 'Il Duce' himself.

> Fascism is a religious conception in which man is seen in immanent relationship with a superior law and with an objective Will that transcends the particular individual and raises him to conscious membership in a spiritual society. (Mussolini, *The Doctrine of Fascism*, in Cohen, 1962: 330)

As Georges Bataille noted long ago, the fascist valorization of the irrational often allowed it to succeed where communism had failed to generate an effective mass movement (cf. Richardson, 1992: 35).

Responding to the calls of discourse for emotional direction and solidarity, fascistic political praxis aimed in a quite self-reflexive way to foster irrational solidaristic ties (*Bruderschaft, Romanita, Volksgemeinschaft* etc.) through civic ritual.[8] Mass political rallies, youth movements, riots and work parties manipulated bodies and symbols in ways that were highly effective in enhancing affiliative sentiments, even though little attention was given to the quality of substantive intellectual argument (cf. Mack Smith, 1983: 127).

Fascist discourses strongly emphasized the importance of action, a relatively insignificant element in the code of democracy, and connected it metonymically to 'force' and 'emotion' whilst opposing it to 'passivity', 'law' and 'reason'.[9] The culture of hard-core fascist groups was dominated by this action principle.

> The SA always appeared as a militant activist group which completely organized the lives of its members. Activism meant: simplification of action, direct physical confrontation with the opponent, direct supervision for success, rejection of mediations, single-mindedness and clarity in orientation, politics as the continuation of adventure/war, proof of reliability (*Kameradenschaft*) as the dominant organizational principle. (Knodler-Bunte, 1977: 46)

However, fascists understood the prevailing social order of liberal democracy as one in which passivity rather than activism reigned. In consequence almost any action was desirable.

> 'Action,' he [Mussolini] used to say enigmatically, is desirable for its own sake 'even when it is wrong'. He admitted that he instinctively resorted to action in moments when he did not know what to do; he had to show he was leading and not being led; he had to go against the current, to give the impression of being always on the move and never indecisive. (Mack Smith, 1983: 114)

But although any action was better than no action, some actions were better than others. Revolutionary fascist action, it was argued, had real world-transforming power. In particular a prevalent apocalyptic narrative associated with the valuation of force over law (see discussion below) directed the imperative for action in a violent and militaristic direction. Fascist discourse repeatedly emphasized the need for heroic, sacrificial, vigorous and virile actions as the best, perhaps only means of attaining salvation in a world collapsing into a nihilistic chaos (cf. Jung, 1947). Violence in particular was praised as possessing purifying and dynamic qualities. Boxing, Mussolini once said, was 'an exquisitely fascist means of self-expression' whilst the sword was mightier than the pen 'because it cuts' (quoted in Mack Smith, 1983: 114). For this reason, mundane political initiatives were often couched in militaristic terms: the Battle for Wheat, a Battle for

Births, Battles against Sparrows, Mice and Houseflies (1983: 115), even a Battle of Talent in the theater (Berezin, 1991: 646). Speed had similar cathectic properties to violence within the fascist mentality. Mercedes and Bugatti racing cars, aeroplanes and Olympic athletes took a central position in the pantheon of fascist achievements. Violence and speed reached their world-historical apotheosis when synthesized in the *Blitzkrieg*. What, after all, can be faster than lightning or more violent than war? With 'action' the shibboleth of fascist praxis, the complexities and nuances of thought and policy (namely rationality and reason) could be put aside as an impediment to simple and direct engagement in world-transforming activity.

Two final points of contrast remain to be made between liberal-democratic civil discourses and those of fascism. Liberal democracy sees 'inequality' and 'hierarchy' as unfortunate but necessary, inevitable or functional consequences of human action. They are the residue left behind by the search to build the good society. In liberal-democratic discourse 'law' provides an essential means of regulating and controlling society. It prevents inequities in the distribution of power from overwhelming the rights and liberties of the individual and provides the basis for contract and the regulation of the distribution of scarce resources. By way of contrast fascist discourses drew upon and went beyond even the absolutist tradition of Bodin, Hobbes and Hegel, rejecting 'the bourgeois notion of universal equality' (Vajda, 1971: 51) and replacing it with a vision of hierarchy both as necessary for national unity and productivity and as a sacred goal of international or interracial struggle (cf. Dandeker, 1985: 360; Eatwell, 1992: 177). In fascist discourses a brutal pragmatism replaced law with hierarchy, and force became the most appropriate way of regulating society. As one commentator on fascism has astutely put it: 'the only "law" to which nations are subject and which also applies to individual subjects is that of the rights of the stronger and fitter power' (Dandeker, 1985: 359). The teachings of Nietzsche (1966) and Darwin (1929), in particular, had drawn attention to the fact that human progress could come only through struggle and that it was the moral duty of the victors to exercise their tyranny and dominion over the vanquished. Might – not reason and thought – produced right.

Fascism desires an active man ... it conceives of life as a struggle, considering that it behooves man to conquer for himself that life truly worthy of him. (Mussolini, *The Doctrine of Fascism*, in Cohen, 1962: 329)

Thus those people who are governed by their men of action and their military leaders win out over those peoples who are governed by their lawyers and their professors. (Maurras, quoted in Nolte, 1969: 111)

> It is evident that the stronger has the right before God and the world to enforce his will ... The whole of nature is a continuous struggle between strength and weakness, an eternal victory of the strong over the weak. All nature would be full of decay if it were otherwise. And states which do not wish to recognize this law will decay. (Hitler 1962: 385)

> Man owes everything that is of any importance to the principle of struggle. (1962: 386)

> We sing of War, the only cure for the world, a superb blaze of enthusiasm and generosity, a noble bath of heroism without which races fall asleep in slothful egoism. (Marinetti, quoted in Oestereicher, 1974: 528)

> War is beautiful because it enriches a flowering meadow with the fiery orchids of machine guns. (Marinetti, quoted in Falasca-Zamponi, 1992: 79)

War, violence and domination – in short, power in its most basic form – were necessary for existence and good. They were creative and purifying, both elevating society and calling the chivalric spirit towards an ethical pursuit of the sacred (Weber, 1964: 40–2). The consequent militarism of fascism extended from the level of grass-roots activism to that of state policy. Originally 'conceived as tightly organized semi-military machines with which state and society were to be conquered', fascist parties could later undertake policies of colonial expansion and total war. This pervasive militarism and predilection for violence, the emphasis on the principle of 'heroic' leadership (Carsten, 1969: 231) and what French fascist Charles Maurras called the 'soldier king', should be understood as a reflection of an underlying code which equated morality and order with hierarchy and force. As Hitler himself put it:

> Strength can only be effective when it is subservient to one will and to one command ... We must train our people so that whenever someone has been appointed to command, the others will recognize it as their duty to obey him ... Germany is no chicken house where everyone runs about at random, cackling and crowing, but we are a people that from its infancy on learns how to be disciplined. (1962: 391)

One consequence of this belief was the widespread use of the military uniform in fascist societies as a means of representing hierarchy, group membership, order and discipline simultaneously (cf. Mack Smith, 1983: 176; Weber, 1964: 39).

Finally, fascism places less stress on the question of autonomy and dependence than liberal democracy, which positioned 'freedom' in a central location in its pantheon of values. When typified as individual liberty, autonomy was held to be incompatible with the need for order and discipline (cf. Mack Smith, 1983: 140; Vajda, 1971: 52). Although fascist discourses occasionally lionized the heroic individual, the main concern of fascism was for freedom at the level of the group united within a totalitarian state that 'expresses and mobilizes the collective national will' (Dandeker, 1985: 357). In particular the members of the moral community were beholden to free themselves from the domination of other groups, a process which would necessarily involve increasing their dependence upon their blood brothers and leaders.

> The new Reich is based on the principle that real action of a self-determining people is only possible according to the principle of leadership and following ... In the theory of the nationalistic Reich, people and state are conceived as an inseparable unity. (Huber, 1962: 370)

> There are no personal liberties of the individual which fall outside of the realm of the state and which must be respected by the state. The member of the people, organically connected with the whole community, has replaced the isolated individual. (1962: 373)

Collective autonomy could only come with the realization of ever greater levels of intragroup solidarity and interdependence along with submission to structures of authority and recognition of the 'leadership principle' (O'Sullivan, 1983: 149ff).

Table 7.2 reconstructs the discussion given above in terms of binary oppositions. This table should be understood as a permutation of the codes of liberal democracy (Table 7.1), which are taken here as the benchmark. Binary distinctions that are upgraded in salience in comparison with liberal democracy are marked with a plus (+) sign, and those that are downgraded are marked with a minus (–) sign. Inversions, that is to say terms which have been swapped from sacred to profane sides of the code, are in italic.

Table 7.2   *Codes of fascism*

Sacred	Profane
Order	Disorder +
Group	*Individual* +
Emotion	*Reason*
Active	Passive +
Power	*Law*
Hierarchy	*Equality*
Exclusive	*Inclusive*
Autonomy	Dependence –

The Discourse of Communism

Parsons (1954a; 1954b) was probably right when he argued that the fascist movement was more radically divergent than communism from the main path of Western development. When we look at the codes of communist civil discourse, we find them to be far closer to those of democratic discourses than to those of fascism. Indeed, it is only in the advocacy of the group over the individual that communist discourses resemble those of fascism rather than democracy. So although communism and fascism may rightly be considered similar in their effects *qua* totalitarian modes of government (Arendt, 1958), in cultural terms they should be considered as distinctive from each other as each is to the codes of democratic civil society.

Communist discourses advocate law, action and inclusion in much the same way as democracy. Law, surprisingly, has a prominent role. Consider for example the extraordinary emphasis given to show trials in dealing with dissent. The positive value given to 'law' in the civil codes of communism makes a dramaturgic effort towards law necessary for elites. Fascist elites, in contrast, were content with abandoning even the pretense of due process. Accountable to a different set of signs (for example an overriding imperative for 'action'), fascists were able to indulge in summary executions, deportations and 'the night of the long knives' style of politics in a more public and open manner. The meaning of 'action' for communism can take various forms. During periods of revolutionary fervor it is elevated to become a key value. In periods of stability, however, there seems to be less stress on radical world-transforming activity and more emphasis on steady progress or strategic withdrawal rather than constant and frenetic activity. In all cases, communist discourses argue that action should be carefully controlled by theory, and never spontaneous or instinctive. Action, in short, was an auxiliary signifier that was subordinate (as we shall see) to reason.

Inclusion, rather than exclusion, was manifested in highly developed affirmative action programs and the meritocratic allocation of personnel. Of course communism's stress on the inclusion of women and other minorities was matched by attempts at the exclusion of the bourgeoisie. However, bourgeois status could normally be lost in the second or third generation. Fascism, on the other hand, extended inclusion only to those selected on the basis of primordial and fundamental ascriptive criteria. Fascism was highly inclusive only as far as this boundary extended and it was a boundary that could not be stretched without risking the contamination of the sacred moral centers of society.

Communist discourses differ from those of liberal democracy in that they elevate reason and equality to centrality as master concepts within their codes. At the same time communism argues for the importance of order, which is closely tied to the idea of rationality in areas such as the planned economy. Where fascist discourses constructed and expressed an affective and fundamentalist radicalism, communist discourses produced the opposite. Marxism can be characterized as 'the extreme of rationalistic radicalism' (Parsons, 1954a: 119). Engels's (1934) distinction between utopian and scientific forms of socialism, and Marx's advocacy of 'scientific socialism', nicely capture the desire of communism to affiliate itself with the sign of rationality. In Marx's own theory a utilitarian model of action drives human progress towards emancipation (Alexander, 1982; Lockwood, 1993) and, in subsequent communist doctrine, reason has been central to the critique of existing society and the design of revolution. Most important of all, reason was to bring order to state socialist society for it would be possible for 'productive forces to dovetail harmoniously into each other on the basis of one single vast plan' (Engels, 1934: 409). The importance of rational planning for communist discourses is nicely captured in the influential policy statements of the Communist International (the Comintern) as well as in the works of Marx and Engels.

> The world system of communism will replace the elemental forces of the world market, of competition and the blind process of social production, by consciously organized and planned production for the purpose of satisfying rapidly growing social needs. With the abolition of competition and anarchy in production, devastating crises and still more devastating wars will disappear. Instead of colossal waste of productive forces and spasmodic development of society – there will be planned utilization of all material resources and painless economic development on the basis of unrestricted, smooth and rapid development of productive forces. (Communist International, 1963 [1928]: 168)

In communist narratives, then, the operation of reason would enable the chaos and anarchy of liberal democracy (capitalism) to be replaced by order. Material, social and mental progress was intimately linked to the processes of planning and control that would replace the chaos of competition and war. According to Marxist eschatology, therefore, the society at the end of history will be a rational society. Emotion and irrationality, on the other hand, are associated with superstition, ideology and mystification – the antinomies of the science of historical materialism.

> The artificial retention of the masses in a state of ignorance ... will have no place in a communist society ... the closest possible cooperation between science and technics, the utmost encouragement of research work and the practical application of its results on the widest possible social scale, planned organization of scientific work, the application of the most perfect method of statistical accounting and planned regulation of

economy ... will release human energy for the powerful development of science and art. (1963 [1928]: 169)

[Communism] will bury forever all mysticism, religion, prejudice and superstition and will give a powerful impetus to the development of all-conquering scientific knowledge. (1963 [1928]: 169)

We should not consider these pronouncements mere wind. Communist societies have historically manifested an extraordinary concern with reason. Consider for example the extraordinary significance of five-year plans and party directives for the development of Soviet and Chinese society. In tandem with this there has been an active tendency to wipe out irrational and informal elements of society through education, collectivization and events like the Chinese Cultural Revolution. Science and technology, seen by fascism as a means to express the irrational and to bring about the desires of the will, are promoted by socialism as ends in themselves, as the very embodiment of communism. As Khrushchev once put it in a press conference: 'We regard communism as a science' (cited in Cohen, 1962: 171). Tokens of this love of science and reason are sprinkled throughout the *parole* of the communist social text: from the massive Soviet space program and excellence in the natural sciences, to showpiece model farms and factories, and even to recreational pursuits like chess – the rational game *par excellence*.[10]

The pre-eminence of reason is similarly manifested in the extraordinary sanctity given to theory. Whereas fascism argued that theory was usually a handicap to action inspired by faith, communist ideology saw theory – usually understood as the detailed study of the classic works of Marx, Lenin, Mao and Engels – as essential to effective action.

'If you must combine', Marx wrote to the party leaders, 'then enter into agreements to satisfy the practical aims of the movement, but do not haggle over principles, do not make concessions in theory.' ... Without a revolutionary theory there can be no revolutionary movement. This cannot be insisted upon too strongly at a time when the fashionable preaching of opportunism is combined with absorption in the narrowest forms of practical activity. (Lenin, 1964)

For this reason Lenin envisaged a vanguard party of intellectuals carefully planning the course of revolution using their knowledge of Marxist theory. Nothing could be more removed from this idea than the fascist pride in the brute force, animal cunning and opportunism of the storm-trooper. The communist coding of violence, war and the brute expression of power similarly reflects this difference. For communist codes, like those of democratic civil society, war and even violent revolution were necessary and temporary evils rather than ends in themselves.

> We are advocates of the abolition of war, we do not want war; but war can only be abolished through war, and in order to get rid of the gun it is necessary to take up the gun. (Mao, cited in Cohen, 1962: 203)

Equality is also an obvious point of difference between liberal democracy and communism. Fascism posited hierarchy and conflict as necessary for salvation. Liberal democracy believes only weakly in the sacred goal of equality, arguing for a formal equality of rights amongst citizens. Communist civil discourses elevated the concept to centrality. Understanding inequality as intensely profane, they argued for the necessity of *substantive* equality in the formation of the classless society that would follow successful revolution.

> Communist society will abolish the class division of society, i.e., simultaneously with the abolition of anarchy in production, it will abolish all forces of exploitation and oppression of man by man … the hierarchy created by the division of labor system will be abolished together with the antagonism between mental and manual labor; and the last vestige of the social inequality of sexes will be removed … under such circumstances the domination of man over man, in any form, becomes impossible. (Communist International, 1963 [1928]: 168)

Communist social organization reflected and enforced this code by means of a centralized, state regulated allocation of facilities. In contrast with democratic society there was remarkable emphasis on uniformity of housing, wages, and transportation.[11] The stress on equality even penetrated to the level of everyday life. For example, communists have often adopted a standard garb such as the blue jacket and pants of Mao's China or the *mono azul* of Republican Spain.

The single greatest point of contrast with liberal democracy, however, lies in the advocacy of the group over the individual.[12] Under communism, fundamental rights, goods and values such as liberty and indeed property, for example, are linked to the collectivity and not the individual. According to communist discourses, salvation was to come to the individual via the recognition of more fundamental collective identities and participation in collective rather than individual action (see Sartre, 1960). The sacred, redeeming status of class consciousness and collective mobilization, which pulled the individual from a morass of solipsistic introspective isolation, were contrasted with the fragmentation of bourgeois individualism (e.g. Lukacs, 1971), its atomization of identity and the chaos of the market. For this reason, communist discourses argued relentlessly for collective solutions to social problems – such as collective farms and communes, collective leadership and even collective artistic collaboration. Because the fundamental good lies in the interests of the group (class) it has been quite legitimate in communism to consider the individual as expendable, the needs of the many outweighing the rights of the few. As with fascism this group focus has been associated with a downgrading of autonomy as a central point in the sign system. The communist citizen is expected to commit themselves wholeheartedly to, and conform with, the group, whilst those able to remain outside established groups and modes of thinking (i.e. the quasi-autonomous) were treated as dangerous and subversive.[13]

In conclusion, we can understand communist discourses as a series of transformations of the same basic set of signifiers that underlie democratic and fascist political discourses. The codes of communist political discourse can be reconstructed as in Table 7.3.

Table 7.3   *Codes of communism*

Sacred	Profane
Order	Disorder
Group	*Individual* +
Reason	Emotion +
Active	Passive
Law	Power
Equality	Hierarchy +
Inclusive	Exclusive
Autonomy	Dependence –

Concluding Remarks: Relativism, Beyond Good and Evil?

> The line dividing good and evil cuts through the heart of every human being ... From good to evil is one quaver, says the proverb, and correspondingly from evil to good. (Alexander Solzhenitsyn, *The Gulag Archipelago*)

Sociological debate is rarely denuded of the influence of non-cognitive criteria, and for this reason particular historical events may influence the intellectual *Zeitgeist* in distinctive ways. The association between intellectual inquiry and the politics of emancipation is to be applauded when the horizons of theoretical inquiry are expanded. But it is necessary to be aware of the paradoxes and dangers of working in such a climate.

Consider the case of civil society theory. Underlying the sociological analysis of civil society is a moral project – the desire to construct a better society from a superior understanding of social institutions. Yet this project cannot be realized if civil society is falsely romanticized or treated only as the object of philosophical speculation. When utopian thinking constructs civil society as radically 'other' to totalitarianism, problems arise in analyzing the continuities, similarities and common historical roots linking disparate political cultures. Theoretical and intellectual possibilities are cut short. For example, the shift from a communist to a democratic political culture is understood almost exclusively in terms of a radical transformation of beliefs rather than as the product of more subtle changes amongst the signifiers of a larger, common political culture. Similarly, there can be little room for complacency once it is understood that the seeds of a totalitarian political culture lie within the concepts and signifiers of civil society itself: a change of emphasis here, an inverted coding there, and the democrat becomes a fascist.

The semiotic approach given here should be understood as a step towards a new, more 'scientific' understanding of civil society – or to be more accurate, civil discourses – which builds upon structural semiotic theory. It is an approach which relativizes and contextualizes the political codes of democratic civil discourse. Although dispassionate and analytical, this approach is not without moral intent. It is an approach very much in the spirit of what Durkheim termed the 'moral science' of social life. It is only from a systematic and comparative study of the various forms of civil society and their discourses that realistic choices can be made about, and within, civil society and its language games under the condition of liberal democracy.

Notes

This chapter originates in a collaborative project with Jeffrey Alexander on the role of binary codes in civil society. I am indebted to Ivan Szelenyi for many hours of discussion about the cultures of communism, fascism and democracy. Steven Jay Sherwood has also been a major influence on my thinking. My thanks to Lyn Spillman and Mike Emmison for providing useful comments on many of the ideas considered here. The usual disclaimers apply.

1 The events of 1989 appear less remarkable with every year that passes. Randall Collins (1992) has correctly pointed out that, far from being aberrant, idiographic events, they can be explained using standard sociological knowledge about regimes and revolutions.

2 I agree with Kumar's observation that debate about civil society has been marked by lack of conceptual clarity. However, his solution – that we abandon the term in favor of more workable concepts like citizenship, the public sphere and the public/private distinction – seems to throw the baby out with the bathwater. 'Civil

society' is useful precisely because it draws our attention to the linkages between such phenomena and suggests that they be studied in a relational manner.

3 Sections of a number of the works consulted for this chapter compared two or more of the 'political ideologies', each one identifying some of the more salient points of agreement or departure between them on an *ad hoc* basis. This activity seemed to be driven by heuristic rather than analytic imperatives (e.g. assisting the novice reader in identifying the qualities and themes of unfamiliar political discourses). The Durkheimian, semiotically informed culture area approach taken here is not only far more systematic, but also makes the relationship *between* ideologies and their resemblances an explicit and central topic for investigation. Not only does the theoretic framework developed here explain the family of civil discourses, their social purpose and their relationships at a formal level, it also provides a platform for the investigation of their historical and social structural roots.

4 Concepts with a master status tend to exert a dominant effect on the character of a political discourse, often overshadowing weaker concepts. In the case of democracy the master statuses of concepts like 'autonomy' and the 'individual' have tended to reduce the significance of 'order' and consequently have served to limit planned state intervention in the public (private) spheres.

5 It is worth noting at this point that some commentators claim that fascism lacks a coherent or clear ideology or is internally contradictory (e.g. Berezin, 1991; Hamilton, 1971). This chapter is in the genre which argues that there is a distinct tradition of fascist thought (Weber, 1964; Cohen, 1962; Nolte, 1969) which underlies the various mass movements commonly dubbed as 'fascist'. Although it is true that fascist discourses were occasionally self-contradictory, this can be attributed to the influence of pragmatic considerations on rhetoric. One would be surprised if one could not find such contradictions, for similar ideological concessions to 'reality' can also be found in democratic discourses. However, the historical evidence is overwhelming that fascist discourses are far from random, but rather are structured by the recurring themes, symbols and concepts of an underlying fascist culture.

6 For a detailed discussion of democratic discourses and a number of historical examples of their role in American politics see Alexander and Smith (1993).

7 The *langue* analogues of 'strength' and 'joy' are 'force' and 'emotion'. Notice that this particular Nazi institution was not called 'strength through reason'.

8 Of course, communist nations have also deployed ritual and symbolism to foster emotional unity. However, in their case the use of ritual has often been something of a last resort following the disappointing failure of the proletariat to respond to the stimuli provided by campaigns of rational indoctrination (study groups, union lectures, subsidized copies of Mao or Marx). In this respect communist parties curiously mirror the ambivalent attitude of the Catholic Church towards the more sensationalistic aspects of Christianity (faith healing, miracles, carnivals etc.).

9 All three discourses in this chapter value activism, reflecting the deep-seated, sacred nature of Judeo-Christian this-worldly activity in Western political culture. However, activism is not a concept universally valued as sacred. Weber's work on comparative religion suggests that some oriental cultures, as well as occidental mystic traditions, valued passivity and contemplation more than activism. We might understand fascist freneticism and mystic withdrawal as limiting cases, with communism and democracy located somewhere on the continuum in between.

10 From 1945 until the collapse of the Soviet Union there was only one non-Soviet world chess champion and around 75% of the world's grandmasters were products of the Soviet chess academies.

11 Of course, the communist elite conferred various privileges upon itself. This does not invalidate the power of the civil discourse of communism. Notice, for example, the way that elites took care to hide their secret excesses (*dachas*, Mercedes automobiles, special shops) from the public – as if they were something of which to be ashamed. Contrast this with the conspicuous consumption indulged in by elites in liberal democracy and fascism (Veblen, 1953).

12 In various places Marx's arguments stress the needs and aspirations of the individual, especially in his discussions of the 'second stage of communism'. Although important theoretical statements, these comments cut across the grain of mainstream communist civil discourse and much of his own writings.

13 A process which helps to explain some of the cultural dimensions of the Soviet persecution of independent kulaks (peasant farmers) and of free-thinking intellectuals throughout the communist world.

References

Alexander, Jeffrey C. (1982) *Theoretical Logic in Sociology*, vol. 2. Berkeley, CA: University of California Press.

Alexander, Jeffrey C. (1991) 'Citizen and Enemy as Symbolic Classification: On the Polarizing Discourse of Civil Society', in M. Lamont and M. Fournier (eds), *Cultivating Differences*. Chicago: University of Chicago Press. pp. 289–308.

Alexander, Jeffrey C. and Smith, Philip (1993) 'The Discourse of American Civil Society: A New Proposal for Cultural Studies', *Theory and Society*, 22: 151–207.

Arato, Andrew (1981) 'Empire vs. Civil Society', *Telos*, 50: 19–48.

Arendt, Hannah (1958) *The Origins of Totalitarianism*. London: Allen and Unwin.

Becker, Howard (1963) *Outsiders*. Glencoe, IL: Free Press.

Benjamin, Walter (1973) 'The Work of Art in the Age of Mechanical Reproduction', in H. Arendt (ed.), *Illuminations*. New York: Schocken Books. pp. 217–51.

Benz, Wolfgang (1990) 'The Ritual and Stage Management of National Socialism', in J. Milfull (ed.), *The Attractions of Fascism*. New York: Berg Publishers. pp. 273–288.

Berezin, Mabel (1991) 'The Organization of Political Ideology: Culture, State and Theater in Fascist Italy', *American Sociological Review*, 56: 639–651.

Bruckner, Peter, Gottshalch, Wilfried, Knodler-Bunte, Eberhard, Munzberg, Olav and Negt, Oskar (1977) 'Perspectives on the Fascist Public Sphere', *New German Critique*, 11 (1): 94–132.

Carsten, F.L. (1969) *The Rise of Fascism*. Berkeley and Los Angeles: University of California Press.

Cohen, Carl (1962) *Communism, Fascism and Democracy*. New York: Random House.

Cohen, Jean (1982) *Class and Civil Society*. Amherst, MA: University of Massachusetts Press.

Collins, Randall (1992) 'The Romanticism of Agency/Structure versus the Analysis of Micro/Macro', *Current Sociology*, 40 (1): 77–97.

Communist International (1963) [1928] 'Programme of the Communist International'. Reprinted in C. Cohen (ed.), *Communism, Fascism and Democracy*. New York: Random House. pp. 167–170.

Dandeker, Christopher (1985) 'Fascism and Ideology: Continuities and Disconti-nuities in Capitalist Development', *Ethnic and Racial Studies* 8 (3): 349–67.

Darwin, Charles (1929) *The Origin of Species*. London: Oxford University Press.

136   *Bifurcating Discourses*

Douglas, Mary (1969) *Purity and Danger.* London: Routledge.

Durkheim, Emile (1964) *The Division of Labour in Society.* New York: Free Press.

Eatwell, Roger (1992) 'Towards a New Model of Generic Fascism', *Journal of Theoretical Politics*, 4 (2): 161–94.

Engels, Fredrich (1934) *Anti-Duhring.* London: Lawrence and Wishart.

Falasca-Zamponi, Simonetta (1992) 'The Aesthetics of Politics: Symbol, Power and Narrative in Mussolini's Fascist Italy', *Theory, Culture and Society*, 9: 75–91.

Freud, Sigmund (1989) *Civilization and its Discontents.* London: Norton.

Gentile, Giovanni (1962) [1928] 'The Philosophical Basis of Fascism', in C. Cohen (ed.), *Communism, Fascism and Democracy.* New York: Random House. pp. 340–4.

Hamilton, A. (1971) *The Appeal of Fascism.* London: Blond.

Hitler, Adolf 1962 [1923] Selections from 'Hitler's Words, the Speeches of Adolf Hitler from 1923 to 1943', in C. Cohen (ed.), *Communism, Fascism and Democracy.* New York: Random House.

Huber, Ernst (1962) [1939] Selections from 'Constitutional Law of the Greater German Reich', in C. Cohen (ed.), *Communism, Fascism and Democracy.* New York: Random House. pp. 369–74.

Jung, Carl (1947) *Essays on Contemporary Events.* London: Kegan Paul.

Keane, John (1988) *Civil Society and the State.* London: Verso.

Knodler-Bunte, Eberhard (1977) 'Fascism as a Depoliticized Mass Movement', *New German Critique*, 25 (2): 161–81.

Kumar, Krishnan (1993) 'Civil Society: An Inquiry into the Usefulness of an Historical Term', *British Journal of Sociology*, 44 (3): 375–95.

Kuper, Adam (1982) *Wives for Cattle.* London: Routledge.

Lenin, Vladimir I. (1964) *What Is To Be Done?* Moscow: Progress.

Lévi-Strauss, Claude (1964) *Le Cru et le Cuit.* Paris: Plon.

Lévi-Strauss, Claude (1966) *The Savage Mind.* London: Weidenfeld and Nicolson.

Lévi-Strauss, Claude (1977)'The Story of Asdiwal', in *Structural Anthropology*, vol. II. London: Allen Lane. pp. 146–97.

Lipset, Seymour Martin (1983) *Political Man.* London: Heinemann.

Locke, John (1946) *The Second Treatise of Civil Government.* Oxford: Blackwell.

Lockwood, David (1993) *Solidarity and Schism.* Oxford: Clarendon.

Lucaks, Georgy (1971) *History and Class Consciousness.* Cambridge, MA: MIT Press.

Mack Smith, Denis (1983) *Mussolini: A Biography.* New York: Vintage.

Nietzsche, Friedrich (1966) *Beyond Good and Evil.* New York: Vintage.

Nolte, E. (1969) *Three Faces of Fascism.* New York: Mentor.

Oestereicher, Emil (1974) 'Fascism and the Intellectuals: The Case of Italian Futurism', *Social Research*, 41 (3): 515–33.

O'Sullivan, Noel (1983) *Fascism.* London: Dent.

Palmieri, Mario (1962) [1936] 'Fascism and the Meaning of Life', in C. Cohen (ed.), *Communism, Fascism and Democracy.* New York: Random House. pp. 344–61.

Parsons, Talcott (1954a) [1942] 'Democracy and Social Structure in Pre-Nazi Germany', in *Essays in Sociological Theory.* New York: Free Press. pp. 104–23.

Parsons, Talcott (1954b) 'Some Sociological Aspects of Fascist Movements', in *Essays in Sociological Theory.* New York: Free Press. pp. 124–41.

Radcliffe-Brown, A.R. (1913) 'Three Tribes of Western Australia', *Journal of the Royal Anthropological Institute*, 43: 143–94.

Radcliffe-Brown, A.R. (1930) 'The Social Organization of Australian Tribes', *Oceania*, 1: 34–63.

Radel, J. Lucien (1975) *Roots of Totalitarianism*. New York: Crane, Russak.

Richardson, Michael (1992) 'Sociology on the Razor's Edge: Configurations of the Sacred at the College of Sociology', *Theory, Culture and Society*, 9: 27–44.

Sartre, Jean-Paul (1960) *Critique de la Raison Dialectique*. Paris: Gallimard.

Schudson, Michael (1989) 'How Culture Works: Perspectives from Media Studies on the Efficacy of Symbols', *Theory and Society*, 18: 153–80.

Smith, Adam (1801) [1759] *The Theory of Moral Sentiments*. London: Strahan.

Smith, Adam (1880) [1776] *The Wealth of Nations*. Oxford: Clarendon.

Smith, Philip (1991) 'Codes and Conflict', *Theory and Society*, 20: 103–38.

Smith, Philip (1994) 'The Semiotic Foundations of Media Narratives', *Journal of Narrative and Life History*, 4: 89–118.

Sorel, Georges (1915) *Reflections on Violence*. London: Allen and Unwin.

Touraine, Alain (1983) *Solidarity: The Analysis of a Social Movement*. Cambridge: Cambridge University Press.

Turner, Victor (1970) *The Forest of Symbols*. Ithaca, NY: Cornell University Press.

Vajda, Mihaly (1971) 'On Fascism', *Telos*, 8 (Summer): 43–63.

Veblen, Thorsten (1953) [1899] *The Theory of the Leisure Class*. New York: New American Library.

Weber, Eugen (1964) *Varieties of Fascism*. London: Nostrand.

Weber, Max (1978) *Economy and Society*. Berkeley, CA: University of California Press.

8

The Racial Discourse of Civil Society: The Rodney King Affair and the City of Los Angeles

Ronald N. Jacobs

Recent theoretical and empirical studies across the social sciences have invigorated an emerging field of 'civil society studies'. Despite this ferment, however, many ambiguities still surround the concept of civil society and its public, discursive organization. Following Habermas (1989) and Parsons (1977), we would expect that civil society consists of a single discourse and a single public sphere. But an increasing number of scholars, influenced by historical studies of particular communities, now argue that civil society consists of multiple public spheres and discourses. In this chapter I examine these competing claims, in a comparison of African-American and 'mainstream' newspaper coverage of the Watts crisis of 1965 and the Rodney King crisis of 1991. I argue that these events were narrated and interpreted differently in the two newspapers, but that they also used a common semiotic system to describe social actors, actions, relationships, and institutions. Furthermore, the different and competing narrations were all socially constructed as a symbolic contest between civil and anti-civil forces, and they all combined the romantic and utopian dimensions of civil society discourse with other contestatory and tragic ones. In other words, while there are multiple public spheres and discourses of civil society, they are organized by a shared cultural environment.

The Cultural Environment of Civil Society

As the civil society concept has moved from the realm of purely normative theory to become more of an empirical tool, it has been modified in several respects. Among these, some of the most important are the recognition that civil society is composed of not one but many public spheres and communities (Calhoun, 1991; 1994; Taylor, 1995); that the study of civil society should supplement its focus on institutions with a consideration of overarching symbolic codes and narratives (Alexander, 1992a; Alexander and Smith, 1993; Jacobs and Smith, 1997); that theories of civil society should dispense with the idea of a 'pre-social self' in favor of a community-situated self (Etzioni, 1995; Walzer, 1995); and that events in civil society should be seen as having a cultural significance of their own (Kane, 1994; Sewell, 1992a). What these revisions of the civil society concept suggest is a model of multiple, overlapping public spheres, all nested within one another. What unites all of them is a shared cultural environment which can guarantee some coordination, inter-subjectivity, and possibly even trust. If there is to be the possibility for the construction of universalistic solidarities beyond the scope of the many different community identities, there must be a common discourse and a 'widest possible' reference public: civil society in its idealized form (Alexander, 1991). While this common discourse will certainly be refracted through the various lenses provided by particular interpretive communities, even the most polarized con-flicts within a society will display a certain set of common commit-ments and a shared language within which social actors express them (Alexander, 1988: 160). This common language is the 'discourse of civil society', which consists of two structural levels: a 'deep struc-ture', or a common semiotic system through which public actors speak and through which public readers interpret what is being communicated; and a 'temporal structure', or a common narrative system through which public actors chart the movement of them-selves, and others, through time. These two cultural environments simultaneously constrain and enable public actions in civil society.[1]

The 'deep structure', or semiotic system of civil society, is described in some detail by both Alexander and Smith in the preceding chapters. I will therefore discuss it in the most rudimen-tary detail possible, concentrating more of my attention on civil society's narrative structure. The semiotic system of any civil society develops through a particular discursive history, resulting in an 'arbitrary' division of the social world into who is deserving of inclusion and who is not (Alexander, 1992a: 291; Alexander and Smith, 1993: 166). Through this historical and cultural process, civil society becomes organized around a bifurcating discourse of citizen and enemy, defining the characteristics of worthy, democratic citizens and also of unworthy, counter-democratic enemies. This 'common code' not only allows for a degree of intersubjectivity among public speakers, but also provides a relatively stable system for evaluating events and persons. Code-like in form, it is based on binary relations of similarity and difference along the dimensions of motives, relationships, and institutions. For each dimension of the code, there is a system of sacred signs and a system of profane signs. The sacred signs exist in relations of similarity to one another, and in relations of opposition to the profane signs (which themselves are understood as similar) . It is this distinction between the sacred and the profane, what Durkheim (1965: 52) called society's most basic classification, that adds an important evaluative dimension to public discourse, helping to communicate information in a forceful and evocative way . Actors, as members of civil society, believe in the sacred side of the code (and thus maintain a modicum of moral reassurance); at the very least, they make their actions and representations accountable in terms of the sacred (Alexander and Smith, 1993: 164–5). For the case of American civil society, the semiotic code is organized around the sacred signs of rational and controlled motivations, open and trusting relationships, and impersonal, rule-regulated institutions. Each of these sacred signs is made meaningful in relation to its binary opposite, and in its relation to other binary pairs added in the process of code making.[2]

While the semiotic system of civil society provides the 'deep structure' necessary for coordinated action in the public spheres of civil society, its narrative structure allows for the construction of common identities, expectations, and solidarities. Narratives help individuals, groups, and communities to 'understand their progress through time in terms of stories, plots which have beginnings, middles, and ends, heroes and antiheroes, epiphanies and denouements, dramatic, comic, and tragic forms' (1993: 156). As studies of class formation (Somers, 1992; Steinmetz, 1992), collective mobilization (Hart, 1992; Kane, 1994), and mass communication (Darnton, 1975; Jacobs, 1996b; Schudson, 1982) have demonstrated, social actions and identities are guided by narrative understandings. Furthermore, by connecting their self-narratives to collective narratives, individuals can identify with such 'imagined communities' as class, gender, race, ethnicity, and nation.[3] As Steinmetz (1992: 505) has noted, these collective narratives can be extremely important for how individuals evaluate their lives, even if they did not participate in the key historical events of the collective narrative.

The narrative structure of civil society consists of a plot, a set of characters, and a genre. *Plot* refers to the selection, ordering, evaluation, and attribution of differential status to events (Steinmetz, 1992: 497–9). A narrative's plot is fluid and complex in its relationship to events; as Eco (1994) has shown, it can 'linger' on a particular event, flash-back to past events, or flash-forward to future events. The basic plot of civil society is the story of integration, participation, and citizenship.[4] In this plot, the *characters* are organized around the opposition between heroes, who fight for the extension of citizenship and rights, and the antiheroes who would restrict citizenship and threaten rights. In this narrative, the citizen is not considered as a diverse and cultural being, informed by a particular lifeworld, by a particular history, or by an embeddedness in particular and multiple communities, but instead as 'universal man' possessing 'natural rights'. Finally, the narrative of civil society is structured by a particular *genre*, which provides a temporal and spatial link between the characters and events of the narrative, and also influences the relationship between the characters, narrator, and reader. The narrative of civil society is structured predominantly by the genre of romance, which provides for a 'theme of ascent' and which is the reason civil society discourse has typically been a utopian one. In romance, as Frye (1957) has described, the hero has great powers, the enemy is clearly defined and often has great powers as well, and the movement takes the form of an adventure with the ultimate triumph of hero over enemy. Romantic genres are viewed by the audience from a perspective of wish-fulfillment, where heroes represent ideals and villains represent threats.

Narratives also enable events to take on a cultural significance of their own. Depending on how they are defined, how they are linked together in a story or plot, and what determines their selection or exclusion into a particular narrative, events can have important consequences for social identities and social actions (Steinmetz, 1992: 497–8). Some events 'demand' narration, and therefore have the power to disrupt prevailing systems of belief and to change understandings about other events in the past, present, and future (Kane, 1994: 504–6; Sewell, 1992b: 438–9). In the modern media age, they become 'media events', announced through an interruption of normal broadcast schedules, repeated analysis by 'experts', and opinion polling about the central characters involved in the crisis (Scannell, 1995; Dayan and Katz, 1992). Drawing on an anthropological perspective and a focus on ritual, Dayan and Katz have examined those celebratory events which demand narration: contests such as presidential debates or Superbowls, conquests such as moon landings, and coronations such as presidential inaugurations. There is still an additional type of event, however, which 'demands narration' in civil society. What I have in mind are those events which get constructed as crises, threatening the romantic and utopian narrative of citizenship, participation, and rights. These events get scripted as a different kind of media event: social dramas testing the ideals of civil society, and demanding the attention of citizens as well as political elites (Turner, 1974: 39). Events such as the Dreyfus affair, Watergate, and the Rodney King beating become important plot elements for the different narratives of civil society and nation, and for this reason can be extremely consequential for collective identities and social outcomes. And while these events frequently also take on a ritualistic dimension, encouraging an eventual emplotment into the romantic narrative of civil society, there are countervailing pressures in real civil societies that continually contest and threaten such a romantic emplotment. It is to these pressures that I turn now.

Discursive Rejections, Exclusion, and Real Civil Societies

While the discourse of civil society may be universalistic, romantic, and utopian, its empirical articulation has everywhere been contested by particularistic, tragic, and dystopian discourses. These competing discourses offer alternative narrations of events, suggesting alternative strategies which are more than mere reaction. As Alexander has noted, 'while the analytic concept of civil society must by all means be recovered from the heroic age of democratic revolutions, it should be de-idealized so that "anti-civil society" – the countervailing processes of decivilization, polarization, and violence – can be seen also as typically "modern" results' (1994: 192). At least three different sources can be identified for these countervailing pressures, described in brief below.

Particularistic Constructions from the 'Center'

The relationship between center and periphery has been one of the most fruitful conceptual sources for post-Parsonian and late-Durkheimian theorists trying to understand the dynamics of integration and exclusion in modern societies. In the original formulation of Edward Shils (1975), the fact that individuals in modern society are oriented toward a common cultural center implies a simultaneous awareness of their own social distance from that center. Only with their symbolic *inclusion* in civil society do they understand their exclusion as 'a perpetual injury to themselves' (1975: 13). As Eisenstadt (1968) has noted in this regard, the goal of participation in civil society does not automatically produce consensus, but can just as easily produce dissensus and conflict. And these conflict-producing symbolic actions are just as often produced from social actors closer to, rather than more distant from, the center. Notwithstanding the universalistic discourse of civil society, all societies were originally composed by a 'core group', whose members are subsequently encouraged to maintain the pre-eminence of certain primordial qualities, and thereby to occupy the 'center' (Alexander, 1988: 83). For example, in Elias's (1978) description of the 'civilizing process' the manners of civility and restraint had the effect of naturalizing both a normative style of interaction and the putative superiority of the courtly society from whence these manners derived. The point is that the romantic and utopian discourse of civil society can be challenged, from the center, by a tragic and dystopian discourse concerning the 'loss of civility'.

Particularistic Constructions from the 'Periphery'
While some challenges to the universalistic discourse of civil society come from those social actors occupying the center, others come from those groups and communities on the periphery. Sometimes this takes a revolutionary form, where those on the periphery deconstruct the universalism of civil society discourse and reconstruct a counter-nationalism seeking to naturalize a different primordial and particularistic origin myth. On other occasions, the expectations provided by civil society's utopian discourse change individual and group definitions of the situation, causing them to see their marginality as both a perpetual injury to themselves and a challenge to the romantic utopia of civil society. This does not lead to a revolutionary strategy, but rather to an activist and inclusionary one. Even though civil rights have not been automatically extended to everyone, have not necessarily yielded social rights, and have not brought substantive status leveling, excluded groups maintain the demand for the inclusion that was promised to them by the discourse of formal and universalistic rights. David Brion Davis (1986: 302) has noted how this exceptionalism of civil society discourse was a resource in the fight against slavery, creating 'a wholly unprecedented ideology that led American blacks of the early 1770s to petition for their freedom'. While thousands of black slaves had risen in revolt against their masters as early as AD 869, those earlier slave revolts never challenged the justice of slavery as an institution. Only with the universalistic discourse of civil society and natural rights were they able to make this strong normative claim on the center.

Particularistic Constructions from Nations and Nation-States
Both of the previous challenges derive in large part from the fact that the romantic and universalistic discourse of civil society, to the extent that it centrally incorporates a discourse of citizenship, presupposes nation-states and national identity. According to Brubaker (1992), citizenship is not only an instrument of participation and integration, but also a means of social closure and exclusion. The combinatorial system of nationhood and citizenship creates resident foreigners, politicizes migration, and often results in diasporic communities of non-citizen non-members whose presence simultaneously reinforces the discourse of civil society and the principle of difference (Brubaker, 1992; Soysal, 1994). And while this process of

social closure is often territorial, creating external enemies, it can also be used to exclude residents (as 'internal enemies'), regardless of whether they are recent migrants or autochthonous groups. The dichotomizing semiotic structure of civil society discourse is easily implicated in this process, providing the basis for excluding resident groups who are defined as 'essentially' profane. This was certainly true in colonial India, where the indigenous populations were coded as 'racially' dependent on community conformity, and therefore unable to exist as autonomous individuals (Chatterjee, 1993). For the case of gender, historical descriptions of women as 'naturally' passive, dependent, and irrational have been linked to the discursive structure of democratic actors in civil society to exclude them from citizenship (Pateman, 1988; Ryan, 1992; Yeatman, 1984). The same has been true for African-Americans, who were repeatedly described by 'scientific' studies as passive and indolent, compared with the 'natural' Caucasian attributes of activity and rationality (Smedley, 1993).

The point is that alongside the universalistic and romantic discourse of civil society there are other discourses, more particularistic, which offer competing narrations for public events. This is of particular importance for crisis, because the competing discourses offer a more tragic genre for understanding social crisis. From the point of view of the civilizing process, crisis can be seen as a tragic breakdown of civility and restraint. From the perspective of the periphery, crisis can be narrated through a tragic deconstruction of the principles of universalism which constitute the romantic promise of civil society. If motivated by the dynamics of social closure which are inherent to the instituted process of citizenship, crisis can be narrated as a referendum on the ability of certain individuals and groups to exercise their citizenship rights in a manner consistent with the semiotic system of civil society. In other words, crisis offers a prime site of contestation for the discourses of civil and anti-civil society.

Narratives of Racial Crisis in Civil Society

I have so far been devoted to a set of arguments concerning the description of the cultural environment of civil society, in both its real and its ideal forms. In the remaining part of this chapter, I want to examine the articulation of these different discourses in actual empirical instances of racial crisis. I focus on two different cases – the Watts crisis of 1965 and the Rodney King crisis of 1991 – and compare how they were reported in the dominant African-American and 'mainstream' newspapers of Los Angeles: the *Los Angeles*

Sentinel and *Los Angeles Times*, respectively. While both news-papers consistently used the sacred side of the semiotic system to describe civil actors and the profane side to criticize anti-civil ones, the narrations of the crises in the two newspapers varied consider-ably, reflecting the influence of other counter-narratives. During the Watts crisis of 1965, the *Los Angeles Times* narrated the crisis largely as a tragic threat to civility and restraint, and coded negatively all attempts to discuss underlying causes. The *Los Angeles Sentinel*, on the other hand, narrated Watts as a threat to the utopian promise of civil society, and focused more on the underlying causes and the anti-civil actions of the police and local politicians. Twenty-six years later, during the Rodney King crisis, both newspapers narrated the crisis as a threat to the utopian promise of civil society. The *Los Angeles Times*, however, reserved the heroic character positions for political elites, while the *Los Angeles Sentinel* was concerned to reserve significant heroic positions for members of the African-American community.

Watts
The Watts crisis began on 11 August 1965, after a white California highway patrolman arrested an African-American, Marquette Frye, on suspicion of drunk driving. While the details which followed this arrest are disputed, what is known is that tensions escalated as a crowd grew to some 250–300 persons, more police arrived, and subsequent arrests were made. Members of the crowd began throw-ing stones as the last police car left the area, setting off a period of rioting that continued for some five days. At the conclusion of these events on 15 August there were 34 deaths, 1,032 injuries, over 4,000 arrests, and an estimated $40 million in property damage.[5] In Los Angeles, the riot shattered the indifference of the white population toward the activities and concerns of the African-American com-munity (Sonenshein, 1993). At the national level Watts, along with the 1964 urban riots in Harlem, Rochester, and Philadelphia, as well as similar events in Chicago in 1965 and Detroit in 1967, was important in redirecting attention away from the civil rights strug-gles of the South and toward the different problems existing in the urban centers of the North and West.

Although Watts was eventually linked to many different narra-tives, including those about the civil rights movement, state politics, national politics, urban policies, and communism, it was initially reported through descriptions of the rioters and their actions. In the *Los Angeles Times*, the rioters were described as 'youthful', 'boast-ful', 'irrational', and 'insane'. Accounts from witnesses described the riot zone as 'terrifying' and 'hysterical'.[6] Others described how the rioters were impeding the rescue work of fire trucks and ambulances, and also through 'false reports designed to lure vehicles into the riot area'.[7] Still others described how 'the rioters were burning their city now, as the insane sometimes mutilate themselves'.[8] These interpretations were not presented as evaluations, but were placed within the descriptive frame of the 'news account', each account attributed to a source. At the same time, however, the polluting, anti-civil discourse of actors and motivations operated to code the rioters as evil. With such a negative coding of the rioters and their actions, accomplished through 'objective' news practices attributed to 'accounts' and 'eyewitnesses', there was a naturalization of support for the police, who were coded positively. This worked initially through the principle of semiotic opposition, where opposition to the rioters also meant opposition to their putative motivation characteristics. Editorial opinion in the *Los Angeles Times* reinforced this opposition early and often, contrasting the forces of order and the forces of disorder.

> Race rioting has brought anarchy to a crowded area of south Los Angeles. Terrorism is spreading. Whatever its root causes, the terror which has gripped the city for three days and three nights must be halted forthwith. If the National Guardsmen belatedly sent to the relief of Chief Parker's outnumbered police, sheriff's deputies and California Highway patrolmen are not enough, additional hundreds must be provided at once ... Only after sanity is restored can there be any meaningful talk about long-range cures of the basic problems involved.[9]

> There are no words to express the shock, the sick horror, that a civilized city feels at a moment like this. It could not happen in Los Angeles. But it did. And the shameful, senseless, bloody rioting continues unabated after the four ugliest days in our history. Decent citizens everywhere, regardless of color, can only pray that this anarchy will soon end. Meanwhile the community, watching, waiting, praying, becomes more aware each moment of the debt owed its heroic law enforcement and fire fighting personnel. These men deserve the highest praise for their splendid efforts under unbelievably difficult conditions.[10]

Note that in these descriptions *citizens* were constructed as desiring a return to order, *without regard to color*: that is, as 'universal man'. In such an interpretive environment there was no possible defense for the rioters, all attempts to stop them were just, and any discussion of the riot's causes were premature and wrong-headed. The rioters were described as lacking in civility and restraint, and those who would support them were therefore supporting the forces of anarchy and evil. This cultural dynamic was reinforced by the efforts of social construction achieved by Los Angeles Police Chief William Parker. Parker claimed that the riots occurred because people lost respect for the law, and he refused to meet with civil rights spokesmen on the grounds that there were no effective leaders.[11] Additionally, Parker blamed 'pseudo-leaders' of the African-American community for influencing the police not to crack down when rioting first broke out, but then not being able to control the rioters themselves.[12] Finally, Parker said that any attempt to blame police for the riots was a 'vicious canard'. The *Los Angeles* Times reported all of these statements uncritically, and reinforced them by linking criticism of the police to 'Communist press agencies' world-wide.[13]

In this developing narrative of the *Los Angeles Times*, where Parker became the heroic figure challenging the antiheroic 'pseudo-leaders' of the African-American community, the civil rights movement itself came to be emplotted into the crisis, as emblematic of a tragic breakdown in civility and social order. Watts quickly became a point of narrative linkage for the *Los Angeles Times* and its public speakers to criticize all forms of civil disobedience, as well as the leaders of the civil rights, student, and anti-war movements.

> Under the leadership of a self-proclaimed peace lover, they have preached non-violence but winked at violence. They have preached love but winked at hate. They have talked about rights but never responsibilities. They have taught their people that law and order are a pedestrian way to achieve results and that civil disobedience is a virtue if it get things done faster.[14]

> It [the rioting] is very much likelier to happen so long as the nation coddles the teachings of the Mario Savios and the Martin Luther Kings, and their disciples who, seeking an honorable motivation for the exercise of their anarchic instincts, walk away from the bloodshed they have caused citing the liturgy of a black mass, which excuses on some ground or other their heinous deeds.[15]

Within this interpretive environment, Watts as a topic of serious discussion was viewed as very dangerous and polluting, used by communists and the fanatical proponents of disobedience. The way this narrative was developing, the crisis of Watts was not one of violence, unemployment, or police brutality; rather, the crisis was the introduction of 'extremist discourse' into the public sphere. In other words, Watts was constructed as a threat to controlled, rational, and civilized behavior, and the rioters were seen as the dependent dupes of extremist discourse propagated by civil rights leaders and communists. For the *Los Angeles Times* and its readers Watts was a tragedy, because it represented a breakdown in civilized society, and because it transformed the heroes of the civil rights movement into fanatical and anti-civil antiheroes. This tragic narration of Watts was reflected in the opinions of white residents in Los Angeles, of whom 74% believed that Watts hurt the civil rights movement, 71% believed that it increased the gap between the races, and 79% supported Chief Parker (Morris and Jeffries, 1970; Sears and McConahy, 1973). This was in marked contrast to African-American opinion in Los Angeles, where 58% of those surveyed anticipated a favorable effect to come from Watts, only 23% expected it to increase the gap between the races, and 76% were critical of Chief Parker (Sears and McConahy, 1973; Tomlinson and Sears, 1970).

While the early *Los Angeles Times* reports constructed Watts as a threat to civilized society, using a tragic narrative of disorder, violence, and fragmentation, early reports in the *Los Angeles Sentinel* were narrated through a much more romantic genre, rejecting the argument that discourse about urban problems was dangerous. These differences in reporting began with the descriptions of the rioting. Rather than describing the rioters through the code of irrationality, the *Sentinel* instead described them as 'lawless' and 'shameful'. While these descriptions were obviously critical in intent, they differed in that they allowed for the likelihood that the rioters had some underlying motivation for their actions. And it was the motivations for these extreme actions which centered the early reports of the *Sentinel*. The initial editorials in the newspaper illustrate the narrative strategy well, where the rioters were criticized, but emplotted into a critique of urban policies affecting the African-American community.

> Basically, we believe that all self-respecting Negro citizens here deplore the burning of buildings, the lootings and shootings and its staggering toll in human lives and property damage which besieged our city last weekend, and also know the need of proper law enforcement to protect all of our citizens ... The incident and the arrests which triggered the riot last Wednesday night were only incidental. Because the psychological fires of frustration had been smouldering in the minds of thousands of deprived citizens in Watts and other areas, and it was going to happen someday, anyhow ... Certainly, it is easy to blame 'criminal elements' or a 'hoodlum fringe,' or even the Communists, when what is called for is some really deep soul-searching.[16]

> They said it couldn't happen here but it did. In this case, the 'they' isn't the undefinable 'group pronoun' of fabricated stories or gossip. They are the leaders of our city government – the Mayor, the Chief of Police, members of the City Council, business and community leaders and just plain everyday citizens who have not been facing up to the facts. People who have been living in a dream world. A world in which they have ignored the fact that we here in Los Angeles have been sitting on a racial tinderbox for at least the last five years! ... The reforms, the programs, the projects, and the grass-roots work which could have been inaugurated to prevent what has been the bloodiest and most disastrous U.S. race riot in

history, never materialized, either because of official non-interest or the simple, isolated, unmovable fact of racial prejudice.[17]

It is notable that these editorials described 'Negro citizens' as distinct from 'everyday citizens', a distinction that pointed to the persistence of marginality and the incomplete realization of the romantic promise of civil society discourse. They also demonstrate a recoding of political elites and 'plain everyday citizens', from reasonably outraged to unreasonable, unrealistic, and exclusionary. Finally, these two editorials demonstrate a reflexive orientation to other public spheres, and a reversal of the narrative lines exhibited in the mainstream Los Angeles media. Where the mainstream media saw danger in 'extremist discourse', the *Sentinel* saw danger in the lack of serious discourse. Where the rioters had been labeled as irrational and unmotivated, they were now symbolized by rational and deep-seated motivations (even if they were still negatively coded as uncontrolled and violent). And where Watts had turned the plot of the civil rights narrative to a discussion of its excesses, for the *Sentinel* it functioned to turn the civil rights narrative to a discussion of its incomplete realization. In other words, the threat to civil society denoted by Watts was the threat from the periphery, where marginality was both a perpetual injury and a challenge to the romantic utopia of civil society. Rather than constructing an opposition between order and disorder, as we saw with the *Los Angeles Times*, the *Sentinel*'s reports mobilized a different opposition: between action and inaction, between reconstruction and blame.

In this narrative environment, where the plot development was in the direction of causes and solutions, news stories about Watts took one of two paths. The first was concerned primarily with the criticism of the Los Angeles Police Department and its chief, and the unrest in Watts was explained as being caused by 'resentment over the tactics of white police officers in minority communities'.[18] From the beginning of its reports about Watts, the sources who were used by the *Sentinel* in its reported speech concentrated on the problem of Chief Parker and the Los Angeles Police Department. Leaders of both the local and national African-American community attributed the cause of Watts to the impure and polluted police department.

Sparked by the Rev. H.H. Brookins, Assemblyman Mervin Dymally and other community leaders, an intensified move to oust Police Chief Parker is gaining momentum. The action, reflecting increasing resentment over the tactics of white police officers in minority communities, was planned as a protest against Parker's attitudes and expressed statements about Negroes. 'Having worked closely with our law-abiding citizens, I am convinced that the removal of Police Chief Parker would be a major factor in curtailing the continued unrest and violence which has brought shame and disgrace to a city destined for greatness,' Dr. Brookins said.[19]

In two conferences at the Governor's office in Los Angeles during the height of the rioting in South Los Angeles, leading members of the community asked 'that Governor Brown remove the national guard from the leadership of Chief Parker and the Los Angeles force, and that the guard be placed under the leadership of a state or federal officer whose very name and presence are not part and parcel of the crisis facing our community'.[20]

These criticisms of the police department emplotted the Watts crisis in the middle of an ongoing crisis of community–government and community–police relations. Here, Watts evinced evidence not of the excesses of civil disobedience, but rather of the lack of real concern for civil rights on the part of local government officials. In this narrative, Los Angeles politicians were linked to heartless and racist policies. Opposed to them were federal officials and community leaders who had long recognized the problems and suggested solutions.

For almost 10 years, warnings that disaster was inevitable have been voiced by sources both within and without the Los Angeles Negro community. Typical of numerous official reports was one that was issued in August of 1963 by the United States Commission on Human Rights which stressed the need for strong measures to relieve police oppression in the Los Angeles ghetto area. And since 1962, civil rights organizations have sought, through non-violent direct action, to dramatize the frustrations and sufferings of the minority community and to give the majority community opportunity to relieve these frustrations before they hardened into feelings of bitterness and rage. With the passage of Proposition 14, with continued unfair employment practices, with heartless delay in the administration of anti-poverty funds, the majority community has replied with a resounding NO, while city officials remained blind and deaf to all complaints of malpractices by the police, answering only with increased police force in the minority community.[21]

The simple and objective facts, and they are plain and ominous to anyone familiar with the area, are that poverty, law enforcement attitudes, and a general feeling of hopelessness, frustration, and being regarded as less than human were the major causes for the riots ... It is apparent at this writing that these points are not clearly understood by the majority of the residents of this city. It is apparent that our Mayor, Samuel Yorty, and Chief of Police, William Parker, either do not want to recognize these facts or recognize them and do not want to give them credence. It is apparent that this is the same feeling of many of our other city, county, and state officials. By their deeds and through their words, it is apparent that they have really not profited from the terrible experience of the tragedy we've all just witnessed and lived through. They are further compounding the crime which they have been guilty of for years: a total apathy and disregard for what have been the area's problems.[22]

What we see in these early constructions of Watts by the *Los Angeles Sentinel* is a challenge from the periphery to the utopian and universalistic ideals of civil society, as well as a romantic hope that the anti-civil antiheroes – local politicians and the majority community – would be superseded by more heroic federal politicians (such as Governor Edmund Brown and President Lyndon Johnson) and empowered African-American leaders. At the same time, however, there was a persistent cynicism in the constructions of the *Sentinel*, due in large part to a reflexive monitoring of the 'mainstream' public sphere.

In sum, the social construction of Watts occurred in a highly polarized environment between the African-American and 'mainstream' presses of Los Angeles. The *Los Angeles Times* constructed the threat by combining the discourses of civil society and civility. In this type of construction, there was strong pressure to shut down all discussion which did not reinforce the putative cardinal virtues of civility and restraint; even Governor Brown and President Johnson were criticized, in fact, for 'glossing over the real reason for the Los Angeles riots'.[23] By contrast, the *Los Angeles Sentinel* constructed the threat by combining the civil society discourse with a deconstruction of perceived false universalisms. In this understanding, white indifference made universalistic citizenship impossible, because there was no honest desire to redress past wrongs.

Rodney King

On 3 March 1991, an African-American motorist, Rodney King, was pulled over for speeding.[24] After a brief chase, King was met by 21 police officers, including members of the California Highway Patrol and the Los Angeles Police Department. In full view of all who were present, King was severely beaten by three white LAPD officers, in the presence of a sergeant and the remaining 17 officers. Unknown to the police officers, the event was videotaped by an amateur cameraman, George Holliday, and sold to a local television station. The videotape, which was broadcast thousands of times, provoked a public crisis over police brutality and racism in Los Angeles. The event contained all the necessary symbolic elements to construct the narrative of crisis as a threat to the utopian discourse of civil society. First, the videotape of the beating – which was recorded by an 'amateur cameraman', an ordinary citizen of civil society – showed visual and technical 'proof' of the event: in a sense, a 'video-text', which itself placed the actors in relations of similarity and opposition to one another. The videotape served a naturalizing function for the subsequent interpretations that would be made. Second, the primary image of the videotape, the brutality of the white officers toward the African-American victim, Rodney King, was easily related to earlier historic images of white police violence against African-Americans. Finally, as we have seen, there was a history of conflict between the police department and minority groups in Los Angeles.

What is immediately noticeable when comparing Watts with the Rodney King beating is the decreasing polarization between the two newspapers, and the increasing willingness of the *Los Angeles Times* to criticize the police. Initial reports in the *Los Angeles Times* represented the beating as a wild deviation and a 'shocking' event. Other reports represented the officers as being irrational and excitable in their work, and as having used their powers illegitimately. Accounts from witnesses reported that the officers were 'laughing and chuckling [after the beating], like they had just had a party'.[25] Similar to the Watts case, these interpretations were not presented as evaluations, but were placed within the descriptive frame of the 'news account', each account attributed to a source. At the same time, the polluting, counter-democratic discourse of civil society was operating within the text: through quotations, editorials, and descriptions. The following descriptions of the event appeared in the first days of the crisis:

> accounts ... suggested that what should have been a relatively simple arrest ... escalated wildly out of control.[26]

> The violent images of white police officers pounding an apparently defenseless black man have raised the ire of civil rights groups.[27]

> The beating of King, videotaped by an amateur photographer, has sparked an outcry over police misconduct in Los Angeles, as well as calls for the resignation of Chief Daryl F. Gates. The images of white police officers pummeling the black motorist with their batons were aired by television stations across the country.[28]

Along with the construction of the event as a crisis came a specification of those violations depicted by the video images: violations of fairness, openness, and justice. News reports described the character attributes of the antiheroic police officers, adding to earlier descriptions of their 'uncontrolled and irrational' motivations. The event of the beating, when linked to the videotape, was understood as a way to expose the evil that existed in the police department. An editorial in the *Los Angeles Times* proclaimed that 'this time, the police witnesses, knowing about the videotape, will probably not compound their offense by lying about what really happened.'[29] This narration, exposing the secrecy and brutality of the officers, was used by local leaders as well as 'objective' news reporters:

> It exploded onto Los Angeles television screens last week. The scene: three Los Angeles police officers involved in a merciless, relentless, brutal beating of a Black man as he lay face down in the ground, while 12 officers observed in tacit approval.[30]

> 'This is not an isolated incident!' thundered José de Sosa, the rally's organizer and president of the San Fernando chapter of the NAACP. 'This is the type of thing that occurs under the cover of darkness throughout our city.'[31]

The police officers were condemned through visual images as well as linguistic discourse. On the one hand, the images of the videotape served to 'naturalize' the relationships between the police officers, brutality, and 'darkness'. On the other, the news reports represented the videotape as a foil to the deceitfulness of the police department. In this double sense, the police officers were symbolically polluted by the videotape. The 'propositional content' (cf. Ricoeur, 1971) of the videotaped event undercoded possible constructions of the crisis as a threat to civility, and instead presented it as encouraging a threat to the romantic aspect of civil society discourse. This does not mean that the event captured in the videotape *determined* the subsequent narration of the crisis. There was no necessary reason why Rodney King could not be described as out of control and irrational, as, for example, television ideologue Rush Limbaugh was to do some time later (see Fiske, 1994: 131). But most news reports did, in fact, begin their coverage with criticisms of the police and their actions.

Still, if it was merely a problem of a few individuals in need of administrative control, crisis need not have ensued. But the Rodney King beating was also constructed as a threat to *institutional* legitimacy, through representations of Police Chief Daryl Gates, who was described as unaccountable, racist, and ego-driven.

> The people of Los Angeles have been unable to hold their chief of police accountable for anything – not his racial slurs or racial stereotyping; not his openly-expressed contempt for the public, juries and the Constitution he is sworn to uphold; not his spying on political enemies or cover-up of that espionage.[32]

> Chief Gates is responsible for inflammatory comments, for the actions of his officers and for the $8 million in taxpayer money paid out last year to satisfy complaints against the department. But because of rigid civil service protections, the police chief is not accountable to the mayor, the City Council or to the city's voters.[33]

With the event having been constructed as a crisis, it began to develop through a tension between romantic and tragic genres. The romantic narrative placed the heroic actors of the local government (the Mayor and the City Council) against the antiheroic ones (Gates and the LAPD). This narrative appeared in both the *Los Angeles Times* and the *Los Angeles Sentinel*. Because Gates refused to hold his police officers accountable for their actions, and because he was coded by the counter-democratic discourse of institutions, the remaining local governmental officials became the defenders of institutional legitimacy more or less by default. This occurred on several different levels. Semiotically, it operated through opposition, where every term implies and entails its opposite. In this case, symbolic opposition to Gates benefited the Mayor and the City Council. Politically, it worked because of the need for an identifiably legitimate authority. This political dynamic was expressed quite well in a *Los Angeles Sentinel* editorial, which argued, 'This community has had enough police brutality and if the chief of police won't stop it, then the commission must, and if not, the mayor and the City Council must take definitive action.'[34]

In the *Los Angeles Sentinel*, however, the romantic form of the crisis narrative differed in important respects from that of the *Los Angeles Times*. An important reason for this was the construction of a second romance in which the African-American community itself was posited as the heroic actor. Employing a style common to the African-American press (cf. Wolseley, 1971), the newspaper invoked the ideals of American society while criticizing actually existing society. In opposition to mainstream society, it represented the African-American community as the true voice of unity and morality, and hence as the only agent able to truly resolve the crisis.

> Rarely, if ever, has an issue so united the Black community in the way the March 3 Rodney King incident has done. The savage beating of King has inspired Los Angeles' Black community to speak with one voice.[35]

> We must not allow ourselves to be set apart in this battle. Justice must be served and we must, at least in part, be the instruments of that justice.[36]

> The African-American community itself has a distinct role in the accountability equation. In fact, the community represents the proverbial bottom line: it is the ultimate determinant of values and enforcers of acceptable standards.[37]

In this romantic narrative, the beating of Rodney King became a transformative event, unleashing the potential power of the African-American community.

In tension with the romantic narratives, both newspapers also drew on the contestatory and tragic discourses of anti-civil society. But the elaboration of these contestatory discourses differed between the two newspapers. In the *Los Angeles Times* the public –

what Sherwood (1994) has called the heroic actor of the 'drama of democracy' – became represented as a series of factions, and it became more difficult to imagine a plot development where a new actor could successfully step in and do battle with Gates and the police department. Within the tragic genre, where the crisis was constructed as a threat to the romantic narrative of inclusion and participation, reaction to the beating was interpreted through a description of class, racial, and ethnic segregation rather than public unity. As an editorial in the *Los Angeles Times* lamented, 'It is profoundly revealing that while middle-class viewers recoiled in horror at the brutal footage, the victim, like many others familiar with police behavior in poor and minority neighborhoods, considered himself lucky that the police did not kill him.'[38]

These types of accounts in the *Los Angeles Times* represented a 'tragedy of fate', in the aporetic sense of resigned acceptance, a tragedy pointing to an evil 'already there and already evil' (Ricoeur, 1967: 313). The tragic frame of the *Los Angeles Sentinel*, however, diverged in important respects from such a tragedy of fate. The *Sentinel* combined elements of tragedy and irony, calling up other recent instances of brutality against African-Americans. News reports in the *Sentinel* juxtaposed the outrage and collective attention about the Rodney King beating with the relative lack of attention concerning another beating case whose trial had begun on the same day. The trial stemmed from the 'Don Jackson case', a 1989 event where two Long Beach police officers were captured on videotape pushing an off-duty, African-American police officer through a plate-glass window, 'followed by the sight of Jackson being slammed onto the hood of their patrol car, after a "routine" traffic stop'.[39] The Don Jackson story served as an important interpretive filter through which to view the Rodney King beating. Other historical events also found their way into the *Los Angeles Sentinel*'s coverage. In a feature interview, Brotherhood Crusade leader Danny Bakewell noted that 'When I saw what happened to that brother on television, I thought I was watching a scene out of the distant past: a Ku Klux Klan lynch mob at work.'[40] By recalling other instances of brutality against African-Americans, writers for the *Los Angeles Sentinel* placed the event of the beating in the middle of a long and continuous narrative, rather than at the beginning of a new one.

While both newspapers constructed the Rodney King crisis as a threat to the utopian ideals of civil society, then, there were significant differences in the character positions used to construct the threat and the addition of historical events to the crisis narrative. In the *Los Angeles Times*, the hope for romantic resolution through political elites was contrasted with the tragic threat of factionalism, in a modified form of the 'loss of civility' thesis. In the *Los Angeles Sentinel*, the hope for romantic resolution through African-American empowerment was contrasted with the tragic threat of white indifference. Similar to the case of Watts, the *Los Angeles Times* operated from an understanding of 'universal citizens', while the *Los Angeles Sentinel* maintained a focus on particularistic citizenship reinforced by white racism and indifference. Thus, when the independent Christopher Commission report was released on 9 July, criticizing the police department and recommending significant reforms, it was incorporated differently into the news narratives of the two presses. For the *Los Angeles Times*, the report was linked to political unity and emplotted as the causal factor for Police Chief Daryl Gates's resignation. For the *Los Angeles Sentinel*, however, the report was constructed as a justification of long-standing community criticisms of police and the expectation of greater African-American participation. Furthermore, while the *Times* followed the event of the Christopher Commission report with reports about police department reforms, the *Sentinel* continued to represent the police department as being exclusive and racist, continued to report about new incidents of police brutality, and continued the narrative line of white indifference. Thus, while the two newspapers initially constructed the crisis through the same threat to the romantic utopian vision of civil society, the *Los Angeles Times* was far less likely to include African-American leaders in heroic character positions, and was far more ready to narrate a successful romantic conclusion without including past and present events of particularistic exclusions. In sum, while there was not as much polarization as during Watts, there were still significant narrative variations between the two newspapers.

Conclusion

While I cannot claim to have provided anything approaching a complete theory of the cultural dimensions of crisis in civil society, the discussions of the Watts and Rodney King cases are suggestive in several ways. The first thing to note is that the semiotic system of civil discourse was used consistently across different events, different historical periods, and different public spheres and communities. Furthermore, the semiotic system of civil discourse was undergirded in all of its forms by a romantic vision of a utopian civil sphere based on citizenship, participation, and rights. Indeed, this brings to mind one of Durkheim's (1965: 470) most important claims: that society is composed not only by its resident, individual members, but above all by the idealized image it forms of itself.

Having said this, however, the narrative elaboration of this idealized image of civil society varied across a number of different dimensions. One dimension had to do with the 'propositional content' of events. Indeed, the visual images of Watts and Rodney King overcoded certain narrations and undercoded others, such that the initial description of the events centered around the rioters and the police, respectively. This does not mean the events determined the narration of the crisis, for, as we have seen, the narrations differed depending on the public sphere in which they took place. Indeed, the actual narrations of Watts and Rodney King depended on how particular events were linked to other public narratives, such as civil rights, urban policies, communism, or police brutality. Narrative constructions were also influenced by the countervailing pressures of anti-civil discourses, such as the 'threat to civility' or the 'tragic indifference of mainstream society'. And there was a further difference in terms of how the heroic character of the civil society narrative – the citizen – was constructed: either as 'universal man', as we saw consistently in the case of the 'mainstream' press; or as community-situated selves, in the case of the African-American press, with differential histories of inclusion and exclusion.

The point is that the discourse of real civil societies is not only composed by its idealized and romantic sources, but also by anti-civil pressures which drive contestatory and tragic discourses in the competition for interpretive authority over public events. Thus, the history of racial exclusion and its narrative emplotment into the multiple public spheres of civil society, combined with the continued demand of excluded groups for the inclusion promised to them by the utopian discourse of civil society (and the narrative emplotment of those efforts), creates a 'racial discourse of civil society'. The same is true for other binary principles of division which have resulted in exclusion, leading to a 'gender discourse of civil society' and a 'colonial discourse of civil society', among others. A complete understanding of the cultural environment of civil society will require a comparative and historical examination of all of these discourses.

Notes

I wish to thank Jeffrey Alexander, Walter Allen, Anne Kane, Andy Roth, Steve Sherwood, Philip Smith and Eleanor Townsley for helpful comments on earlier drafts of this chapter.

1 For the case of material social structures, this dynamic is well understood through the structuration theory of Giddens (1984). For cultural structures it is acknowledged less often, although recent theoretical and empirical work has begun to change this. See, for example, Alexander (1992b; 1996), Alexander and Smith (1993),

158   *Bifurcating Discourses*

Berezin (1994), Ellingson (1995), Jacobs (1996a; 1996b), Kane (1991), Sewell (1992b), Smith (1991), Somers (1992; 1995), and Wagner-Pacifici (1986; 1994).
2 The analytical process of code making is described in great detail by Eco (1979).
3 The idea of imagined communities is borrowed from Anderson (1983).
4 Others have discussed this in far greater detail than I have space for here. See, for example, Cohen and Arato (1992: 415–20, 440–63), Marshall (1964), and Parsons (1977).
5 More detailed descriptions of the events surrounding the Watts uprisings can be found in McCone (1969) and Fogelson (1969).
6 *Los Angeles Times*, 14 August 1965: A8.
7 *Los Angeles Times*, 13 August 1965: A1.
8 *Los Angeles Times*, 15 August 1965: A1.
9 *Los Angeles Times*, 14 August 1965: A1.
10 *Los Angeles Times*, 15 August 1965: A1.
11 See *Los Angeles Times*, 13 August 1965: A3; 14 August 1965: A1.
12 *Los Angeles Times*, 15 August 1965: A4.
13 *Los Angeles Times*, 15 August 1965: A2.
14 *Los Angeles Times*, 18 August 1965: B5.
15 *Los Angeles Times*, 20 August 1965: B6.
16 *Los Angeles Sentinel*, 19 August 1965: A6.
17 *Los Angeles Sentinel*, 19 August 1965: A7.
18 *Los Angeles Sentinel*, 19 August 1965: A1.
19 *Los Angeles Sentinel*, 19 August 1965: A1.
20 *Los Angeles Sentinel*, 19 August 1965: A9.
21 *Los Angeles Sentinel*, 26 August 1965: A6.
22 *Los Angeles Sentinel*, 2 September 1965: A7.
23 *Los Angeles Times*, 29 August 1965: G6.
24 For a more detailed discussion of events related to the Rodney King crisis in 1991, see Jacobs (1996a).
25 *Los Angeles Times*, 6 March 1991: A22.
26 *Los Angeles Times*, 7 March 1991: A21.
27 *Los Angeles Times*, 7 March 1991: A22.
28 *Los Angeles Times*, 9 March 1991: B1.
29 *Los Angeles Times*, 9 March 1991: B7.
30 *Los Angeles Sentinel*, 14 March 1991: A1.
31 *Los Angeles Times*, 10 March 1991: B1.
32 *Los Angeles Times*, 12 March 1991: B7.
33 *Los Angeles Times*, 13 March 1991: B6.
34 *Los Angeles Sentinel*, 7 March 1991: A8.
35 *Los Angeles Sentinel*, 14 March 1991: A1.
36 *Los Angeles Sentinel*, 28 March 1991: A7.
37 *Los Angeles Sentinel*, 11 April 1991: A6.
38 *Los Angeles Times*, 14 March 1991: B5.
39 *Los Angeles Sentinel*, 7 March 1991: A1.
40 *Los Angeles Sentinel*, 14 March 1991: A5.

References

Alexander, Jeffrey C. (1988) *Action and its Environments*. New York: Columbia University Press.

Alexander, Jeffrey C. (1991) 'Bringing Democracy Back In: Universalistic Solidarity and the Civil Sphere', in C. Lemert (ed.), *Intellectuals and Politics: Social Theory in a Changing World*. Newbury Park, CA: Sage. pp. 157–76.

Alexander, Jeffrey C. (1992a) 'Citizen and Enemy as Symbolic Classification: On the Polarizing Discourse of Civil Society', in Marcel Fournier and Michele Lamont (eds), *Where Culture Talks: Exclusion and the Making of Society*. Chicago: University of Chicago Press. pp. 289–308.

Alexander, Jeffrey C. (1992b) 'Analytic Debates: Understanding the Relative Autonomy of Culture,' in J. Alexander and S. Seidman (eds), *Culture and Society: Contemporary Debates*. New York: Cambridge University Press. pp. 1–30.

Alexander, Jeffrey C. (1994) 'Modern, Anti, Post, Neo: How Social Theories Have Tried to Understand the "New World" of "Our Time" ', *Zeitschrift fur Soziologie*, 23 (3): 165–97.

Alexander, Jeffrey C. (1996) *Neofunctionalism and After*. London and New York: Blackwell.

Alexander, Jeffrey C. and Smith, Philip (1993) 'The Discourse of American Civil Society: A New Proposal for Cultural Studies', *Theory and Society*, 22: 151–207.

Anderson, Benedict (1983) *Imagined Communities: Reflections on the Origin and Spread of Nationalism*. London: Verso.

Berezin, Mabel (1994) 'Theatrical Form and Political Meaning: State-Subsidized Theater, Ideology, and the Language of Style in Fascist Italy', *American Journal of Sociology*, 99 (5): 1237–86.

Brubaker, Rogers (1992) *Citizenship and Nationhood in France and Germany*. Cambridge, MA: Harvard University Press.

Calhoun, Craig (1991) 'Indirect Relationships and Imagined Communities: Large-Scale Social Integration and the Transformation of Everyday Life', in P. Bourdieu and J.S. Coleman (eds), *Social Theory for a Changing Society*. Boulder, CO: Westview. pp. 95–121.

Calhoun, Craig (1994) 'The Public Good as a Social and Cultural Project'. Unpublished manuscript.

Chatterjee, Partha (1993) *The Nation and its Fragments*. Princeton, NJ: Princeton University Press.

Cohen, Jean and Arato, Andrew (1992) *Civil Society and Political Theory*. Cambridge, MA: MIT Press.

Darnton, Robert (1975) 'Writing News and Telling Stories', *Daedalus*, 104 (2): 175–93.

Davis, David Brion (1986) *From Homicide to Slavery: Studies in American Culture*. New York: Oxford University Press.

Dayan, Daniel and Katz, Elihu (1992) *Media Events*. Cambridge, MA: Harvard University Press.

Durkheim, Emile (1965) *The Elementary Forms of the Religious Life*. New York: Free Press.

Eco, Umberto (1979) *A Theory of Semiotics*. Bloomington, IN: Indiana University Press.

Eco, Umberto (1994) *Six Walks in the Fictional Woods*. Cambridge, MA: Harvard University Press.

Eisenstadt, S.N. (1968) *Max Weber on Charisma and Institution Building*. Chicago: University of Chicago Press.

Elias, Norbert (1978) *The Civilizing Process, vol. 1: The History of Manners*. Oxford: Basil Blackwell.

Ellingson, Stephen (1995) 'Understanding the Dialectic of Discourse and Collective Action: Public Debate and Rioting in Antebellum Cincinnati', *American Journal of Sociology*, 101 (1): 100–44.

Etzioni, Amitai (1995) 'Old Chestnuts and New Spurs', in A. Etzioni (ed.), *New Communitarian Thinking: Persons, Virtues, Institutions, and Communities*. Charlottesville, VA: University Press of Virginia. pp. 16–36.

Fiske, John (1994) *Media Matters: Everyday Culture and Political Change*. Minneapolis, MN: University of Minnesota Press.

Fogelson, Robert (1969) 'White on Black: A Critique of the McCone Commission Report on the Los Angeles Riots', in R. Fogelson (ed.), *Mass Violence in America: The Los Angeles Riots*. New York: Arno. pp. 111–44.

Frye, Northrup (1957) *Anatomy of Criticism*. Princeton, NJ: Princeton University Press.

Giddens, Anthony (1984) *The Constitution of Society: Outline of the Theory of Structuration*. Cambridge: Polity.

Habermas, Jurgen (1989) *The Structural Transformation of the Public Sphere*. Cambridge: Polity.

Hart, Janet (1992) 'Cracking the Code: Narrative and Political Mobilization in the Greek Resistance', *Social Science History*, 16 (4): 631–68.

Jacobs, Ronald (1996a) 'Civil Society and Crisis: Culture, Discourse, and the Rodney King Beating', *American Journal of Sociology*, 101 (5): 1238–72.

Jacobs, Ronald (1996b) 'Producing the News, Producing the Crisis: Narrativity, Television, and News Work', *Media, Culture & Society*, 18: 373–97.

Jacobs, Ronald and Smith, Philip (1997) 'Romance, Irony, and Solidarity', *Sociological Theory*, 15 (1): 60–80.

Kane, Anne (1991) 'Cultural Analysis in Historical Sociology: The Analytic and Concrete Forms of the Autonomy of Culture', *Sociological Theory*, 9: 53–69.

Kane, Anne (1994) 'Culture and Social Change: Symbolic Construction, Ideology, and Political Alliance During the Irish Land War, 1879–1881'. PhD dissertation, University of California, Los Angeles.

Marshall, T.H. (1964) *Class, Citizenship, and Social Development*. Chicago: University of Chicago Press.

McCone, John A. (1969) 'Violence in the City – An End or a Beginning? A Report by the Governor's Commission on the Los Angeles Riots', (1965), in R. Fogelson (ed.), *Mass Violence in America: The Los Angeles Riots*. New York: Arno. pp. xi–110.

Morris, Richard T. and Jeffries, Vincent (1970) 'The White Reaction Study', in N. Cohen (ed.), *The Los Angeles Riots: A Socio-Psychological Study*. New York: Praeger. pp. 480–601.

Parsons, Talcott (1977) *The Evolution of Societies*. Englewood Cliffs, NJ: Prentice-Hall.

Pateman, Carole (1988) *The Sexual Contract*. Stanford, CA: Stanford University Press.

Ricoeur, Paul (1967) *The Symbolism of Evil*. Boston: Beacon.

Ricoeur, Paul (1971) 'The Model of a Text: Meaningful Action Considered as a Text', *Social Research*, 38: 529–62.

Ryan, Mary (1992) 'Gender and Public Access: Women's Politics in Nineteenth-Century America', in C. Calhoun (ed.), *Habermas and the Public Sphere*. Cambridge, MA: MIT Press. pp. 259–88.

Scannell, Paddy (1995) 'Media Events', *Media, Culture and Society*, 17: 151–7.

Schudson, Michael (1982) 'The Politics of Narrative Form: The Emergence of News Conventions in Print and Television', *Daedalus*: 97–112.

Sears, David O. and McConahy, John B. (1973) *The Politics of Violence: The New Urban Blacks and the Watts Riot*. Boston: Houghton Mifflin.

Sewell, William H., Jr (1992a) 'Introduction: Narratives and Social Identities', *Social Science History*, 16 (3): 479–89.

Sewell, William H., Jr (1992b) 'A Theory of Structure: Duality, Agency, and Transformation', *American Journal of Sociology*, 98 (1): 1–29.

Sherwood, Steven (1994) 'Narrating the Social', *Journal of Narratives and Life Histories*, 4 (1–2): 69–88.

Shils, Edward (1975) *Center and Periphery: Essays in Macrosociology*. Chicago: University of Chicago Press.

Smedley, Audrey (1993) *Race in North America: Origin and Evolution of a Worldview*. Boulder, CO: Westview.

Smith, Philip (1991) 'Codes and Conflict: Toward a Theory of War as Ritual', *Theory and Society*, 20 (1):103–38.

Somers, Margaret (1992) 'Narrativity, Narrative Identity, and Social Action: Rethinking English Working-Class Formation', *Social Science History*, 16 (4): 591–630.

Somers, Margaret (1995) 'What's Political or Cultural about Political Culture and the Public Sphere? Towards an Historical Sociology of Concept Formation', *Sociological Theory*, 13 (2): 113–44.

Sonenshein, Raphael (1993) *Politics in Black and White: Race and Power in Los Angeles*. Princeton, NJ: Princeton University Press.

Soysal, Yasemin (1994) *Limits of Citizenship: Migrants and Postnational Membership in Europe*. Chicago: University of Chicago Press.

Steinmetz, George (1992) 'Reflections on the Role of Social Narratives in Working-Class Formation: Narrative Theories in the Social Sciences', *Social Science History*, 16 (3): 489–516.

Taylor, Charles (1995) 'Liberal Politics and the Public Sphere', in A. Etzioni (ed.), *New Communitarian Thinking: Persons, Virtues, Institutions, and Communities*. Charlottesville, VA: University Press of Virginia. pp. 183–217.

Tomlinson, T.M. and Sears, David O. (1970) 'Negro Attitudes toward the Riot', in N. Cohen (ed.), *The Los Angeles Riots: A Socio-Psychological Study*. New York: Praeger. pp. 288–325.

Turner, Victor (1974) *Dramas, Fields and Metaphors*. New York: Cornell University Press.

Wagner-Pacifici, Robin (1986) *The Moro Morality Play: Terrorism as Social Drama*. Chicago: University of Chicago Press.

Wagner-Pacifici, Robin (1994) *Discourse and Destruction: The City of Philadelphia versus MOVE*. Chicago: University of Chicago Press.

Walzer, Michael (1995) 'The Communitarian Critique of Liberalism', in A. Etzioni (ed.), *New Communitarian Thinking: Persons, Virtues, Institutions, and Communities*. Charlottesville, VA: University Press of Virginia. pp. 52–70.

Wolseley, Roland (1971) *The Black Press, U.S.A.* Ames, IA: Iowa State University Press.

Yeatman, Anna (1984) 'Gender and the Differentiation of Social Life into Public and Domestic Domains', *Social Analysis: Journal of Social and Cultural Practices*, 15: 32–49.

PART III

ARBITRARY FOUNDINGS

9

Neither Faith nor Commerce: Printing and the Unintended Origins of English Public Opinion

David Zaret

The current revival of interest in the eighteenth-century idea of civil society (for example, Alexander, 1991; Cohen and Arato, 1992; Calhoun, 1994; Jacobs, 1996; Seligman, 1993; Somers, 1993) leads inevitably to another old idea, namely public opinion. Civil society refers to a societal community whose axial principle of solidarity demarcates it from political and economic realms based on power and money. This implicates a central place for public opinion in politics because opinion is held to be the principal link between the liberal-democratic state and civil society. This conceptual framework informs prior work on democracy that is both empirical and normative in nature, such as T.H. Marshall on citizenship rights or Jürgen Habermas on the public sphere. The normative authority of open debate in a public sphere is not merely one attribute of liberal democracy but rather a precondition for many others, such as the franchise (Habermas, 1989; Marshall, 1966).

Beyond this point, however, little consensus exists over the origins of a public sphere in political life. When did public opinion begin to mediate between the state and civil society? To pose this question is, in effect, to inquire into the origins of democracy. Currently, wildly inconsistent answers exist with regard to the timing and causes of the birth of public opinion in political life. Work on England as a paradigmatic case places the birth of the public sphere from the late sixteenth to the late eighteenth centuries and cites capitalism and/or

Protestantism as principal causes of this development. Conspicuously absent from this work is inquiry into communicative issues that are, after all, central to any definition of civil society. Though discussions of the modern public sphere often include references to media, genre and multiple audiences (see, for example, Jacobs, 1996: 1238–9), this is not the case for research on the origins of the public sphere, in which sociologists take elite writings by Protestant theologians and/or Enlightenment philosophers as valid indicators of communicative practices in the early modern public sphere (for example, Bendix, 1978; Cohen and Arato, 1992; Habermas, 1989). What is needed, then, is attention to popular aspects of communicative change.

The communicative development analyzed in this chapter is the cultural impact of print technology on a traditional instrument of communication, the petition. I assess the causal relevance of print technology for the public sphere by examining how prior norms of secrecy and privilege in political communication were superseded in the English Revolution (1640–9). At the beginning of the seventeenth century, political communication existed but was severely restricted by norms of secrecy and privilege. For example, disclosure of parliamentary debates was a crime, and popular participation in political discourse was mostly limited to the receiving end of symbolic displays of authority. Yet by the end of the century, a privileged place for public opinion appears in liberal-democratic conceptions of political order, such as those advanced by Locke. How and why did participants in the English Revolution challenge norms of secrecy and privilege in political communication? Posing the question in this manner focuses our attention empirically on the impact of print technology on existing modes of communction. At this time, sermons, newspapers, pamphlets, petitions, and official proclamations conveyed political messages between the center and the periphery. Other, more expressive vehicles for political communication included royal processions, festive rites of status inversion and riots. Petitions, however, were a principal means by which individuals and localities sent requests for favors, grievances and other messages to the political center.

Petitions are an ancient and extremely widespread form of communication. Ancestors of electronic petitions on today's Internet are preserved in papyri records of antiquity, in civil pleadings and requests for favors and exemptions from taxes. This broad range of application also appears in the early Middle Ages, in the widespread use of Merovingian and Carolingian petitionary formulas (Koziol, 1992: 23–58). The evolution of medieval governance provided institutionalized means for sending petitions to monarchs; much of their daily work, in England, involved hearing petitions. Parliaments evolved out of the assemblies of notables convened to hear and judge petitions. Traditions governing petitions provided an outlet for peasant grievances in Tokugawa Japan and old regime Russia (Mitsuru, 1982: 154–5; Verner, 1995: 66). Petitioning, then, was a venerable practice when, in the early modern era, it was put to new uses as a vehicle of popular mobilization in early modern revolutions, most notably in the French Revolution. Results of the final stage in reporting grievances, the *cahiers de bailliage*, were collected and printed in 1789. French historians have produced an elaborate historiographic literature over the content and implications of the more than 30,000 preliminary *cahiers de doléances*, those drawn up at the local level (see Chartier, 1987: 110–44; Tackett, 1986: 257–70). Petitioning was practiced not only by opponents of the *ancien régime* but also by Catholics opposed to the de-Christianization policies of the Jacobins (Desan, 1990: 124–35). It was a feature of other early modern revolutions (for the Dutch Patriot Revolution, see te Brake, 1989) and subsequent popular movements that petitioned against slavery and for electoral and social reform (for a review, see Tarrow, 1994: 41–2).

In this chapter, I explore the impact of printing on petitioning in the English Revolution and analyze the emergence of a public sphere in politics as an extension and reworking of traditions governing petitions. These traditions regulated the form and content of communication by petition as a privilege (in the medieval sense) that exempted petitioners from secrecy norms that otherwise prohibited popular discussion of political matters. The traditional petition referred local grievances to central authority but did not load its message with normative claims about the 'will of the people'. In the English Revolution, petitions violate these rules and begin openly to lobby Parliament on pending business – a gross violation of secrecy norms. In this instance, innovative practice preceded theoretical novelty. The extension and reworking of communicative traditions in petitions was an unreflective development; that is, it occurred before political philosophy or religion supplied a formal justification for placing appeals to public opinion at the center of political life. Proximate causes of this practical innovation derive from technical and economic aspects of printing: respectively, increased ability to reproduce texts and competitive economic forces in printing. The causal relevance of capitalism and religion is mediate, determined by complex links to these technical and economic aspects of printing. In addition, use of printed petitions as a political tool involved organizational innovation: voluntary associations gathered for the purpose of organizing petitions, a task that traditionally was led by local elites in counties, guilds and municipalities. Thus, the birth of the 'party' is intertwined with petitioning.

Theoretical Issues

Sociological interest in public opinion is not new, though recent events have renewed interest in old questions about the cultural underpinnings of democracy. The relationship between institutionalization of democratic governance and a supportive culture for citizenship as a means to participate in the pluralist pursuit of utility was a central theme in functionalist analyses of the development of civic culture, psychological modernity, and value generalization. Applications of this perspective to early modern England describe the rise of 'civic consciousness' and 'legal-rational order' (Hanson, 1970; Little, 1970). Other theoretical perspectives that derive more directly from Weberian (for example, Bendix, 1978; Kallberg, 1993) and Marxist (Gould, 1987; Habermas, 1989) traditions have also influenced current work on democracy's cultural preconditions.

Applied to the case of England, sociological analyses produce inconsistent conclusions on the origins of the public sphere. Disagreement exists not only over the relative importance of capitalism and Protestantism but over precisely what in either of these developments had democratic implications for a public sphere. Neglect of communicative developments underlies this inconsistency. A speculative mode of inquiry is the inevitable consequence of devoting little attention to communicative practices that are, after all, central to any definition of the public sphere.

Ever since Marx, class-centered models have exercised considerable influence in sociological studies of democracy, which today are not confined to avowedly Marxist accounts. Contemporary sociologists of all persuasions complacently assume the explanatory adequacy of pointing out a connection to capitalism as a means for explaining the origins of the public sphere. Although the ever-rising bourgeoisie remains the preferred choice, sociological accounts cite virtually every class between the very top and bottom as principal actors in the creation of the liberal-democratic public sphere (for a review of the literature, see Zaret, 1996: 1500–1). Currently, applications of any class-centered account to the English Revolution confront the formidable obstacle of the now-not-so-new revisionist history, with its devastating, empirical attack on sociological suppositions about the centrality of class for democratic development. In the English Revolution, little evidence supports this supposition and more specific ones on the centrality of the bourgeoisie in revolutionary politics (1996: 1506–7). Sociological work on the English Revolution that invokes these suppositions can fairly be charged with failing to take account of more than two decades of historical research on the English Revolution. Fortunately for proponents of class-centered accounts, the most important study of the origins of the public sphere, Jürgen Habermas's *Structural Transformation of the Public Sphere* (1989), locates its origins well after the English Revolution has run its course. The continuing importance of this early work by Habermas derives from its historical and institutional model of the public sphere, for which England is the paradigmatic case. Habermas's historical-institutional account stands in sharp contrast to prior writings by critical theorists, whose descriptions of the eclipse of reason derive from interpretations of broad movements in social and political theory. For this reason *Structural Transformation* remains a key point of reference in debates over current prospects for the public sphere, though the discrepancy noted years ago by Cohen (1979: 71) – between lively debates over Habermas's analysis of the decline of the public sphere and passive acceptance of his account of its capitalist origins – is still evident.

Habermas's analysis anticipates a fusion of Marxism and structural functionalism. Joining class-centered and differentiation perspectives, it describes how parcelized sovereignty in feudalism, with its conditional restraints on property, was superseded by structural transformations in early capitalist development that differentiated a private realm, civil society, from a public realm of sovereign authority. In this development, the public sphere emerges as the mediator between these private and public realms.

> The bourgeois public sphere may be conceived above all as the sphere of private people come together as a public; they soon claimed the public sphere regulated from above against the public authorities themselves, to engage them in a debate over the general rules governing relations in the basically privatized but publicly relevant sphere of commodity production. (1989: 27)

The hallmark of this public sphere is more rational, critical habits of thought, which make it 'a sphere of criticism of public authority ... The medium of this political confrontation was peculiar and without historical precedent: people's public use of their reason' (1989: 27, 51). Habermas traces institutional autonomy of the public sphere to its differentiation from the economy and the state, whose principal consequence is the public sphere's capacity to support rational and critical discourse. 'The rational-critical debate of private people in the *salons*, clubs, and reading societies was not directly subject to the cycle of production and consumption, that is, to the dictates of life's necessities' (1989: 160). Here Habermas develops an old theme in critical theory: Adorno, Horkheimer and Marcuse had attributed the capacity for critical reason to bourgeois culture's isolation from material civilization (see Zaret, 1992).

Differentiation is, of course, a central theme in functionalist and neo-functionalist explanations of the public sphere. In this line of work, universalistic values in public discourse facilitate social integration under conditions of growing system differentiation. What principally distinguishes this view from the one advanced in critical theory is emphasis on the religious, specificially Protestant origins of the public sphere. But what, it may be asked, in Protestantism leads to democracy? Answers to this question are as wide-ranging as those offered for the class origins of the public sphere: the priesthood of all believers, justification by faith, the communion of the saints, covenant theology, Presbyterian ecclesiology, predestination, the sanctity of conscience, and more (for references, see Zaret, 1989). The same variability evident in sociological references to the class character of early democratic culture also appears in references to democracy's religious sources. Along with every class between the very bottom and top, nearly every conceivable aspect of early Protestantism has been invoked in sociological work on the origins of a public sphere in politics. This variability derives from two sources. First, too much speculative latitude exists in exegetical accounts of reflective writings by Enlightenment philosophers and Protestant divines – the principal source used in prior work on the early public sphere. Second, speculation is inevitable where attribution of causes invokes such broadly conceived variables (capitalism, Protestantism).

I should emphasize that these preliminary reflections do not presuppose the irrelevance of capitalism and religion. Rather, they suggest a better way to explore their causal relevance. I should also acknowledge that prior sociological work does not uniformly ignore communicative issues. In his analysis of the public sphere, Habermas refers to the importance of 'the press' for 'the new domain of a public sphere whose decisive mark was the published word' (1989: 16, 24). Bendix (1978: 256–8, 261–7) devotes more attention to this point in his remarks on 'intellectual mobilization' where he describes book publishing and literacy, and outlines their importance for the spread of Protestant and democratic ideas. These and other scholars (for example, Calhoun, 1988; Mayhew, 1984) treat communicative change too narrowly, assessing it as a factor that merely facilitates other changes by disseminating new ideas more rapidly and to a broader, socially diverse audience. But as Eisenstein (1980: 691–2) has shown in her analysis of the impact of early modern printing on learned culture, novelty in the mode of communication can have intimate links with novelties in its content. The cultural impact of printing goes beyond issues of access and distribution. The analysis advanced in this chapter upholds this point by showing how communicative change in print culture not only supplied a new way to transmit ideas to a public but also created novel practices that simultaneously constituted and invoked the authority of public opinion in political discourse.

Finally, the account advanced here revises prior work on the origins of public opinion in showing that this development was unintended and occurred initially at the level of unreflective practice, without the aid or anticipation of supportive theories. The absence of such theories, and the persistence of old traditions that placed deference and patronage at the core of politics, explain the ambivalent reactions of contemporaries toward political appeals to public opinion. Under the impact of printing, traditional practices, such as petitioning, were transformed in directions that implicated public opinion as the ultimate source of normative authority for setting a legislative agenda. Printing not only increased the scope of political communication but altered its content, orienting it to an anonymous body of opinion, a public that was an unelaborated object of discourse as well as a collection of persons engaged, as writers, readers, printers and petitioners, in political debates. That this development was not the outcome of democratic creeds is shown, below, by the uniform distribution of novel petitioning practices among all parties in the English Revolution, most of whom disavowed anything resembling a democratic creed.

Secrecy, Privilege and Political Communication

Prior to the English Revolution, the absence of anything resembling appeals to public opinion in politics derives from norms of secrecy that strictly limit political communication. In theory, no public space for political discourse exists outside Parliament, where a customary right of free speech in the fifteenth century had evolved into a formal privilege under the Tudors. Confined to Parliament, this freedom is (in the medieval sense) a privilege demarcated by secrecy norms, whose violation, even by MPs, is a punishable offense. For commoners, norms of secrecy reflect an unchallenged assumption, no different in early Stuart England than under Elizabeth, when Thomas Smith explained that commoners 'have no voice or authority in our commonwealth, and no account is made of them but only to be ruled' (quoted in Hill, 1974: 186). Religion (Puritan or otherwise) supplied no reason to dissent from this view: Hooker repeats Calvin's strictures that 'private men' have no right to engage in public discussion of government (Hooker, [1593] 1845: I.102; Calvin, [1536] 1962: II.656–7). This outlook reflects political and religious assumptions of an early modern world that put deference and patronage at the core of politics. The old idea that irrationality inversely correlates with social rank, a central theme in organic and patriarchal conceptions of politics, received added support from the Protestant tradition that emphasized the corruption of reason.

Of course, some political communication occurred. In contrast to reflections upholding norms of secrecy and privilege in political communication, several practices afforded limited opportunities for political communication in pre-revolutionary England. After all, political communication in some form is as old as kingship, implicit in its commemorative architecture, coinage and coronation rituals. But these practices limit communication to symbolic displays of authority, to a cultural frame of reference for understanding recip-rocal claims between subjects and rulers. Other practices involved more than symbolic displays and facilitated substantial opportunities for sending messages from the periphery to the political center. Yet these practices, which include crowds and riots, elections, petitions and newsletters, were tightly circumscribed. The scope of discussion in these practices was inversely related to accessibility: discussion was most restricted where popular access was greatest (see Zaret, 1994: 180–4). Political communication was hardly unknown in pre-revolutionary England, but it was denied in theory and, in practice, its scope was inversely related to accessibility. No type of political communication permitted unrestricted access to open discussion of political matters in a public space.

Petitions and Medieval Precedent

Though they precluded popular discussion of political matters, norms of secrecy did permit expressions of grievance. The petition was the principal vehicle for this mode of communication, and it was used for every conceivable grievance. Traditions governing use of petitions existed in medieval society, where parliaments met as high courts that received and tried petitions. These were juridical in nature; they voiced grievances over miscarriages of justice or requested relief from taxes, forest laws and feudal obligations. England was no different from other European societies, though, unlike France, nearly all petitions on private grievance after the mid thirteenth century went to the central government. In the early seventeenth century, petitions were objects of popular knowledge, and well suited to a hierarchical world in which deference and patronage functioned like money. The word 'petition' was a common figure of speech, used literally and metaphorically to signify deferential request for favor or redress of a problem. Letter writers seeking office or advancement called their request a petition. On Sundays clerics explained that prayer was a petition to God and the faithful were humble petitioners. Worldly petitions went to parliaments and kings. When summoned, a parliament began with a medieval ritual, the appointment of receivers and triers of petitions. Petitions to kings requested office, alms or relief from debt, delay of justice or imprisonment. They were received by secretaries of state (if the petitioner had influence or money) or the court of requests (from poor suitors). This last point calls attention to popular access to petitioning. Rich and poor alike petitioned; it was a popular activity because it provided a substitute for the proximity and influence available to those with court connections. When the plague threatened London in 1625, Sir Edward Coke argued that Parliament, then in session, should establish no committees to receive petitions because of 'the danger of infection by drawing the meaner sort of people about us' (Great Britain, Parliament, [1625] 1873: 11–12).

At the outbreak of the English Revolution in 1640, the right to petition was widely recognized and held equally applicable to individuals, Parliament and other collectivities, who used petitions to express public and private grievances, request favors, and enter pleas in juridical proceedings between private parties. For expressing grievance, petitions were held to be an undisputed privilege of all subjects, even when it proved troublesome to petitioned authorities. In 1646, the right to petition was invoked in heated debate by MPs over a Presbyterian petition that openly challenged Parliament's right to rule the Church. Some saw this as contempt of Parliament, but other MPs argued 'that they [the petitioners] ought not be so charged for all the subjects may petition and show their reasons why freely' (Harington, [1646–53] 1977: 15). Confronted by insurgent royalist movements in 1648, Parliament instructed a committee to frame an order against 'all tumultuary meetings under pretence of petitions, with an assertion of the subject's liberty to petition in a due manner'. A royalist petition from Essex defended the right to present 'just desires of the oppressed in a petitionary way (the undoubted right of the subject) and the very life of their liberty itself' (Great Britain, Parliament, 1646–8: v. 563, 567; 669f.12[20], 1648).

The right to petition derived from medieval traditions. Neither constitutionalism nor liberal democracy informs discussions of the subject's right to petition and the duty of officials to receive or forward them. Responding to criticism of his role in forwarding a petition to Parliament from a parish for the right to select a minister, a commander of a parliamentary garrison wrote to the woman who owned that right, requesting that 'your ladyship ... not blame your servant in doing his duty by tendering their petition as a neighbor and countryman he is bound to do' (Luke, [1644–5] 1963: 237–8). Radical petitions against bishops and episcopacy were defended with the claim that 'freedom ... to make our grievances known is a chief privilege of Parliament.' Agitators in the New Model Army invoked the rhetoric of 'privilege' to defend their right to petition Parliament for redress of grievances; but the customary language used here also appears on the other side, when royalists protested efforts by Parliament to stop petitions in favor of the King and/or the Episcopal Church (see Zaret, 1996: 1512). A staple feature of royalist ideology is the charge that the Long Parliament aimed at 'arbitrary rule' when it interfered with royalist petitioning. In equivalent formulations by royalists, army agitators, and Puritans on the right to petition, 'liberty' and 'freedom' have the medieval denotation of privilege or immunity. In petitioning, 'the indisputable right of the meanest subject' (E341[5], 1646: 6), petitioners enjoy immunity from norms of secrecy and privilege that otherwise excluded them from political communication. Women and radical supporters of Parliament used traditional arguments to justify their participation in petitioning. Male and female petitioners on behalf of radical Leveller causes invoked the religious metaphor, noted earlier, that compared prayer to petitions, arguing that 'those in authority can in nothing more resemble God than in their readiness to hear and receive the complaints and petitions of any that apply themselves unto them' (E579[9], 1649: 1). Female Levellers requested that Parliament not 'withhold from us our undoubted right of petitioning, since God is ever willing and ready to receive the petitions of all ... The ancient laws of England are not contrary to the will of God' (669f.17[36], 1653). Thus contemporaries understood the right to petition in terms of medieval tradition and not a liberal-democratic conception of right.

Though sanctioned by medieval tradition, English petitions were subject to restrictions on their content and the practices used to collect them. Similar restrictions existed elsewhere, e.g. in peasant petitions in Tokugawa Japan (Mitsuru, 1982: 154–5) and in old regime petitions in France and Russia (Desan, 1990: 124–5; Verner, 1995: 66). Like other medieval rights, the right to petition was hedged with restrictions that reflected assumptions about the social importance of deference and patronage. Though no formal law defined their restrictions, three sets of limits can be inferred from prevailing practice and from negative reactions to 'seditious' or 'factious' petitions (for references see Zaret, 1996: 1513–17). First, petitions neither invoke nor imply normative claims for 'the will of the people'. Permissible messages from the periphery to the political center conveyed by petition did not include claims about the supremacy of popular will over the petitioned authorities. This point dovetailed with secrecy norms: petitions could not lobby Parliament because it was a violation of parliamentary privilege to inform outsiders about debates and speeches in Parliament. Second, deferential and juridical rhetoric in petitions portrays grievance as an apolitical conveyance of information and petitioners as 'humble' or 'poor' suitors. Petitioners 'pray' for relief from grievances but do not prescribe a solution, leaving that to the wisdom of the invoked authority. This appears in a petition to the King from London citizens in September 1640 (Rushworth, 1721: iii.1264). Demands for convening a Parliament had grown rapidly since the dissolution of the Short Parliament, in May, and the subsequent military fiasco that, by August, resulted in a Scottish army of occupation in the northern part of the realm. To support their request that the King convene Parliament, the 'humble petitioners' recite grievances about taxation, religion and the alarming military situation; and they report that they have found 'by experience that they are not redressed by the ordinary course of justice'. They advance their request for a Parliament so that thereby 'they may be relieved in the premises'. (This last phrase is still a term of art used by lawyers!) Beyond signaling deference, this rhetoric conceals the intent to lobby by way of petition, that is, to promote a preferred solution to a grievance. This would be presumptuous and signal contempt of authority. Petitions submitted a problem to a petitioned authority; petitions did not presume to instruct or otherwise lobby those in authority. 'We come,' declared London apprentices in a petition for peace in 1643, 'to embowell our grievances ... before you, not presuming to dictate to your graver judgments' (669f.6[101], 1643). This deferential and juridical rhetoric portrayed expressions of grievance in petitions as neutral flows of information, devoid of implications for subordinating politics to popular will.

Finally, an additional set of restrictions reinforced the first two restrictions by further separating a legitimate petition from an ideological statement. For example, the central role of local elites in organizing petitions helped to maintain apolitical appearances. Petitions were issued by local corporate entities, especially when they raised grievances of a public nature. Though the right to petition pertained to individuals as well as to collectivities, it was more closely associated with guild halls, wardmoots, municipal common councils, assize and quarter sessions for petitions over public issues. Private persons who issued such petitions were liable to the accusation of 'faction', no small matter in a society where the ideal of organic unity made faction (or, in modern parlance, party) tantamount to sedition. This accusation was less likely where petitions advanced purely private interests. But where grievance took on a public complexion, its expression in a petition by local authorities on behalf of a collectivity, as the unanimous view of a guild, county or city, sustained its appearance as an apolitical conveyance of information. Other restrictions stipulated that grievances should be local and neither critical of existing laws, indicative of discontent with authorities, nor made public. This last point highlights differences between traditional petitioning and the public sphere. The traditional right to petition did not create a public sphere but constituted a privileged space in which petitioners communicated directly to those in authority. Communicative rules for petitioning permitted expressions of grievance, but only in a restricted form that has little in common with modern conceptions of the public sphere as a forum for political debate. Restrictions on communication by petition were well suited to a society where political conflict and factions were understood as deviant behavior.

What remains to be explored, then, are changes in petitioning that create public opinion as a political factor in the English Revolution. A public sphere emerged in the 1640s when new uses for petitions eliminated traditional restrictions on petitioning. Printed petitions from private associations of individuals simultaneously constituted and invoked public opinion as a means for lobbying Parliament and discrediting political adversaries.

Petitions and Printing

Historians have long recognized the importance of petitions, both as a topic and as a resource in the study of the English Revolution. Much has been written on the content of petitions, the social composition of petitioners, the organization of petitioning, and the probative value of petitions as indicators of local opinion (for a review, see Zaret, 1996: 1503–6). However, historians have not devoted much attention to changes that distinguish petitioning before and during the English Revolution, and the role of printing in this development, when violation of traditional rules that restricted expressions of grievance quickly led to new communicative practices. Petitions shed apolitical appearances and became a modern political weapon, a communicative device used by private, voluntary associations of individuals who put appeals to public opinion at the core of political conflict. Printing is the most evident difference between petitioning before and during the English Revolution. From the adoption of printing in England up to 1640, only few instances exist where a petition was printed. After 1640 the attack on prerogative and ecclesiastical courts at the outbreak of the English Revolution led to collapse of the control over printing that had been vested in those courts. All sides quickly grasped the tactical importance of printing, and used it to publish broadsides, declarations, pamphlets, newspapers and petitions.

Petitioning in the English Revolution occurred at all levels, coming from wounded soldiers, parishes, cities, counties, the army, guilds, and private factions. In 1641, well before political uses of petitioning had been fully developed, a contemporary observed that 'no time nor history can show that such great numbers of oppressed subjects of all sorts ever petitioned' (Oxinden, [1607–42] 1932: 286). The Long Parliament opened, in 1640, with agreement over the validity of requests for modest religious and political reforms (respectively, limiting the power of bishops and the necessity for parliamentary consultation in fiscal and foreign policy). MPs, who would later take different sides, presented county petitions that recited extensively solicited grievances. Agreement dissipated when subsequent petitions, in 1641–2, sided with Parliament or King, some with as many as 20,000 signatures, though 3,000–10,000 signatures was more usual. In the winter of 1642–3 rival petitions appear on behalf of peace and war policies. More partisan petitions, in the summer of 1643, represented different factions on the parliamentary side, which subsequently came to include Presbyterians, independents, army activists, Levellers and others.

That most of these petitions appeared in print reflects popular interest in them. This prompted printers to print petitions, Parliament to order their publication, and journalists to report them. The very act of printing a petition after its presentation to Parliament signals a departure from tradition. This violates the requirement that expressions of grievance in petitions take the form of apolitical flows of information from the periphery to the political center of the nation. No reason exists to print a petition other than to invoke a segment of public opinion as a piece of political propaganda. By publicizing petitions, printing transformed them, orienting their production to readers of printed texts as a means to influence public opinion. This new use of petitions, as an instrument designed to influence the opinion of a large anonymous audience of readers, a public, explains why their printed form often contains accounts of local circumstances surrounding the adoption of a petition or its reception by Parliament.

For political elites in Parliament, printed petitions created an appearance of support for their policies. In managing a conference between the Lords and the Commons, John Pym read supportive county petitions and then had his speeches and the petitions printed. Coordination of parliamentary maneuvers and petitioning was a political art practiced to perfection by Pym. For activists outside Parliament, printed petitions invoked the authority of opinion to justify efforts to lobby MPs. A petition from an Essex parish against their superstitious vicar was printed as a broadside, with a notice 'To the Courteous Reader', pointing out the relevance of this case for the general proposition that 'Prelates have been the original cause of all the divisions and schisms in the church' (669f.4[28], 1641). Though supporters of the Long Parliament first adopted the practice of printing petitions for public consumption, this was not inspired by uniquely Puritan or parliamentary convictions. The other side was equally adept at this practice. Royalist activists promoted petitions and rushed them into print in order to influence public opinion. The editor of a printed collection of petitions that advocated repression of sectaries, Sir Thomas Aston, declared his intent in publishing this collection is to 'show that the way is open. And since noise and number are taken into consideration, the forwardness of assailants [i.e. Puritan petitioners] will ... put shame upon the defendants to be so far behind' (E150[28], 1642: Sig. A2v). In addition to ideological conviction, purely economic motives among printers who hoped to profit from sales of hot items are another reason why more than 200 petitions and collections of petitions were printed between April 1641 and April 1643, which included publication of many unauthorized and forged petitions (see Zaret, 1996: 1527).

Printed petitions appeared individually and in collections with other petitions. Often a petition first appeared as a broadside, designed to be affixed to a public place, then in a quarto format (a pamphlet). Petitions presented to Parliament were covered by newspapers that, after 1641, appeared in regular weekly editions. It is important to note that popular interest in petitions did not depend on the ability to read them. Petitions were read aloud and discussed in churches and taverns, often in conjunction with efforts to obtain signatures to them. This popular access to printed petitions and other political materials was unprecedented. Prior to 1640, contemporaries used scribal modes of transmission and relied on personal connections and private letters to obtain documents such as speeches by MPs and parliamentary petitions to James and Charles.

Not only did printing make petitions more accessible to a popular audience, it also transformed the process of petitioning, facilitating massive petitions campaigns that, on short notice, covered London or an entire county. In 1645, Presbyterian activists in London circulated a printed petition with blank spaces in the title where the name of a particular ward could be inserted (669f.10[37], 1645]). Printing quickly became a tool for the art of petitioning because it made petitions a weapon that could respond rapidly to unfolding political developments. From printing presses issued small 'tickets', such as one in July 1643 from a nascent independent party announcing a petition for more active prosecution of the war against the King that could be signed at the Merchant Taylors Hall from 4 a.m. until 8 p.m. An account of this petition-in-progress, which substantially reproduced the ticket, was available to readers of the newspaper *Special Passages* (E61[3], 1643; E61[9], 1643: 7). Petitions were now printed for the use of petitioners, often with instructions about gathering signatures and meeting to present the signed petitions in a procession to Parliament. Copies of the *Humble Petition of Many Thousand Poore People* contain the following line at the bottom: 'For the use of the petitioners who are to meet this present day in More Fields, and from thence to go to the house of Parliament with it in their hands' (669f.4[54], 1642). Similar instructions appear on petitions by Anabaptists, Levellers and royalists (for references, see Zaret, 1996: 1529). Appended to a petition from female Levellers in London and adjacent boroughs, who request release of six imprisoned radical leaders, are these instructions:

> All those women that are aprovers hereof are desired to subscribe it, and to deliver in their subscriptions to the women which [*sic*] will be appointed in every ward and division to receive the same; and to meet at Westminster Hall upon Monday the 23 of this instant April 1649, betwixt 8 and 9 of clock in the forenoon. (E551[14], 1649: 14)

Printing was essential for massive petition campaigns. As many as 500 copies of a petition were printed specifically for gathering signatures (669f.12[20], 1648; H.M.C. Portland, 1891: 453).

But in addition to heightened access to petitions – for potential readers and signatories – printing also inspired change in the content of petitions. This aspect of printing has received little attention in prior work, where printing's implications for democratic politics in the English Revolution are conceived solely in terms of access. Printing's relevance for alterations in the content of political messages derives from its imposition of dialogic order on conflict, a consequence of increased ability to produce and reproduce texts. Printing encouraged readers to interpret conflict between King and Parliament, and subsequently among parliamentary factions, as an ongoing debate in printed texts that simultaneously referred to and excerpted from prior texts. Printed political texts invited readers to compare texts. Though they prompted readers to arrive at 'correct' conclusions, printed political texts derived rhetorical force from the presupposition that they reliably reproduced prior texts. One not untypical example appears in a preface to a Puritan tract: 'A petition for peace is presented to the Parliament by some thousands of citizens; the petition finds a peaceable answer; and that answer (as I shall now set forth) is opposed by an unpeaceable reply' (E101[23], 1643: 1). The same dialogic order also appears in printed materials, petitions and controversial pamphlets, by royalists (see Zaret, 1996: 1530). Dialogic order also arises in printed petitions that refer to prior petitions from the same party that had met with a less than favorable reception. This self-referential quality appears in many Leveller petitions (1996: 1531), such as those issued in 1649 whose title page describes them as petitions from 'presenters and pro-moters of the late large petition of September 11' (this had requested abolition of the Lords, religious toleration, and a trial for the king). The title page of another Leveller petition in 1649 lists requests advanced in three prior petitions, dating back to 1647, intended to secure 'the people's rational and just rights and liberties, against all tyrants whatsoever, whether in Parliament, Army or Council of State' (E574[15], 1649). So one consequence of the use of printed petitions as political tools is references to unmet requests advanced in former petitions, which pushed petitioning in the direction of lobbying.

Printing's imposition of dialogic order on conflict prominently appears in 'cross-petitions'. Cross-petitions, often with impressive numbers of signatories, promptly challenged claims advanced in a prior petition, often in print only a few days, to be representative of local opinion (see Zaret, 1996: 1531–2). Cross-petitions appeared in 1641 as supporters of the established Church attacked Puritan petitions for abolition of bishops and ceremonial 'corruptions'. Subsequent cross-petitions gave voice to rival views over the militia in the spring and summer of 1642, and later that winter over demands for 'accommodation' in peace petitions that delineated royalist and parliamentary positions. On the parliamentary side, growing conflict between Presbyterians and independents produced a new spasm of cross-petitions, a complex, multi-party affair with contributions from the New Model Army, Levellers, and resurgent royalists whose petitions protested 'arbitrary authority' in the centralized controls imposed by Parliament via county committees. Newspapers advanced the imposition by printing of dialogic order on political conflict in reports on petitions-in-progress. As conflict escalated between independents and Presbyterians in 1646, *The Scottish Dove*, a partisan Presbyterian diurnal, reported on the progress of a Presbyterian petition in London; then it observed, 'There is a cross-petition framed ... by another party in and around the City ... There are many thousand hands gather all about the suburbs ... especially at conventicles and private meetings' (E339[13], 1646: 676). News reports of petitions exhibited a high degree of circumspection when petitions provoked negative reactions from Parliament, but readers would find something about these developments.

Printing was certainly not the sole source of a capacity to construct public life in terms of ideological conflict, for this can also arise under scribal modes of communication. Still, printing made this capacity available to a remarkably diverse audience that was not possible under scribal modes of communication (see Zaret, 1994). Moreover, printing motivated readers and writers (and petitioners) to orient their efforts to this capacity. On all sides petitions refer to claims advanced in print and thereby pushed political communication in new directions, in which a public became associated with a capacity for rational thought and broad legitimacy for establishing a legislative agenda. Proliferation of printed political materials was both a cause and a consequence of the growing importance attached to appeals to public opinion. At bottom, this development derives from economic and technical aspects of printing – from, respectively, commercial motives that ensured a plentiful supply of printed political materials and the ease with which texts could be reproduced. This development cut across ideological and religious lines, for the imposition of dialogic order appears in petitions from all principal parties to the English Revolution.

The Authority of Public Opinion

Innovative use of petitions for political communication led to the invention of public opinion in politics in a distinctively modern guise, where public opinion is both nominal and real. Nominally, it is a fiction, collectively constituted by its invocation in political discourse; yet real individuals participate in political discourse as writers, readers, printers and petitioners. Appeals to public opinion in printed texts simultaneously constitute it and invoke its authority as the ultimate ground of legitimacy for the purpose of broadly setting a legislative agenda. So far, we have seen how appeals to public opinion arise out of transformations in petitioning wrought by economic and technical aspects of print culture that I have just described. What remains to be assessed is the authority that contemporaries attribute to opinion in politics. Novel views on this subject appear in debates over the representative qualities of petitions, in tactical efforts to defend or attack opinions invoked in printed petitions. Remarkably modern ideas on the role of reason and consent in the public sphere appear in debates on the issue of representation in competitive appeals to public opinion by petitions and cross-petitions.

At the same time, however, ambivalence bordering on denial marks contemporary reaction to new uses for petitions as a means to invoke public opinion for the purpose of lobbying Parliament. Reluctance to acknowledge the legitimacy of this development flows not only from traditional norms of secrecy and privilege in political communication but also from more general precepts about deference and hierarchy in politics. The invention of public opinion in innovative petitioning represents a case where an innovation is disclaimed by its practitioners. The absence of a philosophic or ideological rationale for placing public opinion at the core of political practice also explains contemporary reluctance to acknowledge communicative innovation. Only at later stages in the revolution, when use of printed petitions was an established political art, did some radicals explicitly affirm the centrality of public opinion in politics (see later in this chapter). Communicative change occurred as contemporaries reworked traditions governing petitions but relied on traditional rhetoric as a means to avoid acknowledging innovation. Even as they imitated Parliament's early success in using printing to publicize petitions, royalist petitions disclaimed any element of innovation, which they attributed to the other side (see Zaret, 1996: 1533–4). But ambivalence and contradiction also marked reactions to innovative petitioning by Parliament and its supporters. A cross-petition in March 1642 from parliamentary activists in London denounced a prior petition organized by the city's royalist Mayor and Recorder: the 'bold publishing in print of the said petition', and the King's approving response, 'was purposely done, wickedly, seditiously, to make divisions.' Presumably none of these lamentable qualities tainted the printing of the counter-petition by Parliament's supporters (669f.3[58], 1642).

Thus, contemporaries on all sides shied away from recognizing innovative aspects of their petitions, preferring instead to invoke public opinion but not acknowledge its legitimacy for the practical purpose to which such invocations in petitions were put by political factions, namely, to lobby political authorities. Expediency and opportunism, dictated by political necessity, are part of these responses to innovations in petitioning. But these responses also exhibit a pattern, one shaped by communicative practices that have run ahead of political and social theory. No formal body of reflection provided a basis for justifying that which was implicit in petitioning activities, namely, invoking the opinion of a public to justify setting a legislative agenda. Instead, contemporaries invoked rhetorical properties to justify their petitions and traditional hierarchical notions to attack petitions by adversaries. Yet novel practices led contemporaries to new ideas that express a surprisingly robust conception of public opinion in political life, which emphasized the importance of informed consent, open debate and appeals to reason in petitioning.

Debates over the validity of rival petitions led partisans on all sides to attach importance to informed consent in signing petitions (see Zaret 1996: 1536–7). Few records exist that shed light on individual decisions to sign a petition, so it is difficult to assess how much weight should be given to informed consent versus manipulation and coercion. Though laypersons often sought advice from their parish minister, and organizers of petitions used ministers as agents for collecting signatures, reports of conflict and abortive petitions indicate that ordinary persons were capable of resisting threats or manipulation by persons in positions of local authority (1996: 1524). Along with informed consent, contemporaries upheld the need for a free and open exchange of ideas in the petitioning process. Unlike a public petition campaign, one conducted in secrecy might facilitate manipulation and deception. This point was made by all factions (1996: 1537). Radical activists attacked an anti-army petition issued by Essex Presbyterians in 1647 who had printed copies quietly sent from London: 'That which is to go under the name of a county or corporation ought to be first publicly propounded to all the inhabitants of that county or corporation, that there may be a general meeting, debates & consultation about the matter' (E384[11], 1647: 7).

Debates over petitions involved the issue of representation and the legitimacy of petitions on public issues from associations of purely private persons. Competitive petition campaigns weakened the traditional stricture that petitions with grievances of a public nature be initiated by local elites in assizes, guilds, and municipal councils. Though this practice persisted, it was increasingly complemented by petitions issued, initially, in the name of 'inhabitants' of a county or city and, later, by factions, such as the Presbyterians, independents, and Levellers. A letter from the Privy Council to the Mayor and Aldermen of London complained about this development when, inspired by the Twelve Peers' Petition in 1640, activists in London circulated a petition:

to which many hands ... are endeavored to be gotten in the several wards ... And we cannot but hold it very dangerous and strange to have a petition framed in the names of the citizens, and endeavored to be signed in a way not warranted by the charters and customs of the city. (Rushworth, 1721: iii.1262)

Similar arguments came from Digby and Hyde, who urged the House not to accept the Root and Branch Petition of 1640, which advocated radical religious reform. Digby would have supported the petition if it followed tradition; if it were intended 'as an index of grievances, I should wink at the faults of it'. When he realized its innovative features, 'I looked upon it then with terror, as upon a comet or blazing star raised and kindled out of the stench, out of the poisonous exhalation of a corrupted hierarchy.' What so alarmed Digby was that the petition expressed the opinion, not of the London Corporation, 'but from I know not what 15,000 Londoners' who presumptuously intended 'to prescribe to a Parliament' (1721: iv.170–2; D'Ewes, [1640-1] 1923: 335).

Competitive petition campaigns also led to new claims for the political authority of opinions advanced in petitions and for reason as the ground of opinion. On all sides, competitive use of printed petitions to invoke public opinion expanded the scope of claims for its authority in politics. Pragmatic developments, at the level of communicative practice, led to new ideas on the authority of public opinion. For example, traditional strictures that precluded petitioning explicitly against a law were violated by petitions that did not come only from radical supporters of Parliament. In 1648, Surrey petitioners for royalist peace proposals defended, against fierce opposition from Parliament, the right to petition 'for redress of grievances, nay, for the removal of things established by law' (E443[8], 1648: 3). Many royalist, Leveller and army petitions advanced an immanent mode of political criticism, which cited presuppositions thought to be binding on all persons, such as the 1628 Petition of Right, to argue against positions taken by Parliament (see Zaret, 1996: 1539). Alongside this immanent mode of criticism in petitions appear novel claims on behalf of reason as the basis for opinions advanced in a petition. Here, then, is a historical precedent for 'people's public use of their reason' which, according to Habermas (1989: 27), only appears in the eighteenth century. In response to pro-Episcopal petitions that claim support from 'the better sort of inhabitants', defenders of petitions against bishops, in 1641, held the relevant issue to be not the petitioners' social status but 'their considerations, what they publish' (E160[2], 1641: 7). Women petitioners published an addendum 'with their several reasons, why their sex ought thus to petition, as well as the men'

(E134[17], 1642). A Presbyterian petition is the topic of a pamphlet that contains a dialogue in which a churchwarden urges a parishioner to sign the petition. After the churchwarden declares, 'it is as harmless a petition as ever was subscribed unto, and many honest and understanding men have subscribed it', the parishioner replies, 'I will not make other men's examples, but my own reason the rule of my actions ... I look upon it as a very dangerous petition' (E340[24], 1646: 3). Leveller writings on petitions consistently upheld the need for critical knowledge of public issues, 'advised deliberate consideration (such as few in this nation are accustomed unto), without which that which is called knowledge or understanding is not true knowledge of understanding' (E373[5], 1646: 2). In 1646, petitioners in Hertford and adjacent counties invoke reason to justify their petition against mandatory tithes. The title page of their defense (E389[2], 1647) proclaims that it was conceived 'by some of the said petitioners ... for the vindication of themselves and their fellows' (a term indicative of humble social status), in which they proved their case 'by good reasons from the word of God, and by evident demonstration of sound reason, sufficient to convince any rational man, unless he have a resolution that he will not be convinced'.

The evidence also suggests that radical participants in competitive petition campaigns began to perceive limitations to petitioning. As a device to organize and invoke public opinion, the petition was inherently reactive. Legitimating even an expanded role for petitioning did not ameliorate structural problems of a government that was not representative. Leveller writers raised this issue when they advanced arguments about how petitions ought to be evaluated by those in authority. Some argued that 'it will not be thoroughly well in England, till Parliaments make answers to petitioners according to the rule of fundamental law' (E684[33], 1653: 13). For Levellers, fundamental law refers to an admixture of natural law and constitutional law. An even more explicit turn to constitutional reform as an alternative to petitioning appears in arguments for the Agreement of the People. Levellers and army agitators offered the Agreement as the basis of a constitutional settlement, 'conceiving it to be an improper, tedious, and unprofitable thing for the people to be ever running after their representatives with petitions for redress of such grievances as may at once be removed by themselves' (Lilburne, [1649] 1944: 160; and see An Agreement, [1649] 1944: 324).

At this point we can detect an emergent liberal-democratic agenda for politics, though this was irrelevant for precipitating the conflict between Parliament and the Stuart monarchy. This agenda was facilitated by innovative petitioning because it provided practical experiences with invoking public opinion and thereby highlighted

the obsolescence of traditional norms of secrecy in political communication. Accordingly, some radicals, such as the Levellers,
quickly moved from promoting the right to petition to grand
schemes for constitutional reform. Thus, innovative communicative
practices had intimate links with novel ideas on the importance of
public opinion in political life that signal the advent of liberal-
democractic conceptions of politics. In conjunction with petitioning,
these ideas appeared inconsistently; but the break with traditional
conceptions of political communication is unmistakable. Constituting and invoking public opinion in printed petitions obliterates
norms of secrecy and privilege; it also advances more optimistic
assessments of human capacity for reasoned discourse that distinguish Lockean liberalism from pessimistic assessments in
Puritanism. Still, few contemporaries at this time were prepared
theoretically to develop liberal-democratic implications of printed
appeals to public opinion, principally because of the persistence of
prevailing assumptions about deference and hierarchy. Innovative
use of petitions was a practical development that initially evolved
with no discernible links to principled attacks on the centrality of
deference and hierarchy in politics. Hence, innovative petitioning
occurred on all sides in the Revolution. Liberal-democratic ideas on
the centrality of public opinion in politics are, then, practically
anticipated by communicative developments. Only later do these
ideas take explicit form, first in radical reforms proposed by
Levellers, later in writings by Locke and others. Yet there, too,
discrepancies between theory and practice persist, though in attenu-
ated form. Locke's writings on the ultimate authority of public
opinion for determining when government has lost legitimacy were
shaped by the monster petitioning campaign, in 1679-80, on the
succession issue (Knight, 1993). But one searches in vain for a
principled defense of free and open communication in writings by
Locke. Freedom of expression and of the press are fundamental to
Locke's conception of legitimate order, but, as Laslett and others
point out, they are never given explicit formulation in his *Two
Treatises of Government*. Prevailing views on the irrationality of
commoners remained an obstacle to explicitly subordinating government to public opinion, though Locke regarded this irrationality as a
contingent and not necessary state of affairs (Laslett, 1960: 85n;
Dunn, 1982: 185–6).

Conclusion

Examination of communicative tradition and change throws new
light on the origins of the liberal-democratic model of the public

sphere. The relevance of tradition – explored in an older line of work that runs from Weber to Hintze and Bendix and portrays democratic citizenship as a historical extension of aristocratic privileges and immunities – appears in this study in the extension of traditional communicative privileges and immunities for petitioners that eventuated in a public sphere. The relevance of communicative change for the public sphere derives from specific economic and technical aspects of printing, respectively, its competitive organization and its technical efficiency (relative to scribal modes of communication) for producing texts. Economic aspects of printing are responsible for the widespread availability of printed petitions: printers reaped profits by seizing opportunities to cater to popular interests. But printing's relevance for change in petitioning that created public opinion as a political factor goes beyond increasing the *scope* of communication and involves change in its *content*. For this, technical implications of the printing are most relevant: the dialogic imposition of order that ideologized conflict, by orienting discourse to an anonymous body of readers, a public, to whom politics appear as a debate where reasons are given for and against different views. Printing's relevance also extends to organizational issues: mobilization of resources to produce printed petitions led to the embryonic party. In the 1640s, petitioning by 'factions', voluntary associations based on shared ideological commitment, developed alongside the older pattern of petitioning based on affiliation by parish, ward, guild, municipality and county. In politics, petitioning became the organizational analogue to sectarianism in religion. Finally, printed petitions display the same complex relationship to public opinion that can be observed in modern media. Petitions represent individual opinions but are also a tool for their manipulation. This complexity reflects the dual nature of public opinion as a nominal and a real entity. Nominally, public opinion is a discursive fiction; *qua* public opinion it exists only when instantiated in political discourse. Yet real individuals participate in political discourse as writers, readers, printers and petitioners. Like today's opinion polls, printed petitions are devices that mediate between nominal and real moments of public opinion.

The centrality accorded to communicative tradition and change in this analysis of the early public sphere militates against prior sociological accounts that (1) minimize or neglect the causal significance of communicative issues, (2) rely, instead, on speculative references to capitalism and/or Protestantism as sources of the public sphere, and (3) use reflective writings by philosophers or theologians as a proxy for communicative practices in popular politics. The analysis in this chapter does not deny the relevance of economic and religious factors but, instead, calls attention to their essentially mediated character. The relevance of capitalism and Protestantism occurs in their links to communicative changes associated with print culture. Empirical study of communicative change affords little support for neo-functionalist speculation on affinities between Protestantism and the liberal model of the public sphere. Religion is hardly irrelevant, especially when one considers that the mobilization of opinion by petitioning in the 1640s occurred in a revolution denominated by religious issues. But the same economic and technical effects of printing animated innovative communicative practices on all sides in the English Revolution: e.g. competitive use of printed petitions to appeal to public opinion, the dialogic imposition of order, and growing scope of authority claimed for opinions advanced in petitions. This is, then, one more argument (see Zaret, 1989) against the widespread supposition that liberal-democratic ideology arose as a secular extension of Protestantism. Elsewhere (Zaret, 1994) I point out that religious dissent in pre-revolutionary England diplays precisely the same economic and technical effects of printing that appear in political discourse in the 1640s. This includes popular access to debates over religious issues – e.g. Puritan demands for liturgical reform – that are marked by the imposition of dialogic order by printing. Religion's relevance for the public sphere emerges out of complex linkages to printing. Beyond this, the affinity alleged to exist between religion and democratic culture is a classic instance of a spurious relationship, where the religious and political variables of interest display the same economic and technical effects of printing.

Much the same point about spuriousness applies to class-centered approaches to the public sphere. Seldom does sociological discussion of the early public sphere fail to reference its 'bourgeois' character (see Somers, 1993: 588), in spite of the stark challenge posed by historical revisionism for claims about the centrality of class for revolutionary politics and democracy in early modern England. According to Calhoun, claims about the specifically 'bourgeois' character of the early public sphere do not imply 'that what made the public sphere bourgeois was simply the class composition of its members. Rather, it was *society* that was bourgeois, and bourgeois society produced a certain form of public sphere' (1992: 7). Elsewhere, Calhoun (1988; 1994: 310) associates this character with 'urbanity' and 'capitalist business relations'. For Habermas, the bourgeois character of the early public sphere is to be found in the economic content of debates which established the public sphere: 'debate over the general rules governing relations in the basically privatized but publicly relevant sphere of commodity production and social labor' (1989:27). Empirical study of communicative change affords no support for any of these claims. Use of printed petitions to constitute and invoke public opinion in the political arena was tied neither to urban areas, predominantly economic debates, nor any social stratum or strata that, however vaguely, can be labeled bourgeois – unless we apply that label to nearly everyone in early modern England. Economic issues are not irrelevant, but the relevance of capitalism, like religion, is mediated by the connection to printing. Competition among printers stimulated publication of printed texts and thereby facilitated markedly increased access to printed political materials, including petitions. But beyond this mediated relationship, the evidence does not support oft-repeated claims about the principal role of capitalism in the origins of a public sphere.

Finally, I suggest that this foray into the past has strong implications for contemporary debates over the future of the public sphere. Study of communicative change in the seventeenth century provides a much-needed corrective to pessimistic assessments of the contemporary public sphere's potential for fostering use of reason in the political life of advanced industrial societies. Long a hallmark of critical theory, this pessimism has been extended in new directions in postmodernist social theories. Most striking about both theoretical positions is the exaggerated sense of novelty attached to communicative developments in the twentieth century that are held responsible for the eclipse of reason in public life. For critical theorists, the extension of commerce into cultural and communicative domains undermines the autonomy of the public sphere, and with it the possibility of critical use of reason in political life. Mass culture in the twentieth century is said to have eroded boundaries between the public sphere and the realm of commodity production. By reversing the differentiation of the public sphere from the world of socially necessary labor, this development is said to have destroyed the capacity of the public sphere to sustain critical uses of reason. This dour parable of differentiation and dedifferentiation in the rise and fall of the public sphere is restated in semiotic terms by postmodernists. Whereas critical theory attributes the eclipse of the public sphere to commercial impulses that dissolve the boundary between it and civil society, postmodernism refers, instead, to textual reproduction as the culprit. Heightened capacity to reproduce texts also leads to dedifferentiation that is similar to the process described in critical theory. However, culture does not collapse into civil society, as critical theory's one-dimensional thesis holds; rather, it explodes in an eruption of signification that engulfs civil society and creates *n*-dimensional worlds of meaning (see Zaret, 1992). For critical theory, communicative change leads to a corrupting commercialism; for postmodernism, it leads to a semiotic dissipation of objectivity.

Both the one- and *n*-dimensional theses of critical theory and postmodernism suffer from the same misapprehension of communicative change. The empirical analysis in this chapter deals with precisely the same communicative developments thematized by critical theory and postmodernism. In following the economic and technical impact of printing on petitioning, we have seen how commerce and textual reproduction were central to communicative developments in the English Revolution that promoted innovative petitioning. Commerce and textual reproduction enhanced popular access, imposed dialogic order on political debates, and thereby constituted a public sphere for critical use of reason in politics. Commerce and textual reproduction laid the groundwork for novel political practices that used reason to invoke the authority of public opinion for setting a legislative agenda. In short, liberal-democratic modernism was a practical accomplishment that sprang from developments that critical theorists and postmodernists hold responsible for the dissolution of modernism and liberal democracy. The force of this observation might be lessened if it could be shown that the relative magnitude of communicative change, in terms of increased commercialism and capacity for textual reproduction, is far greater in the twentieth than the seventeenth century. Yet this seems unlikely when one considers the point of departure for communicative developments in the earlier period: scribal modes of transmission and norms of secrecy. A historically balanced assessment of communicative change would acknowledge the intrinsically positive features of commerce and technical ability to reproduce texts as a corrective to one-sided views on their negative consequences that fuel the unwarranted pessimism of hypercritical theories.

References

References first list seventeenth-century petitions and pamphlets by their British Library shelf-marks. A microfilm edition of this material, organized according to these shelf-marks, has been issued by University Microfilms International and can be found in major research libraries. For seventeenth-century texts, I use original punctuation and spelling of titles; extracts quoted in the chapter are modernized. London is the place of publication unless otherwise indicated.

E61[3] (1643) [announcement of petition].
E61[9] (1643) *Special Passages*, no. 1.
E101[23] (1643) anon., *Accomodation Cordially Desired*.
E134[17] (1642) *A True Copie Of The Petition of the Gentlewomen and Tradesmens Wives*.

E150[28] (1642) *A Collection Of sundry Petitions Presented to the Kings most Excellent Majestie.*

E160[2] (1641) *The Petition For The Prelates Briefly Examined.*

E339[13] (1646) *The Scottish Dove*, no. 136, May 28 to June 3.

E340[24] (1646) *A New Petition ... to back the late City Remonstrance.*

E341[5] (1646) *A Glasse for Weak ey'd Citizens.*

E373[5] (1646) William Overton, *A Word in Season.*

E384[11] (1647) *A New Found Strategem Framed In The Old Forge of Machivilisme.*

E389[2] (1647) *The Husbandmans Plea Against Tithes. Or, Two Petitions.*

E443[8] (1648) *A Declaration Of the Knights, Gentlemen, and Free-holders ... of Surrey.*

E551[14] (1649) *To The Supreme Authority of the Nation. The humble Petition Of divers ... Women.*

E574[15] (1649) *The Remonstrance Of many Thousands of the Free-People.*

E579[9] (1649) *To The Commons of England, Assembled in Parliament.*

E684[33] (1653) *The Onely Right Rule For Regular Laws and Liberties.*

669f.3[58] (1642) *A true Coppy of the Petition of the Lord Maior ... and ... Common Counsell.*

669f.4[28] (1641) *To Parliament ... The humble Petition of ... Chigwell.*

669f.4[54] (1642) *To The Honorable the House of Commons ... the humble petition of many thousand poor people.*

669f.6[101] (1643) *The Humble Petition of the Well-Affected Yong Men.*

669f.10[37] (1645) *To The Right Honorable the Lords & Commons.*

669f.12[20] (1648) *To the Right Honorable both Houses of the Parliament.*

669f.17[36] (1653) *Unto every individual Member of Parliament.*

Alexander, Jeffrey (1991) 'Bringing Democracy Back In: Universalistic Solidarity and the Civil Sphere', in Charles Lemert (ed.), *Intellectuals and Politics*. Newbury Park, CA: Sage.

An Agreement ([1649]1944) *An Agreement Of The Free People Of England*, in William Haller and Godfrey Davies (eds), *The Leveller Tracts*. New York: Columbia University Press.

Bendix, Reinhard (1978) *Kings or People?* Berkeley, CA: University of California Press.

Calhoun, Craig (1988) 'Populist Politics, Communications Media and Large Scale Societal Integration', *Sociological Theory*, 6: 219–41.

Calhoun, Craig (1992) 'Introduction', in Craig Calhoun (ed.), *Habermas and the Public Sphere*. Cambridge, MA: MIT Press.

Calhoun, Craig (1994) 'Nationalism and civil society', in Craig Calhoun (ed.), *Social Theory and the Politics of Identity*. Oxford: Blackwell.

Calvin, John ([1536]1962) *The Institutes of the Christian Religion*. London: James Clarke.

Chartier, Roger (1987) *The Cultural Uses of Print in Early Modern France*. Princeton, NJ: Princeton University Press.

Cohen, Jean L. (1979) 'Why More Political Theory?', *Telos*, 40.

Cohen, Jean L. and Arato, Andrew (1992) *Civil Society and Political Theory*. Cambridge, MA: MIT Press.

Desan, Suzanne (1990) *Reclaiming the Sacred: Lay Religion and Popular Politics in Revolutionary France*. Ithaca, NY: Cornell University Press.

D'Ewes, Symonds ([1640–1]1923) *The Journal of Sir Symonds D'Ewes*. New Haven, CT: Yale University Press.

Dunn, John (1982) *The Political Thought of John Locke*. Cambridge: Cambridge University Press.

Eisenstein, Elizabeth (1980) *The Printing Press as an Agent of Change*. Cambridge: Cambridge University Press.

Gould, Mark (1987) *Revolution in the Development of Capitalism*. Berkeley, CA: University of California Press.

Great Britain, Parliament ([1625]1873) *Debates in the House of Commons in 1625*. London: Camden Society.

Great Britain, Parliament (1646–8) *Commons Journal*, vol. 5.

Habermas, Jürgen (1989) *Structural Transformation of the Public Sphere*. Cambridge, MA: MIT Press.

Hanson, Donald W. (1970) *From Kingdom to Commonwealth: The Development of Civic Consciousness in English Political Thought*. Cambridge, MA: Harvard University Press.

Harington, John ([1646–53]1977) *The Diary of John Harington, M.P.* Taunton: Somerset Record Society.

Hill, Christopher (1974) *Change and Continuity in 17th-Century England*. London: Nicolson.

H.M.C. Portland (1891) *Calendar of the Manuscripts of the Duke of Portland*, vol. 1. London: HMSO.

Hooker, Richard ([1593]1845) *Works*. Oxford: Oxford University Press.

Jacobs, Ronald N. (1996) 'Civil Society and Crisis: Culture, Discourse, and the Rodney King Beating', *American Journal of Sociology*, 101 (5): 1238–72.

Kallberg, Stephen (1993) 'Cultural Foundations of Modern Citizenship', in Bryan S. Turner (ed.), *Citizenship and Social Theory*. London: Sage.

Koziol, Geoffrey (1992) *Begging Pardon and Favor*. Ithaca, NY: Cornell University Press.

Knight, Mark (1993) 'Petitioning and the Political Theorists: John Locke, Algernon Sidney and London's "Monster" Petition of 1680', *Past & Present*, 138: 94–111.

Laslett, Peter (1960) 'Introduction', in Peter Laslett (ed.), *Locke's Two Treatises of Government*. Cambridge: Cambridge University Press.

Lilburne, John ([1649]1944) *Englands New Chains Discovered*, in William Haller and Godfrey Davies (eds), *The Leveller Tracts*. New York: Columbia University Press.

Little, David (1970) *Religion, Politics and Law*. Oxford: Blackwell.

Luke, Samuel ([1644–5]1963) *The Letter Books of Sir Samuel Luke*, ed. H.G. Tibbutt. Bedford: Bedfordshire Historical Record Society.

Marshall, T.H. (1966) *Citizenship and Social Class*. New York: Anchor.

Mayhew, Leon (1984) 'In Defense of Modernity', *American Journal of Sociology*, 89: 1273–1305.

Mitsuru Hashimoto (1982) 'The Social Background of Peasant Uprisings in Tokugawa Japan', in T. Najita and J.V. Koschmann (eds), *Conflict in Modern Japanese History*. Princeton, NJ: Princeton University Press.

Oxinden, Henry ([1607-42]1932) *The Oxinden Letters*, ed. D. Gardiner. London: Constable.

Rushworth, John (1721) *Historical Collections of Private Passages of State*. London: L.C. Thomason.

Seligman, Adam B. (1993) 'The Fragile Vision of Civil Society', in Bryan S. Turner (ed.), *Citizenship and Social Theory*. London: Sage.

Somers, Margaret (1993) 'Citizenship and the Place of the Public Sphere', *American Sociological Review*, 58: 587–620.

Tackett, Timothy (1986) *Religion, Revolution, and Regional Culture in Eighteenth-Century France*. Princeton: Princeton University Press.

Tarrow, Sidney (1994) *Power in Movement*. Cambridge: Cambridge University Press.

te Brake, Wayne (1989) *Regents and Rebels: The Revolutionary World of an Eighteenth-Century Dutch City*. Oxford: Blackwell.

Verner, Andrew (1995) 'Discursive Strategies in the 1905 Revolution', *The Russian Review*, 54: 65–90.

Zaret, David (1989) 'Religion and the Rise of Liberal-Democratic Ideology in Seventeenth-Century England', *American Sociological Review*, 54: 163–79.

Zaret, David (1992) 'Critical Theory and the Sociology of Culture', *Current Perspectives in Social Theory*, 12: 1–28.

Zaret, David (1994) 'Literacy and Printing in the Rise of Democratic Political Culture in Seventeenth-Century England', *Research on Democracy and Society*, 2: 175–211.

Zaret, David (1996) 'Petitions and the "Invention" of Public Opinion in the English Revolution', *American Journal of Sociology*, 101: 1497–555.

10

Mistrusting Civility: Predicament of a Post-Communist Society

Piotr Sztompka

Trust as a Resource of Civil Society

In one of the earliest comments on the anti-communist revolution of 1989 in Eastern-Central Europe, Ralf Dahrendorf suggested that the clock of transition runs at three different paces. 'The hour of the lawyer' is the shortest; legal changes may be enacted in months. 'The hour of the economist' is longer; dismantling command economies and establishing functioning markets must take years. But the longest is 'the hour of the citizen'; transforming ingrained habits, mental attitudes, cultural codes, value systems, pervasive discourses. This may take decades and presents the greatest challenge (Dahrendorf, 1990).

The insight that the quality of the citizens, the 'human factor', will ultimately be decisive in the battle for democracy, occurred a decade earlier to those 'organic intellectuals' (to use A. Gramsci's phrase) who allied themselves with political opposition in the 1980s. At that time, the old and entirely forgotten sociological notion was dug out, revived and inserted into the mainstream of public discourse. It was the concept of 'civil society'. The history of democratic opposition in Poland, Hungary, and Czechoslovakia may be written as the history of struggle for civil society, so fragile or almost entirely destroyed under the communist regime (Garton Ash, 1989: 194; 1990; Tismaneanu, 1992; Szacki, 1994: 112).

In the course of struggle and accompanying intellectual debates, the concept of civil society acquired three distinct meanings, attributable to the three theoretical traditions from which it was extracted. The first may be called the *sociological* concept, with antecedents in the classical theories of human groups, those of Ferdinand Tönnies or Georg Simmel (even though those authors did not use the term itself). Here civil society is the synonym for community (*Gemeinschaft*) or mezzo-structures – the intermediate sphere of human groups between the micro-level of the family, and the macro-level of the nation-state. From that perspective the main weakness of communist society was defined as the 'sociological vacuum, that exists between the level of the primary group and the level of the national society' (Nowak, 1981: 17). The same meaning of civil society may be found in recent sociological literature, when it is conceived as 'the totality of social institutions and associations, both formal and informal, that are not strictly production oriented nor governmental or familial in character' (Rueschemeyer et al., 1992: 49).

When the concept was used with this connotation the ideological message was clear: to overcome state monopoly, authoritarian control, totalitarian 'colonization of the life-world' (Habermas, 1987). In this respect the struggle was highly successful. Long before 1989, there had appeared a dense network of unofficial, sometimes illegal, associations, discussion clubs, voluntary organizations, self-education groups, trade unions, culminating in the social movement Solidarity. And since 1989, we have witnessed a true explosion of such intermediate bodies, now official, legitimate and recognized. Suffice it to mention that more than 100 political parties have registered in Poland since that date, some 20 of which entered the first democratically elected parliament. The foundations and other non-governmental organizations (NGOs) number in the thousands. In this sense, the civil society was reconstituted, sometimes even overblown. It will take some time before it regains normal proportions. Yet certainly, the 'sociological vacuum' is no longer there.

But there is another sense of the concept, which was also revived by Eastern European intellectuals. It is the *economic concept*, related to the classical heritage of Karl Marx and Max Weber. Here, civil society refers to the autonomous sphere of economic activities and relationships, the 'mode of production' rooted in private ownership, moved by entrepreneurial initiative, pervaded by rational calculation and aimed at individual profit. The actors operating in that sphere are labeled the 'bourgeois' in traditional language, or the 'middle class' in modern terminology.

In the hands of democratic opposition, the ideological message implied by such a concept was to overcome the command economy centrally controlled by the state, and eliminate the privileged status of state property as the dominant mode of ownership. In this respect, too, the battle has been considerably successful. After 1989, individual, private property regained its full legitimacy: the policy of privatization has already transferred large chunks of state capital into private hands. There was an outburst of entrepreneurial activities, initially in the domain of small-scale trade, financial operations, and short-term investments, aimed at quick profit, but clearly evolving in the direction of serious, long-range ventures of larger scale. Just to mention some numbers, in Poland within two years about 88% of retail trade has been put into private hands, and more than a half of GNP is already produced by the private sector. In 1993 the private sector accounted for 59% of employment, and taking into account an extensive 'gray sphere', around two-thirds of the population are employed outside the public sector (Poland, 1994: 127). The market already exists, and a sizable middle class has emerged. Thus the civil society, in the second meaning of the term, has been at least partly reconstituted.

The picture becomes more complex when we move to the third meaning of the concept. This may be called the *cultural concept*, derived from the heritage of Alexis de Tocqueville and Antonio Gramsci. Here civil society indicates the domain of cultural presuppositions, ingrained 'habits of the heart', values and norms, manners and mores, implicit understandings, frames and codes – shared by the members of society, and constraining (or facilitating) what they actually think and do. It is the sphere of Durkheimian 'social facts'. Robust civil society is synonymous with axiological consensus and developed emotional community, bound by the tight network of interpersonal loyalties, commitments, solidarities. It means mature public opinion and rich public life. It means the identification of citizens with public institutions, concern with common good, and respect for laws. In modern sociology, such a neo-Durkheimiam, culturalistic interpretation of civil society is put forward by Jeffrey C. Alexander: 'Civil society is the arena of social solidarity that is defined in universalistic terms. It is the we-ness of a national community, the feeling of connectedness to one another that transcends particular commitments, loyalties, and interests and allows there to emerge a single thread of identity among otherwise disparate people' (1992: 2).

The communist regime has never succeeded in fully destroying the civil society understood in this way (in the Polish case, one may even say that it stopped trying quite early, around 1956). But whatever remained of civil society was nevertheless pushed underground, became the 'civil society in conspiracy', directly opposed to the state and its institutions. Nowhere and never before has the opposition of civil society and the state, the people and the rulers, 'we' and 'them', been so clear-cut and radical. In the case of Poland the polarization was enhanced by a sequence of historical circumstances: more than a century (from 1794 to 1918) of partitions among neighboring foreign powers, then Nazi occupation (1939–45), and then Soviet domination (1945–89) – producing a strong stereotype of the state as something entirely alien, imposed and hostile. The idea of a nation, a cultural, linguistic or religious community rooted in sacred tradition, was opposed to the state, oppressive machinery of foreign domination. Instead of the hyphenated idea of a nation-state, we had two, not only separate, but mutually opposed concepts: the nation and the state.

In the period after World War II, and particularly in recent decades, this strongly embedded archetype has produced a double effect. The first was an affirmation and idealization of the 'private'. Most of the people have retreated into the familial sphere, where they cherished and cultivated national traditions, went to church, and silently complained about the regime. It was their authentic civil society. Most of that was not a true social entity; it had only a virtual reality, existing in imagination, memories, thoughts and dreams. The hard reality required that most of the people had to enter the public sphere for professional, occupational, career reasons – and then, in public roles, they opportunistically played by the imposed rules, only to escape back as soon as possible, more or less ashamed, to their private, imaginary enclaves.

The second, concomitant effect was the negation of the 'public'. Any deeper association with state institutions, politics, regime – like taking governmental office, accepting position in the parliament, enrolling in the ruling party – was considered as polluting, stigmatizing, sometimes akin to treason. Therefore those for whom passive withdrawal ('internal emigration') was not enough, and who wanted to participate in authentic political life, had to constitute it outside official politics. The leaders of democratic opposition have couched characteristic notions: 'non-political politics' (Konrad, 1984; Havel, 1988; 1989), 'parallel polis' (Benda et al., 1988), 'alternative society', 'the power of the powerless' (Michnik, 1985), 'the strength of the weak' (Geremek, 1992). As Andrew Arato described the discourse characteristic for Polish oppositionists: 'one point unites them all: the viewpoint of civil society against the state – the desire to institutionalize and preserve the new level of social independence' (1981: 24). In the Polish case, the emergence of alternative society was facilitated by the Catholic Church, the only large-scale organization which managed to stay outside state control, and which provided ready-made organizational networks, the symbolic rallying point for anti-state sentiments, and even the buildings open for conspirational meetings and educational enterprises.

The 'civil society in conspiracy', at the beginning restricted to narrow groups of activists, started to grow in the 1970s, and it exploded in the phenomenon of the massive social movement Solidarity in the 1980s. 'What Solidarity was able to provide, on a heroic scale, was the structure and practice of a social movement whose hallmarks were national mobilization and monolithic solidarity' (Kumar, 1992: 15). It strengthened the association of civil society with spontaneity, self-organization, massive activism, mobilization from below, autonomy and independence from the state, with a strong anti-étatist orientation. In conspiracy, in the period of struggle it had proved immensely successful. But then the glorious year 1989 came and civil society came out of conspiracy, entering the world of normal politics. Its success pre-empted its continued viability. As Krishan Kumar puts it:

> The strengths of its period of opposition became the weaknesses of its period of rule, and of its relevance as a general model of civil society ... It has in any case proved impossible to depart too far from its basic conception of civil society: as an organization (or 'self-organization') of society *against* the state. (1992: 15–16).

I wish to examine the hypothesis that the key to rebuilding robust civil society (in the cultural sense) is the restoration of trust in public institutions, public roles, and political elites, as well as in the viability of a new political and economic order. Trust is a powerful cultural resource, a precondition for proper and full utilization of other resources, like entrepreneurship, citizenship, and legalism, and for full exploitation of institutional opportunities provided by the emerging market, democratic polity and pluralistic thought (Sztompka, 1993).

The Prolegomena to the Theory of Trust

Socio-individual praxis is always oriented toward the future, and shaped in its course by anticipations of future relevant conditions. Such conditions may appear in two forms: as natural environment and social milieu. Natural and social environments threaten human agents with certain dangers and risks to which they have to adapt or respond. Thus, the future of society is always an area of complexity and uncertainty. Trust helps to reduce complexity and alleviate uncertainty (see Luhmann, 1979), by taking some aspects of the future for granted, 'bracketing them', and proceeding as if everything was simpler and more assured. Trust is the resource for dealing with the future.

Trust deals in this manner primarily with *socially* generated aspects of the future, with the social environment of action. When we speak of the social environment we have in mind other people and their actions. People live and act in the world constituted of other people and their actions. The others – like ourselves – are free agents, and may take a variety of actions. Some of them will be beneficial for us, some will be harmful. We cannot know in advance which actions others will choose. There is always a risk that they will decide on harmful and not beneficial actions. The risk grows as potential partners become more numerous, heterogeneous, distant from ourselves – in short, when our social environment becomes more complex. 'In conditions of increasing social complexity man can and must develop more effective ways of reducing complexity' (Luhmann, 1979: 8). Most often the risk produced by a complex environment is unavoidable, because to go on living we have to carry interactions nonetheless. So we make bets about future actions of others: we give or withdraw trust.

I propose the following definition: *trust is the bet on future contingent actions of others*. This brief formula has a number of implications.

First, trust refers to human *actions* and not to natural events. With reference to future natural events we express hope rather than trust. Compare two statements: 'I hope that the earthquake will not strike'; 'I trust the fire brigades to be well prepared for that eventuality.' Or another pair: 'I hope the weather will be fine'; 'I trust the meteorological forecast for tomorrow.' Hope describes our attitude towards events beyond human control, which neither we, nor apparently anybody, can influence, and to which people may only adapt once they occur. Trust describes our attitude towards events produced by human actions, and therefore at least potentially subject to our control, to the extent that we may monitor and influence the actions of others. To put it in more general terms, the concept of trust belongs to the *agency-focused discourse*, the concept of hope to the *fate-focused discourse*.

Second, both trust and hope are directed towards *uncertain* events, i.e. those of which we do not have full cognitive grasp. We cannot seriously say 'I trust the sun will rise tomorrow', or 'I hope the night will come.' Common experience as well as astronomical knowledge convince us that those are certainties. Uncertainty of natural events implies impersonal dangers; uncertainty of social conditions produces humanly created risks. Trust is expressed in risky situations, hope in dangerous situations. Risk is a concept belonging to the discourse of agency, and danger to the discourse of fate.

Third, the uncertainty of future social conditions derives from the *contingent* actions of others; it means actions in which they exercise freedom of choice. Trust expresses our expectation of some outcomes, among many options that others may have. If actions are not contingent, but fully enforced, coerced by other people or by myself, there is no place for trust. It would not be natural to say: 'I trust my slave to serve me' (as if he had a choice), or 'I trust the convict to remain in prison' (as if there was another option).

Fourth, the trust is vested in the actions of *others*. Normally I don't put trust into my own actions, I simply do them. It wouldn't sound natural to say 'I trust I will brush my teeth this evening' (because I will if I want). The exceptions are those conditions of affection, intoxication, incapability etc. when I lose control over my own will, and appear to myself as somebody else. This may be expressed in saying: 'I cannot trust myself not to hit him', or 'I cannot trust my driving today', or 'I trust I will be able to walk after that disease.' Here I myself become a quasi-other whose actions I endow with trust or distrust.

Fifth, trust is a *bet*, and that means two things. On the one hand, it means the commitment through some actions of my own. I 'place a bet', I 'make a bet', by engaging in some activity: marrying a woman I trust, voting for a politician I trust, buying from a salesman I trust, lending to a partner I trust. On the other hand, trust means the expectation with certain probability that the actions of others will be beneficial for me: that my wife will take care of the household, that a politician will lead, that the salesman will not cheat me, that the debtor will be solvent. When expectation of beneficial actions is not joined by active commitment, by the 'bet', there is only confidence, and not trust. Confidence is the passive, detached estimation of beneficial outcomes, resulting from the actions of others: 'I have confidence that the politicians will somehow prevent nuclear war'; 'I have confidence that ecological catastrophe will somehow be averted.' Thus, confidence belongs to the family of concepts focused on fate, rather than agency.

Sixth, the *content* of the bet may involve more or less demanding expectations. Trust implies that the others will be trustworthy, i.e. their future conduct will exhibit some combination of the following traits (ordered along growing strength of expectations):

1 regularity (orderliness, consistency, coherence, continuity, persistence), and not randomness or chaos
2 efficiency (competence, discipline, consequentiality, proper performance, effectiveness), and not futility or negligence (Barber, 1983)
3 reliability (rationality, integrity, e.g. considering arguments, honoring commitments, fulfilling obligations), and not voluntarism or irresponsibility
4 representativeness (acting on behalf of others, representing their interests), and not self-enhancement
5 fairness (applying universalistic criteria, equal standards, due

process, meritocratic justice), and not particularistic bias (favoritism, nepotism)

6 accountability (subjection to some socially enforced standards, rules, patterns), and not arbitrariness

7 benevolence (disinterestedness, help, sympathy, generosity), and not egoism (Barber, 1983).

Trust may be vested in various social objects, constructed at various levels of generality:

1 In the social order as such, or its particular form: 'America is a great society', 'Democracy is the only equitable regime.' This kind of trust may be called *generalized*. It provides the people with 'ontological security', i.e. 'confidence in the continuity of their self-identity and the constancy of surrounding social and material environments of action' (Giddens, 1990: 92).

2 In all the institutional segments of society, e.g. economy, science, education, medicine, justice, and the political system: 'The German economy works', 'The Swedish medical system is highly developed.' This kind of trust may be called *segmental*.

3 In expert systems, i.e. 'systems of technical accomplishment or professional expertise that organize large areas of the material and social environments in which we live today' (Giddens, 1990: 27), such as transportation, telecommunications, defense arrangements, financial markets, computer networks. The principles and mechanisms of their operation are opaque and cryptic for the average user. And yet, in our time we could hardly survive without using – and trusting – them. This form of trust may be called *technological*.

4 In concrete organizations, e.g. a particular government, corporation, university, hospital, court of law. This may be called *organizational* trust, and when it refers to political organizations – government, police, army, legal system, parliament, civil service – it is one form of the public trust.

5 In products, i.e. all kinds of goods satisfying various human needs. Trust in this case may refer in a general way to goods of a certain type ('corn flakes are healthy'), or to goods made in a certain country ('Japanese machines are highly dependable'), or in more concrete fashion to products of a certain firm ('I buy IBM only'), or even creations of a specific author ('If this is by Le Carré it surely will be an exciting book'). Let us call it *commercial* trust.

6 In social roles performed by incumbents of specific positions, e.g. attorneys, judges, medical doctors, priests, and representatives of similar professions. Trust is granted here irrespective of concrete

personal qualities, to all incumbents at a par. Thus it may be called *positional* trust.

7 In persons. Here trust depends on perceived individual competence, fairness, integrity, generosity and similar virtues. It reaches its peak in the case of persons considered as eminent, great heroic, ascribed with charisma. Let us refer to that primordial form of trust as *personal*. When the persons are public but are treated on their own, individual merits, as Mitterrand, Clinton, Walesa, and not just presidents, it is another form of public trust. When on the other hand we endow with trust of this type those persons present in our private individual micro-settings – friends, family members, co-workers, business partners etc – it will be a form of private trust.

If in a given society trust is typically vested in one selected kind of object, we shall call it *focused*. For example, there are societies which exhibit considerable trust in the interpersonal, intimate, private relations, and have deep distrust in the more abstract institutions. But trust (or distrust) may also be *diffused*, occurring more or less consistently at all levels. Metaphorically, we speak about the climate or the atmosphere of trust, or distrust, pervading the whole society. If that happens, the consequences for the whole social life are very profound. Trust (or distrust), widely shared and manifested in all areas of social life, turns into a normative expectation, becomes embedded in a culture, and not only in individual attitudes. When the *culture of trust* or the *culture of distrust* appears, the people are constrained to exhibit trust or distrust in all their dealings, independent of individual convictions, and departures from such a cultural demand meet with a variety of sanctions.

Social life does not allow for a vacuum. If trust decays, some other social mechanisms are apt to emerge as functional substitutes for trust, satisfying the universal needs for orderliness, predictability, efficiency, fairness etc. Some of them are clearly pathological.

The first reaction is *providentialism*: the regression from the discourse of agency toward the discourse of fate. The supernatural or metaphysical forces – God, destiny, fate – are invoked as anchors of some spurious certainty. They are thought to take care of a situation about which nothing can be done, as it is entirely prede-termined. For the people, it remains to 'wait and see'. This 'vague and generalized sense of [quasi] trust in distant events over which one has no control' (Giddens, 1990: 133) may bring some psycho-logical consolation, repress 'anxiety, angst and dread', but at the social level it produces disastrous effects: passivism and stagnation.

The second, quite perverse substitute for trust is *corruption*

(Elster, 1989: 266). Spreading in a society, it provides some misleading sense of orderliness and predictability, some feeling of control over chaotic environment. Bribes provide a sense of control over decision makers, and the guarantee of favorable decisions. 'Gifts' accepted by medical doctors, teachers, bosses are to guarantee their favors or preferential treatment. The sane tissue of social bonds is replaced by the net of reciprocal favors, 'connections', barter, sick 'pseudo-*Gemeinschaft*' (Merton, 1968: 163) of bribe-givers and bribe-takers, the cynical world of mutual manipulation and exploitation (see Gambetta, 1988: 158–75 on the Italian mafia).

The third mechanism is the overgrowth of *vigilance*, taking into private hands the direct supervision and control of others, whose competence or integrity is put into doubt, or whose accountability is seen as weak, owing to inefficiency or lax standards of enforcing agencies. If businessmen do not trust their partners, the handshake will no longer do. They will draw meticulous contracts, insist on bank guarantees, and count on litigation if partners breach trust. But enforcing agencies may themselves be distrusted. If the police force is judged as inept, private security agencies are employed. If banks cannot elicit debts, private debt collecting agencies appear, which occasionally resort to force. If medical doctors are not trusted, a patient will check diagnosis with a number of them.

The fourth mechanism may be called *ghettoization*, i.e. closing in, building unpenetrable boundaries around a group in an alien and threatening environment. The diffuse distrust in the wider society is compensated by strong loyalty to tribal, ethnic or familial groups, matched with xenophobia and hostility toward foreigners. People close themselves in ghettos of limited and intimate relationships, isolated and strictly separated from other groups, organizations and institutions. By cutting the external world off, they reduce some of its complexity and uncertainty. For example Polish emigrant groups in the US, arriving in the first half of the twentieth century, have never been able to assimilate and still tend to live in closed communities, cultivating traditions, religious faith, native language, customs. This may be explained by the culture of distrust arising in relatively uneducated, poverty stricken groups coming from pre-industrial settings and finding themselves in an entirely new and alien social environment (see Thomas and Znaniecki, 1918–20).

The fifth reaction may be called *paternalization*. When the 'culture of distrust' develops, with existential 'angst and dread' becoming unbearable, people start to dream about a father figure, a strong autocratic leader (Das Führer or Il Duce), who would purge with an iron hand all distrustful ('suspicious', 'alien') persons, organizations and institutions, and who would restore, if necessary by force, the semblance of order, predictability and continuity in social life. When such a leader emerges he easily becomes a focus of blind, substitute trust.

The sixth reaction may be called *externalization* of trust. In the climate of distrust against local politicians, institutions, products etc., people turn to foreign societies, and deposit their trust in their leaders, organizations or goods. By contrast, they are often blindly idealized, which is even easier because of the distance, the selective bias of the media, and the lack of direct contrary evidence. In this vein we believe in foreign economic aid or military assistance, the exceptional merits of American democracy or the unfailing quality of Japanese cars.

The Syndrome of Distrust in Post-Communist Society

Let us turn now to more concrete social realities, and apply these conceptual distinctions to the case of post-communist societies in Eastern-Central Europe.

Endemic distrust, appearing at all levels and in all regions of social life, remains a reality six years after the fall of real socialism. Evidence for that can be sought in two directions. First we may examine some *behavioral indicators*, what people do or are ready to do: more precisely, typical modes of actual or intended conduct, which inferentially would signify a lack of trust. Second we may examine *verbal indicators*: straightforward declarations, evaluations of various aspects of social life, elicited by surveys and opinion polls, in which various types of distrust find more direct articulation. The evidence refers exclusively to the case of Poland, but I suppose similar tendencies could be spotted in other countries of post-communist Europe.

Perhaps the strongest *behavioral indicator* of generalized distrust in the viability of one's own society is the decision to emigrate. This is the clearest form of the 'exit option' (Hirschman, 1970) which people take when life conditions become unbearable and no improvement is in sight. The stream of refugees fleeing East Germany in 1989, or the 'boat people' escaping Haiti, Cambodia, Vietnam, and Cuba, or Mexicans slipping through the American border, show that those people have lost 'internal trust' in the political or economic system of their own society. At the same time, the functional substitute of 'external trust' develops: either in the vague, diffuse notion of 'the free world', 'the West' etc., or in the more specific idea of an intended, most attractive country of immigration (be it the US, Canada, Germany etc.). Now look at the Polish case. Long after 1989, when all previous political motivations are no longer present, a considerable stream of emigrants is still flowing out of Poland, coming especially from higher educated groups and professionals (doctors of medicine, engineers, artists, musicians, sportspeople etc.). In the American 'visa lottery' Poles consistently get the largest quotas, which indicates that the number of applicants is also the largest. And even more tellingly, survey data show that 29% of citizens, i.e. approximately one in three, seriously consider emigrating (*Central and Eastern Eurobarometer*, March 1993).

The phenomenon akin to emigration, just another variant of the 'exit option', is the withdrawal from participation in public life, and the escape into the closed, private world of the family, friendship circles, work groups, or voluntary associations. In those 'ghettos' people find 'horizontal trust', compensating functionally for the lack of 'vertical trust' in institutions. During the communist period it was referred to as 'internal exile'. But some symptoms of that seem to continue. One is electoral abstention. In the first democratic presidential elections in Poland, almost 50% of citizens chose to abstain; later in municipal elections the overall participation was around 34%, falling to 20% in cities. In the area of economic conduct it is characteristic how extended families or kinship networks are mobilized to provide capital or labor for entrepreneurial ventures. In a relatively poor country, it is quite striking how enormous amounts of money can be raised in philanthropic actions, as long as they are defined as spontaneous and private, and not run by the government. The same people who donate large sums to the 'Great Orchestra of Festive Help' (a nationwide telethon to raise money for sick children) will use all their wits to evade taxes.

Pervasive distrust may alternatively be manifested by the 'voice option' rather than the 'exit option'. Those who do not want to emigrate, or to become passive, take to collective protest. The number of 'protest events' is a good sign of public distrust. Of course this must be accompanied by some level of trust in the contesting groups or movements and their potential efficacy. Distrust in official politics is substituted functionally with trust in 'alternative politics' from below. The life of post-communist society is rich in protest events. In the case of Poland, we observe repeated waves of strikes, street demonstrations, protest rallies, marches, road blockades, prolonged fastings, expressing generalized distrust in government or more specific distrust in concrete policies.

Distrust may be spotted when we examine forms of behavior directed toward the more distant future. If the image of the future is unclear or negative we observe the presentist orientation: concern with the immediate moment, to the neglect of any deeper temporal horizon. Some authors refer to contemporary Poland as a 'waiting society', showing 'reluctance to plan and think of the future in a long time perspective' (Tarkowska, 1994: 64–6). Evidence of such attitudes is found when we turn to some prevailing types of economic behavior. One of them is conspicuous spending on consumer goods, to the neglect of investing. Most people are still reluctant to invest in private business; only 14% consider it seriously, and only 7% are ready to invest in stocks (*Gazeta Wyborcza*, 30 April 1994). But even among those who decide to invest a characteristic pattern appears. It is striking that most investments still go into trade, services, and financial operations, rather than production or construction (Poland, 1994: 125). This reflects the uncertainty about legal regulations, terms of trade, and consistency of economic policies. Another sign of economic distrust is to be found in saving decisions: 59% of the people declare that saving is entirely unreasonable (*Gazeta Wyborcza*, 18 October 1994). Among the minority of those who do save, foreign currency is still considered more dependable by a large segment of the population, in spite of low interest rates. Approximately 36% of all savings are put into foreign currency, most of that in US dollars and Deutschmarks (*Gazeta Wyborcza*, 3 April 1994), and 25% of Poles believe that saving in dollars is the best defense against inflation (*CEBOS Bulletin*, January 1994). This is another symptom of externalization of trust.

If we look at consumer behavior, the externalization of trust becomes obvious. People consistently prefer foreign over local products, even of comparable quality, and even if local prices are lower. This refers equally to agricultural products, food, clothing, technical equipment, all the way up to automobiles.

Institutional distrust in the economic area may be indicated by the typical behavior of investors on the stock exchange, a new institution in the Polish economy. Most investors completely disregard 'fundamental analysis' based on objective indicators of performance reported by the firms, using at most the 'technical analysis' of price curves, according to some fashionable magical recipes ('Elliott waves' are particularly in vogue). Investors seem to rely on the wildest rumors, and exhibit pervasive suspicion of all official pronouncements, statistical data, and economic prognoses.

In the area of services, the distrust in public institutions is glaring. If the choice is available, people most often prefer private over public services. When socialized, state-run medicine lost its monopoly, a large proportion of patients switched immediately to private doctors and their clinics, in spite of high expenses. More and more private schools at elementary and secondary level are draining students from public education, in spite of excessive tuition. This is slowly extending to the level of higher education, where even highly prestigious state universities are abandoned by some students in favor of new private establishments. The ruling assumption seems to be that the only dependable guarantee of good services is money.

Generalized distrust in the social order and public safety is visible in the spread of all sorts of self-defense and protective measures. Vigilance develops as the functional substitute for trust. The sales of guns, gas pistols, personal alarms, the installation of hardened doors, specialized locks and other anti-theft devices at home and in cars, the training of guard dogs, have all grown into a flourishing business. There has been an eruption of private institutions and organizations, making up for the undependable operation of state agencies: private security guards, detective agencies, debt collectors etc. We also observe the growth of voluntary associations aimed at the defense of citizens against abuse: consumer groups, tenants associations, creditor groups, taxpayers' defense organizations and the like.

Let us move now to direct opinions, evaluations, and projections, in which people verbally exhibit some measure of distrust.

At the most general level, the best *verbal indicator* of trust is the appraisal of systemic reforms, their success up to now, and their future prospects. Unfortunately, only 29% of the citizens unconditionally approve reforms, while 56% declare distrust (*Central and Eastern Eurobarometer*, February 1993). In another poll 58% of the respondents appraise the current political and economic situation as deteriorating (*Gazeta Wyborcza*, 22 February 1994). When asked about more specific dimensions of reforms, only 32% declare that democracy is a good thing, while 55% are dissatisfied with democratic institutions (*Central and Eastern Eurobarometer*, February 1993). Similarly, only 29% believe that privatization brings 'changes for the better' (*Gazeta Wyborcza*, 17 April 1994). When pressed about the concrete changes, which after all did take place, the respondents show a strikingly negativistic bias, perceiving mostly the dark side of reforms. As crucial changes, 93% indicate the growth of crime, 89% the appearance of economic rackets, 87% socioeconomic distance and growing polarization into rich and poor, 57% reduced social security and care for the needy, 62% weakened mutual sympathy and helping attitudes among the people (*Gazeta Wyborcza*, 17 June 1994).

Another indicator of generalized trust is the comparison of the present socioeconomic situation with the past. Again, distrust clearly prevails. Asked about their own, personal condition, 53% feel that they are living worse than before (*Gazeta Wyborcza*, 17 June 1994). Appraising the situation of others, around half of the respondents believe that people were generally more satisfied under real socialism. This surprising result is confirmed by three independent polls, estimating the percentages at 52%, 48%, and 54% (*Gazeta Wyborcza*, 28 June 1994).

When thinking about their society in the future, people are even more pesssimistic. Only 20% trust that the situation will improve, 32% expect a turn for the worse, and 36% hope that it will at least remain unchanged (*Gazeta Wyborcza*, 17 April 1994). More concretely, in respect of the overall economic situation, 62% believe that it will not improve (*Central and Eastern Eurobarometer*, February 1993), and 55% expect the cost of living to rise (*CEBOS Bulletin*, January 1994). A confirmation of distrust in the future is found in the list of problems that people worry about: 73% indicate the lack of prospects for their children as something that worries them most (*CEBOS Bulletin*, January 1993).

More concrete institutional and positional distrust takes many forms. Politicians are treated with greatest suspicion; 87% of a nation-wide sample claim that they take care only of their own interests and careers, and neglect the public good (*Gazeta Wyborcza*, 11 July 1994). If anything goes wrong in society, 93% of the people declare that 'the politicians and bureaucrats are guilty' (Koralewicz and Ziolkowski, 1990: 62). Moreover, 48% see public administration as pervaded by corruption, and only 8% perceive corruption in private businesses (*Gazeta Wyborcza*, 19 March 1994). The veracity of those in high office is also doubted: 49% of citizens do not believe information given by the ministers (*Gazeta Wyborcza*, 25 March 1994), 60% are convinced that data on levels of inflation or GNP growth released by the state statistical office are false (*CEBOS Bulletin*, January 1994). Not much trust is attached to fiduciary responsibility (Barber, 1983) of government or administration: 70% believe that public bureaucracy is entirely insensitive towards human suffering and grievances (Poleszczuk, 1991: 76). Fairness and justice are found to be absent in public institutions: 71% say that in state enterprises 'good work is not a method of enrichment' (Koralewicz and Ziolkowski, 1990: 55), and 72% believe that people advance not because of success in work but owing to 'connections' (Poleszczuk, 1991: 86). This extends to the courts of law: 79% claim that verdicts will not be the same for persons of different social status (1991: 88). The police are considered with the traditional lack of confidence, and hence public security is evaluated as very low: 56% of the people try to avoid going out after dark (*Polityka*, 14 May 1994) and 36% do not feel safe in the streets at all, day or night (*CEBOS Bulletin*, November 1993). To the question 'Is Poland an internally safe country?', 67% respond in the negative, and only 26% feel secure (*Gazeta*

Wyborcza, 21 March 1994). Even the Catholic Church, traditionally the most trusted of all public institutions, seems to be affected by the climate of distrust, especially when it takes a more political role: 54% disapprove of such an extension of the Church's functions, and 70% would like the Church to limit its activities to the religious area (*Gazeta Wyborcza*, 10 May 1994). It seems as if any contact with the political domain is polluting.

The mass media, even though much more independent and not linked directly to the state, do not fare much better. Apparently they have not yet regained trust, which was devastated by their instrumental role under real socialism: 48% of the people still do not believe the TV, and 40% distrust the newspapers (*Central and Eastern Eurobarometer*, February 1993).

The obverse side of the strong internal distrust in its many manifestations is the emphasis on external trust toward the West. It has been found that 49% of the people are aware of European integration treaties, and 48% declare a positive view of the European Union and its policies. As much as 80% would like Poland to join the European Union, and 43% opt for doing it immediately (*Central and Eastern Eurobarometer*, February 1993). The support for joining NATO is even stronger, as the result of pervasive external distrust toward Russia and other eastern neighbors of Poland.

In the generalized climate of distrust, a vicious self-fulfilling mechanism starts to operate. To trust those who are deemed untrustworthy is clearly irrational. It is more rational to be distrustful in an environment devoid of trust. Those who manifest trust will not only lose in the game, but will be censured for stupidity, naivety, credulity, simple-mindedness. Cynicism, cheating, egoism, evasion of laws, outwitting the system, turn into virtues. And that cannot but lead to even deeper corrosion of trust.*

Toward the Recovery of Trust

The main issue of policy is how to break that vicious, self-enhancing sequence, and how to reverse it. Directly targeting distrust by moralizing, preaching, convincing people of the benefits of trust is very limited in its effectiveness in a situation in which preachers are

---

*In the case of post-communist transition the speed of events clearly overtakes the publishing process. At the moment when this book comes out the diagnosis based on the data for the early nineties doesn't seem so gloomy anymore. There are already clear signs of the consistent recovery of trust, in all respects mentioned above.

not trusted either. Thus the only viable policy is the indirect approach: consistent democratization and persistent improvement of democratic mechanisms. Restoration of trust must be brought about by consistent governmental policies. The battle should be fought on six fronts.

First, *against tentativeness and for certainty*. Consistency and irreversibility of pro-democratic policies must be safeguarded. They must be followed according to a clear pattern, blueprint or logic. They must document the unwavering, reform-oriented will of the authorities, by means of creating *faits accomplis* and pre-commitments. Hesitation, *ad hoc* reversals, slow downs on the democratic course must be avoided. People must feel that the authorities know what they are doing and where they are going, that they have a clear program and execute it persistently. The atmosphere of tentativeness, of trial and error, of another grand 'political experiment' must be eliminated, even if that provides the politicians with easy excuses for their failures. Jon Elster makes an excellent point: 'The very notion of "experimenting with reform" borders on incoherence, since the agents' knowledge that they are taking part in an experiment induces them to adopt a short time horizon that makes it less likely that the experiment will succeed' (1989: 176).

Second, *against arbitrariness and for accountability*. The key to that is the rule of law, constitutionalism, judicial control, as well as the efficiency of enforcement agencies of all kinds. In legislation and application there must be no place for voluntarism, arbitrariness, *ad hoc* action, opportunistic stretching or modifying of laws. The immutable principles of the constitution must precisely define the foundations of social and political organization, and include provisions preventing easy amendments. It must have the air of eternity. The laws must be binding for all citizens irrespective of their status. Enforcement of laws and citizens' obligations must be rigorous and must not allow of exceptions. Strong measures must be taken against crime.

Third, *against insecurity and for personal rights*. Fundamental rights of citizens have to be assured, and among them the right to private property. Consistent privatization and constitutional affirmation of private property are perhaps of key importance. Clear and precise financial laws, banking statutes, trading codes must safeguard the security of investments and economic transactions. Strict and consistent currency policies must restore the faith in local money.

Fourth, *against secrecy and for visibility and familiarity*. Governmental actions must be made as open and transparent as possible.

An efficient media policy aiming at that must be worked out and implemented. Pluralistic independent media and autonomous institutions for gathering statistical data, census offices, and reform watch centers must be developed. The politicians must be made more personal and familiar by disclosing some aspects of their private lives. Continuous polling, monitoring and reporting of public moods must become the rule. Survey results feed back to the public and eliminate the lack of awareness of the opinions of others, the pattern of 'pluralistic ignorance', so detrimental to trust.

Fifth, *against monocentrism and for pluralism.* There is a need for consistent decentralization, delegating competences to local authorities and providing local units with autonomy and self-rule. Only when people feel that some public issues really depend on them will they develop public responsibility and loyalty to institutions. 'Political systems that leave more decisions to the individual ... can generate more trust' (Elster, 1989: 180). Pluralism must also refer to political allegiances, consumer choices, cultural preferences. The larger and more variable the field for trusting commitments, the stronger the mobilization for trust.

Sixth, *against ineptitude and for integrity of personnel.* People arrive at judgments about the political, economic or other 'expert systems' and institutions by encountering their representatives: ministers and mayors, clerks and mailmen, bus conductors and airline hostesses, secretaries and teachers, doctors and nurses. All of them operate at 'access points' to the systems (Giddens, 1990: 90). Their demeanor may exude trust – when they show professionalism, seriousness, competence, truthfulness, concern for others, readiness to help. On the other hand, any bad experiences at 'access points', any frustrating contacts – even when vicarious, through the media, and not personal – are immediately generalized to the whole system (1990: 90–1). Extensive training, meticulous screening, and highly selective recruitment to all positions of high social visibility – including first of all the political offices – are prerequisites for generalized, institutional and positional trust.

None of these policies is easy to implement. But one thing is certain: without political will and determination in this direction the crisis of trust that we observe at present in post-communist societies will not be overcome.

Note

Several arguments and data presented in this chapter have been used by myself in two earlier articles: 'Vertrauen: Die Fehlende Ressource in der Postkommunistichen

Gesellschaft', in B. Nedelmann (ed.), *Kolner Zeitschrift für Soziologie und Sozialpsychologie, Sonderheft 35/1995*, September 1995, pp. 254–76; and 'Trust and Emerging Democracy: Lessons from Poland', *International Sociology*, 11 (1), March 1996: 37–62.

References

Alexander, J.C. (1992) 'Democracy and Civil Society'. Mimeo, UCLA, Los Angeles.

Arato, A. (1981) 'Civil Society against the State: Poland 1980–81', *Telos*, 47: 23–47.

Barber, B. (1983) *The Logic and Limits of Trust*. New Brunswick, NJ: Rutgers University Press.

Benda, V. et al. (1988) 'Parallel Polis or an Independent Society in Central and Eastern Europe: An Inquiry', *Social Research*, 55 (1–2): 211–46.

CEBOS Bulletin, periodical of the Center for the Study of Social Opinions at Warsaw.

Central and Eastern Eurobarometer, Commission of the European Communities publication, Brussels.

Dahrendorf, R. (1990) *Betrachtungen uber die Revolution in Europa*. Stuttgart: Deutsche Verlag-Anstalt.

Elster, J. (1989) *Solomonic Judgements*. Cambridge: Cambridge University Press.

Gambetta, D. (ed.) (1988) *Trust: Making and Breaking Cooperative Relations*. Oxford: Basil Blackwell.

Garton Ash, T. (1989) *The Uses of Adversity*. New York: Random House.

Garton Ash, T. (1990) *We, the People: The Revolution of '89*. Cambridge: Granta.

Gazeta Wyborcza, a popular Polish daily edited by A. Michnik.

Geremek, B. (1992) 'Civil Society and the Present Age', in *The Idea of Civil Society*. National Humanities Center. pp. 11–18.

Giddens, A. (1990) *The Consequences of Modernity*. Cambridge: Polity.

Habermas, J. (1987) *The Philosophical Discourse of Modernity*. Cambridge, MA: MIT Press.

Havel, V. (1988) 'Sila bezsilnych' ('The Power of the Powerless'), in *Thriller i inne eseje (Thriller and Other Essays)*. Warsaw: Nowa. pp. 92–7.

Havel, V. (1989) *Living in Truth*. London: Faber and Faber.

Hirschman, A.O. (1970) *Exit, Voice, and Loyalty: Responses to Decline in Firms, Organizations, and States*. Cambridge, MA: Harvard University Press.

Konrad, G. (1984) *Antipolitics*. New York: Harcourt Brace Jovanovich.

Koralewicz, J. and Ziolkowski, M. (1990) *Mentalnosc Polakow (Mentality of the Poles)*. Poznan: Nakom.

Kumar, K. (1992) 'Civil Society: An Inquiry into the Usefulness of an Historical Term'. Mimeo, University of Kent at Canterbury.

Luhmann, N. (1979) *Trust and Power*. New York: Wiley.

Merton, R.K. (1968) *Social Theory and Social Structure*, 2nd rev. edn. New York: Free Press.

Michnik, A. (1985) *Letters from Prison and Other Essays*. Berkeley, CA: University of California Press.

Nowak, S. (1981) 'A Polish Self-Portrait', in *Polish Perspectives*. pp. 13–29.

Poland (1994) *Poland: An International Economic Report 1993/1994*. Warsaw: Warsaw School of Economics.

Poleszczuk, A. (1991) 'Stosunki miedzyludzkie i zycie zbiorowe' ('Interpersonal

Relations and Collective Life'), in M. Marody (ed.), *Co nam zostalo z tych lat (What Has Remained of Those Years)*. London: Anex.

Polityka, a leading political weekly magazine in Poland.

Rueschemeyer, D., Stephens, E.H. and Stephens, J.D. (1992) *Capitalist Development and Democracy*. Cambridge: Polity.

Szacki, J. (1994) *Liberalizm po komunizmie* (*Liberalism after Communism*). Krakow: Znak.

Sztompka, P. (1993) 'Civilizational Incompetence: The Trap of Post-Communist Societies', *Zeitschrift fur Soziologie*, 2: 85–95.

Tarkowska, E. (1994) 'A Waiting Society: The Temporal Dimension of Transformation in Poland', in A. Flis and P. Seel (eds), *Social Time and Temporality*. Krakow: Goethe Institut. pp. 57–71.

Thomas, W.I. and Znaniecki, F. (1918–20) *The Polish Peasant in Europe and America*, vols. I–V. Boston: Badger.

Tismaneanu, V. (1992) *Reinventing Politics: Eastern Europe from Stalin to Havel*. New York: Free Press.

11

The Public Sphere and a European Civil Society

Víctor Pérez-Díaz

'Generalists' versus 'Minimalists'

In this essay, I discuss some topics which are related to current problems in the process of development of a European public sphere, which is a key component of a European civil society in the making. The difficulties arise from the fact that (a) European society is composed of national societies whose citizens' attention is focused mainly on matters of political responsibility and economic policy at a national level; (b) explicit pro-European discourse is not consistent with the actual politics of the main political actors; and (c) it is not easy to articulate narratives that could help in building up a feeling of belonging to a European 'community'. Such is the subject matter of the following sections. However, the present section is devoted to providing a better understanding of the development process by placing it within the framework of a general discussion of the relationship between the concept of the public sphere and that of civil society (taking careful note of the different uses of this term). I conclude by suggesting that the difficulties alluded to should, in fact, be considered as opportunities or challenges.

The recent uses of the term 'civil society' come mainly from three sources, which are connected to three different archaeological strata in the term's modern intellectual history. Firstly, there are those theorists who use the term in ways which are fairly close to that of the Scottish philosophers of the eighteenth century. They adopt a broad view of civil society (or 'civil society *sensu lato*') as the ideal type of a society characterized by a set of *sociopolitical* institutions such as the rule of law, limited and accountable public authority, economic markets, social pluralism and a public sphere. They could be called 'generalists' and include, for instance, Ernest Gellner (1994) and myself (Pérez-Díaz, 1993; 1995). Secondly, there are those who use the term to denote the non-governmental components of civil society *sensu lato* (namely, the economic markets together with associations and a public sphere). Those in favor of using the term in the sense of a 'non-governmental civil society' (such as Keane, 1988) may have been influenced by the use of the term (or its conceptual equivalents) in the nineteenth century, either by the Marxist tradition (which focused on markets and social classes) or by the sociological tradition (which focused on social solidarity and associations: Gouldner, 1980). Thirdly, in the twentieth century, we find several authors who prefer to use the term in an even more restricted way and focus on *some* non-governmental components of civil society *sensu lato*, excluding both the economy and the state. Those working within the Marxist tradition (such as Cohen and Arato, 1992) were inspired by Gramsci and Habermas; those working in the sociological tradition (such as Alexander, 1994) by Parsons and possibly Gouldner. They share the common trait of referring to a 'civil society' which is reduced to a peculiar combination of associations (or social movements) and the public sphere. (I say 'peculiar' in so far as they tend to neglect *individual* players in the public sphere, and they tend to consider associations and social movements only or mainly in their capacity as players in the public sphere.) If I refer to those who use the term 'civil society' in its widest sense as 'generalists' (myself included), I would call those of the third category (who refer to 'civil society *qua* the public sphere') as 'minimalists' or 'sociocultural minimalists'. I shall now center my attention on some aspects of the contrasting views of generalists and minimalists.

Between generalists and minimalists, more than a mere verbal or terminological discussion (which is better avoided, if possible), there are substantive disagreements concerning their subject matter. As a generalist, I tend to focus on the *systemic links* among the different components of civil society in its broadest sense. These occur between the spontaneous (or nomocratic: Hayek, 1979) orders of economic markets, social pluralism and the public sphere (where autonomous agents exchange resources, social identities and arguments, and coordinate their activities) on the one hand, and a public authority subject to the rule of law (and responsive to the markets, associations and public opinion) on the other. These links can be followed in all directions. The *nomoi* or rules of the orders are implemented by means of a set of institutional mechanisms which include a public authority (willing and ready to apply legitimate violence to impose these rules) and informal sanctions (or 'culture', in the language of the neo-institutionalists: North, 1990) such as the approval, or disapproval, expressed by public opinion. In turn, the public sphere refers to the proper conditions in which the public authority can use its powers, to the rules of politics and of the economy, and to the identity (and the boundaries), of the community, which is the social referent of both the public authority and the rules. Of course, the basic premise of the search for systemic links between the various components of civil society is that civil society, as an ideal type, has a systemic character and therefore its different parts tend to fit together. This premise goes back to what is usually referred to as the 'naive' view which tended to prevail among the Scottish philosophers of the eighteenth century. Though they were well aware of the tensions existing in the commercial societies of their time, they envisioned a civil society in which '(civic) virtue' and 'wealth' went hand in hand. To their way of thinking, the tensions were not internal contradictions which would destroy the system (*à la* Marx), but practical problems which could be overcome. Tensions could degenerate into endemic difficulties and permanent distortions of the ideal character, but there was no historical law or inner logic leading inexorably in that direction. As I see them, these theorists were 'possibilists' or 'indeterminists' (Pérez-Díaz, 1995). At the same time, I see a partial confirmation of the systemic nature of civil society in that the existing societies to which we could point as approximations to the ideal type, such as the United Kingdom or the United States, have been able to adjust themselves to the dramatically changing circumstances of the last two to three centuries while maintaining the essentials of civil society's institutions. This is indicative of the remarkably adaptive capacities of their sociopolitical systems.

By contrast, most minimalists tend to reject such a systemic link among the diverse components of what I call civil society. Most are inclined to see fundamental conflicts between the economic markets, the state and what they call 'civil society', and I call the public sphere (which, in order to avoid verbal misunderstandings, I shall refer to as the public sphere from now on). Particularly those who belong to the more recent Marxist tradition (and those neo-functionalists who feel closer to a critical or conflictual view of the modern world) tend to think of the public sphere not merely as different from, but as fundamentally opposed to, the modern market economy and the modern state. They appear to combine Weber's view of a clash between conflicting gods with Marx's search for systemic contradictions in the modern world. They overemphasize the repressive nature of a market economy and a bureaucratic state, while they underscore the 'liberative potential' of the public sphere.

The (Marxist or critical) minimalists' views on the liberative potential of the public sphere seem to have undergone substantial changes over the course of time. Initially, these theorists believed that the public sphere would provide the foundations for transforming the state and the economy. Later on, they embraced a more defensive (and pessimistic) view of the public sphere as a bulwark of resistance to the combined encroachments of the state and capitalism (in Habermas's language, 'the system'). This change in attitude may have reflected a displacement of feelings of powerlessness from one historical terrain to another. Superficially, the change may have corresponded to the theorists' loss of heart, sensing the increasing difficulty of defeating capitalism as they faced up to its resistance to its own demise as well as the readiness of workers to accommodate to it. Thus, they developed a theory of late organized capitalism in which a conflation of 'evil forces' (of commercial, political and media conglomerates) almost succeeded in crushing people's resistance and lulling their critical dispositions, converting them into a mass of acquiescent consumers. Nevertheless, we may speculate that, at a deeper level, the minimalists' retreat into a more defensive position was influenced by another factor. This consisted of them projecting onto capitalist societies the powerlessness which they felt when confronted by the socialist systems in Eastern Europe – systems which were so very close to an almost total fusion of political, ideological and economic hierarchies (the Caesaro-Papism-Mammonism referred to by Gellner, 1994: 4) and which appeared so impervious to change from within.[1] In fact, the transformation of these socialist societies (such as the Soviet Union) came at the end of a period of systemic drift, and were the result not so much of concerted action by political elites and collective movements as a combination of external pressures and (internal) institutional and cultural weaknesses (hence, the ideological collapse of the socialist establishment almost overnight). Under these circumstances, the critical intellectuals were witnesses to (or participated in) social movements which initiated crucial changes and then retreated into a defensive position (as happened to Solidarnosc after the military coup in 1981).

A more complex (and more optimistic) version of minimalism is to be found in Alexander's (1993; 1994) work. He seems to be in search of some middle ground between Parsons's understanding of the market order and universalistic bureaucratic state structures, and the position adopted by Cohen and Arato, which makes that of Parsons look like a Hegelian apology for the established order of, in this case, the American system (Alexander, 1993: 800). On the one hand, Alexander (1993: 802) suggests that there is a liberative potential in market economies and bureaucratic state structures; on the other, he criticizes Keane's 'non-governmental civil society' on the grounds that, by placing together 'privately-owned, market-directed, voluntarily run (and friendly-run) organizations', he wishes to conflate phenomena which are 'by no means theoretically complementary and pragmatically congenial' (1994: 17). This may be construed as meaning that, according to Alexander, there is no systemic link between the realm of a market economy and that of the sociocultural arrangements of the public space (not to mention the realm of public authority or the state). Indeed, it seems that the main thrust of Alexander's attack on the broader concept of civil society (and of his *plaidoyer* for a more delimited understanding of the term) is that the public sphere (in his terms, 'civil society') should be marked off as responding to a logic of its own, which is that of 'a sphere of universalizing social solidarity' (Alexander 1994: 6, 18).

I have a number of difficulties with the minimalists' view of civil society *qua* public sphere. I do not mind their use of the terms as much as their implications for a public sphere whose links to the other components of civil society have been drastically loosened. My difficulties are analytical and empirical on the one hand, and normative on the other. On analytical and empirical grounds, my objections have to do with the substantive contents of the public sphere as regards politics and the economy, as well as regards its community of reference and the formation of people's capacities in order for them to participate actively in it.

First, I think that the development of a public sphere is so intimately connected to discussion of the economy (rules of the markets and economic policy) and of the proper role and perform-ance of the public authority (and its administrative staff) that severing the link between them would deprive the public space of most of its contents and reduce it to an empty shell. Empirically, it seems easy to demonstrate that the very emergence of civil societies (that is, of actual societies close to the ideal type), dating back to the seventeenth and eighteenth centuries, depended on debates on tax policies and the proper limits and conditions of the public authority, which were conducted with determination and persistence for a certain period. This continues to be true of today's civil societies in which most civic debate still dwells on similar matters.

Second, the development of a public sphere also depends on the development of a feeling of belonging to a particular community. Even though we may talk of civil society as an ideal type, the fact is that we can only observe a plurality of particular civil societies, distinct from one other and with recognizable boundaries (between members and non-members). Much public debate evolves around the expression of feelings of belonging to a particular community. Such feelings are rooted in people's shared experiences (past and present) of mutual need and mutual obligation, that arise in the context of economic and political exchanges and other social activities. These experiences are also shaped and given meaning by narratives (with some mythical components) which usually refer to a 'country' or a 'nation' (or some other form of a 'primordial' or 'quasi-primordial' community). These narratives provide the basis for a number of rituals and ceremonies which appeal to and reinforce people's feelings of loyalty and attachment to that particular community, and of fellowship towards each other. In civil societies, the identity of a particular community is also partly defined by the institutions of the rule of law, an accountable public authority and individual freedoms. However, whatever the strength of the civil identification of the community may be, it coexists with that of the particular memories and feelings to which I have just referred.

Each community demands not just people's loyalty, but loyalty *intense enough* for these people to be willing and ready to risk their lives and property on behalf of it. Sometimes this means that they must be ready either to die or to allow their children to die for it. Even if there is no imminent danger of death, concern for the public good as expressed by debate and participation in the public sphere is supposed to be a significant and (to some degree) a passionate endeavor for a critical mass of concerned citizens, in the absence of which a civil society cannot be expected to endure.[2] Feelings of intense attachment to a particular community and the corresponding appeal to extraordinary sacrifices on its behalf imply an understanding of the community as having a 'sacred' character. They also imply that politics are premised on beliefs and rituals that amount to some form of 'religion', the ultimate avatar of which, under modern conditions, seems to be 'civic (or civil) religion', with its blend of universalistic and particularistic elements. A civic religion makes as much for fulfillments of civic duty, such as dying on the battlefield in defence of one's country, which is greeted by ritual ceremonies of dignified pain and awe, as for transgressions of the basics of civil life, such as treason in time of war, which is greeted with horror and intense moral indignation. It seems as if some form of civic religion goes together with the various forms of civil societies, and we should not forget that Pericles's funeral oration in honor of the first Athenian citizens to be killed on the battlefield in the Peloponnesian wars is one of the best expressions ever of the beliefs on which civil society is founded (Thucydides, 1972 [*c.* 404 BC]: Book 2).

Finally, the full development of a public sphere depends on people's cultivation of certain habits and dispositions which, in turn, may be fostered by their practical involvement in the workings of markets and liberal polities. Most minimalists take a hyper-rationalist view of the public sphere as one in which rational arguments are exchanged among a community of conversants who abide by some of the cognitive and moral rules of the communicative game. These include formal logic and the general principles governing people's access to the public space. In my view, however, even more important than formal, explicit acceptance of the rules by the conversants is their actual acquisition of habits and dispositions. These include self-confidence in making decisions and accepting personal responsibility for them (Oakeshott, 1991: 364); toleration of others, which is balanced by a readiness to check violence from whatever quarter it may come; and resistance to the abuse of authority. These habits and dispositions cannot be the result of the communicative experience *per se*, nor can they be acquired by rational persuasion. They are the result of practical experience, and they are acquired by means of repeated activities of the proper kind. The point is that, in the long run, markets and liberal polities have proved to be institutions which have demanded, and provided incentives for, the right kinds of practical experience and the necessary activities, which are performed on an everyday, routine basis by large segments of the population; and they have proved to do so much better than their historical alternatives (such as command economies and authoritarian polities). Thus, for instance, Bailyn's (1967) discussion of the American colonists suggests that the development of civic capacities for debate and intervention in collective business depended upon the colonists' prolonged training in the practices of deliberation and argument as well as their ability to summon up the moral and emotional resources needed to engage in an argument, reach a personal conclusion and stick to it in the face of social pressure. This training was acquired by the colonists' involvement in markets and political assemblies, as well as in congregational religion.

On normative grounds my objections to the minimalists follow on from a moral commitment to a *civitas* understood as a community of free individuals, who are well advised to keep a critical eye on all kinds of big organizations while at the same time accepting their duty to act as responsible citizens. From this viewpoint, I have no basic objection to introducing a note of caution about, and a commitment to making a realistic assessment of, the degree to which state and business organizations cooperate with each other with a view to exploiting and manipulating the public, and also train their employees in the habits of uncritical obedience. However, in doing so, we should be careful of going to extremes. We must not fail to look on big organizations of all kinds with caution: states, parties, business firms, unions, media organizations, churches, cultural, consumer, ecological and feminist associations and many others. None can be considered above suspicion. But we would be going too far if we overlooked the other half of the picture: the liberative potential that these organizations may possess as well as the degree of freedom of their individual units (the possibilities of 'fight and flight' in respect of organizational constraints) and, therefore, the degree of indetermination in organizations' internal workings and strategic conduct.

However, from the moral commitment to a community of individuals and citizens there follows not only the above (negative) attitude of generalized and limited suspicion towards big organizations but also the (positive) disposition to participate in the public arena. From this viewpoint, I contend that there is an inherent danger in the position of the sociocultural minimalists of its leading (paradoxically) to a society of irresponsible citizens. By reducing people's expectations and aspirations as regards shaping the rules of the market economy and the state, those in favor of a strategy of civic retrenchment seem to advocate a new version of Epicurean morality. Epicure's garden has become Habermas's lifeworlds. Their implicit argument seems to be: 'let us cultivate our garden (where we may enjoy a well protected existence), while engaging in occasional *razzias* into the foreign territory of the state and the economy (where the production and distribution of material resources take place and the rules of coexistence are implemented, allowing for the cultivation of the garden to proceed in peace).' Thus, the choice of cultivating the garden, together with the refusal to accept the burden of responsibility for the economic and political system that makes it possible, suggest a low level of either rational understanding or practical morality or both. The minimalists appear to view the present economic and political circumstances as though they had a distinct similarity to those of the late Roman Empire: in Hegel's words, a soulless mechanism. But this view does not do justice to the possibilities and promise of the post-1989 world, when we took a giant step forwards by getting rid of the totalitarian nightmares of our century. I believe that this is a time, not for Epicurean morality, but rather for a new breed of Stoics, of active citizens of the world.

However, it may well prove that today's Europeans have first to learn how to be good citizens of the European community in order to become good citizens of the world (or, of particular societies 'within the Great Society': Hayek, 1979: 47). In the following sections I shall apply some of the above considerations to the case of the European public sphere as a crucial component of European civil society. The scale and complexity (which is inherent in the aggregation of several national civil societies) of the European case cannot be adequately examined within the limits of this essay; nevertheless, it may be worthwhile taking inspiration from the work of our Scottish forerunners and trying our hand at observing and analyzing a new form of civil society *in statu nascendi*, while playing our part in it as citizens of the new community.

The Public Sphere and the Construction of a European Civil Society

The construction of European (political) unity has been proposed as a task that should be undertaken by today's Europeans with the utmost determination, to judge by the vehemence and reiteration with which it is proposed to us. Many journalists, politicians, intellectuals, clerics and civil servants (of both the 'right' and the 'left') consider it their duty to remind us that this unity is desirable and even inevitable. But, for some reason, their exhortations seem to meet with only limited success. The public listens to them, acknowledges their sermons and then proceeds to something more urgent or more interesting that rapidly becomes the focus of its attention.

The truth is that the subject of European unity has been relatively absent from the everyday conversation of the majority of Europeans for a very long time (though the signs are that this is no longer the case). This fact is of prime importance because it indicates how far they are from having laid the foundations of the edifice. They have a few important elements, some arches, part of the roof, some Roman tiles, a stork's nest, a baroque façade; and they have plastered up the advertisements, kitted out the tourist guides (with uniforms and regulations), built the roads and set up the coach services. There is even a motley crowd wandering around the site. But this crowd talks intermittently and out of turn. It needs to listen and converse.

A continuous, ongoing, unending civic conversation involving a 'critical mass' of concerned European citizens in regard to matters of institutional design, policy and collective identity is a necessary condition for building whatever European political construction may be possible. A public space or public sphere is a crucial building block of that construction, and the counterpart for a common public authority, in the larger framework of a European civil society that would allow for a lively internal pluralism.

For centuries, Europe has been accustomed to alternating between unity and fragmentation, continually reinventing her unity in plural forms. This internal plurality has been her sign of identity since the world of the Romans and the world of the Germanic tribes merged at the end of what we have since called the ancient world. The relative homogeneity of European cultural and socioeconomic systems has always been under enormous pressure and has never led to stable political unity. The tension between the Papacy and the

Empire soon changed this unity into a longed-for but impossible aspiration; and its impossibility was accentuated by the emergence of powerful national states, against the backcloth of the broad dispersion of territorial powers and personal jurisdictions.

In the modern era, Europe has been the scenario of recurrent attempts at hegemony which, at their height, have not survived the passage of two, three or, at the very most, four generations. What, from the point of view of the protagonizing nations, were the hegemonies of *pax Britannica, rayonnement* or *siglos de oro* were transformed, in the eyes of their antagonists, into more transient and hazardous achievements, full of pretentiousness and fueled by dreams of a somewhat illusory greatness which proved extremely dangerous for the freedom of all the others. As a result these hegemonic attempts have always provoked defensive alliances against them in the face of which they have usually succumbed. Each nation has had its moment of glory which has generally proved to be threatening to all the rest. Only in the course of time, once the danger has passed, has it been possible to soften the memory of these experiences. In this way, in the kaleidoscope of European memory, the terrible magnificence of the great, historic nations has become grist for the tourist mill; and the flower of their chivalry arrayed in knightly splendor has become cardboard cut-out horses decked out in tinsel on a merry-go-round, their only charms residing in the evocations of childhood.

The kind of political unity which Europe has embraced over and over again, throughout her history, has been the soft kind of relative equilibrium among the powers; this has created a moderately stable framework for the incessant struggle for cultural and economic domination among her many components, embarked upon a constant round of imitation and challenge among themselves. But although the experiment in the construction of European unity over the last 40 years has gone a long way beyond this traditional balance of power it is, however, curious to observe that, in spite of the wishes expressed by so many of her political leaders, the general public is reluctant to contemplate the creation of a European state as the ultimate goal of this process of construction, and neither the institutions nor the sentiments of the majority of Europeans seem to respond to a project of strong political unity of this nature. In reality, this process seems better fitted to what would be the construction of a European civil society than a European state.

As already indicated, by 'civil society' I mean an ideal type referring to a set of political and social institutions, characterized by limited, responsible government subject to the rule of law, free and open markets, a plurality of voluntary associations and a sphere of free public debate. The European situation only partly corresponds to the ideal type; but sufficiently so in order for its application to be of some value. European public authority is limited since, fundamentally, it is a directorate of (formally) sovereign public powers operating on the logical basis of an equilibrium of power by which each one limits the others; to which some supranational or transnational organisms of unequal importance have been added. Markets make up a fundamental part of the European system and they are basically free and open (although the sectors in which European public authorities intervene are of considerable relevance, in particular the agricultural sector). The *dramatis personae* of the voluntary associations which operate at a supranational or transnational level are increasingly numerous, influential and diverse (in the form of businesses, academic networks, religious associations, policy networks and/or lobbies, etc.). As regards the public sphere, it is perhaps the least developed component of the four.

Nevertheless, the public sphere is decisive in the formation and development of a civil society because it is within this sphere that the problem arises (and is eventually solved) of deciding whether members of a society are simply free individuals who pursue their own private interests or whether they are, at the same time, citizens who engage actively in debate on public affairs, on institutional matters and matters of policy and identity, and form opinions about them. It is the latter of these two alternatives which provides the basis for democracy because it establishes the ground rules for the proper relations between politicians and citizens, because it identifies the issues of common concern, and because it allows the development of feelings of collective identity and of belonging to a political community (both of which are conditions prior to democracy itself).

In fact, feelings of belonging to a civil society are encouraged by participation in the debate, as much within primary circles like the family, friends or the work group as within the framework of wider social movements or organizations, and even in forums of generalized communication. Discussion about the common good may be the foundation of community, even when this communication expresses diversity of opinion (which is normally the case), if it tends to ratify everyone's interest in certain common themes and reinforce feelings of belonging to the same entity, at least under certain conditions. However, the reasoning must not incline towards arguments for the exclusion from the community of those who hold a different position. It is perhaps possible to build a political community in which the decisions of a charismatic or traditional leader are endorsed by popular acclaim with a minimum of articulated public discussion; but it is quite impossible to build a civil society without an abundance of it.

Current Difficulties for the Development of the European Public Sphere: The Public's Focus on Political Responsibility and Socioeconomic Policy

One of the difficulties of articulating either a civic conversation or a European public sphere at present arises from the fact that European unity does not seem to be a matter which excites much interest or attention among Europeans today. Their main interest lies in matters which are oriented more towards their nation-states than towards Europe. The contents of domestic debates suggest the crucial importance of two topics: that of the relation between the public authority and the citizens, and that of socioeconomic policy. There cannot be a vigorous European public sphere unless these topics become a central part of the European debate and political process.

Let us take, first, the question of the crisis of relations between political parties and public opinion, which many commentarists believe it has been possible to observe in Europe for some time past. In some countries, this crisis has recently taken on a dramatic complexion. In Italy it has led to the substitution of the majority of the traditional political class (over the last 50 years) for another of a different order. For decades the Italians had lived with a party system whose corruption they were aware of but took philosophically: they knew about the irregular financing of their political parties but this did not prevent them voting for them with regularity. Perhaps they thought that it was the lesser evil because the party system was compatible with a high degree of prosperity and freedom (which a non-democratic, fascist or communist system would threaten); and that, to some extent, it was merely a logical extension of a somewhat lax lifestyle as regards abiding by the rules, whatever they were. Political and economic arrangements had always been made in this way to some extent, at least in large areas of the country. As a result, corruption had come to be looked on as a natural course of action and it was felt to be something that Northern Europeans, although they could not understand it very well, could, in practice, tolerate and learn to live with.

For some still mysterious motives it seems that this ambiguous self-complacency has abruptly disappeared. What began as a limited investigation into abuses in the north of Italy evolved, thanks to the Lombard League, into an explosion of indignation with spectacular electoral results, and thanks to the efforts of a network of magistrates, into an operation (*mani pulite*) exposing relations between the state, the parties and businessmen: in particular, the mechanisms for financing the political parties. The Italians have had to reinvent their state and their political regime, and in the process of doing so, they have had to create new parties and articulate a somewhat different political discourse with new ground rules.

The Spanish political crisis of 1993–6 bears a certain resemblance to the Italian one. Spain completed her transition to democracy within two to three years of Franco's death and consolidated it a few years later (when she could act without fear of a military coup or a guerrilla or an anti-establishment movement destroying it). But the institutionalization of democracy, that is, the interiorization of the ground rules as habitual behavior on the part of its agents, has been much less easy to achieve. In Italy, it has not been fully achieved even after 50 years; and, in a manner of speaking, the Italians have had to reconstitute their republic anew. In Spain, 20 years after the transition, the climate of corruption has generated a grave political crisis.

Whatever its outcome, I wish to underline the cathartic function of a political crisis for the citizens of a country. They discover that they can no longer maintain their indifference or unconcern for public affairs. The question of political corruption follows them wherever they go, arising spontaneously in conversation. Politics, at its most basic, has become part of their lives and it arouses relatively intense and somewhat disagreeable feelings in them. They are overcome by feelings of indignation or depression which they would probably prefer not to experience. In short, they have not been free to choose whether or not to take an interest in public affairs; they have simply found themselves unable to avoid them. It is almost as if they feel that they and their personal identity are implicated in these arguments: for this reason they react so emotionally.

Possibly they believe that they are affected by the question of corruption because it projects an image of a corrupt country of which they form a part, and that is humiliating. They have to admit that they already knew that it was corrupt, and that they have done little or nothing about it. They probably also know that, to a lesser degree, they and everyone else have conformed to the general standard and bent the rules too. Thus their anger towards those caught *in flagrante* is part of a phenomenon of ambivalence and the outward projection of the contempt which they may feel towards themselves (which makes these feelings rather more complicated than merely moral indignation or cynicism). In short, countries which are experiencing these spasms of doubt about their public institutions expend a large part of their emotional energies on themselves; and the ordering of this institutional, cultural and interior disorder logically occupies a great deal of time.

If this were simply a localized phenomenon, we could dismiss it as an exception. But it is not. What has happened in Italy and Spain could probably happen in other countries which have recently embraced democracy, like Greece or the countries of Central and Eastern Europe which, in recent decades, have existed for most of the time under totalitarian regimes and, previous to that, under authoritarian and clientelistic ones. The transformation of these countries into civil societies with transparent, universal rules for political and economic life requires the setting up of institutions (above all of a microsocial nature) which are difficult to design and attend to with sustained attention for a long enough period. If the problem of these nations could be defined simply as a problem of making the transition to and consolidating democracy, and introducing the fundamentals of a market economy (and a regime of private property), it would not be necessary to go into these details. But civilization rests on details. The first step may be to rewrite the books with the new ground rules (constitutions and laws), to make the necessary speeches and start the ball rolling. The next step is to attain a certain quality in the actual functioning of political, social and economic life, which can be a lot more arduous.

Is it possible to imagine a remotely similar situation occurring in the nucleus of the liberal democracies of Great Britain, Central Europe or the Scandinavian countries? Maybe not with the pathological features of the southern countries (although we should not overlook the amnesty which the French political parties granted themselves on matters of corruption in 1989), but there does exist the same lack of confidence in relations between the political class and society, a problem of almost 20 years' standing. The myth of the 'good old times', of stable relationships apparently brimming with confidence among the diverse social groups and political parties (presumably), refers to the 1950s and (almost) the 1960s. The following decades have seen a relatively volatile vote from many groups, the emergence of alternative social movements, feelings of malaise with the established parties, the redefinition of the messages of those parties, and the restlessness of public opinion. It has seemed obvious to many that, in such large and complex societies as our own, there is no room for direct democracy (not even at intervals, as occurs to some extent in Switzerland); nevertheless, it is no less obvious that the classic formula of representative democracy, in which a country delivers its political decision-making capacity into the hands of its representatives, who are usually incorporated into political parties, does not correspond to the sentiments prevalent among the European public at present.

To some extent this problem causes the introversion of public opinion, not its extroversion: attention centers on obliging politicians to put their house in order in each country. This preference on the part of the public is usually at variance with that of the political class in a number of European countries; this was made quite clear when the Treaty of Maastricht was ratified and one sector of public opinion condemned its politicians for their apparent neglect of domestic problems. Moreover, this disparity is comprehensible because today these problems are serious and urgent ones which concentrate the attention (and emotions) of the public on the performance of their national governments.

It is obvious that, in general, political discussions in almost all countries are centered on their own affairs; a glance through any European newspaper demonstrates this quite clearly, not only from the relative length of the articles but also from their rhetorical tone. What is central and what is peripheral is taken for granted: each country is the center of its world. The language employed leaves no doubt about what inflames the passions of the readers and what merely attracts polite attention. Each country would appear to be deeply enamored of itself (some of them indulging in an intense love/hate relationship) while it observes with emotional distance the fortunes of all the rest, and in the meantime works out and weighs up its agreements and disagreements with them. It takes an interest in its neighbors, but keeps its heart to itself.

The critical problems of today do no more than confirm these priorities for the immense majority of the public in each country – above all, if we take into account the definition of the situation which is proposed to them by the various political parties that need their electoral support. The economic crisis is still, and above all else, a matter to be dealt with by this or that domestic economic policy. It is said that soon the monetary policies of European countries will be a joint affair. Meanwhile, each country appears to be convinced that its government is responsible for the progress of its own economy; and the central bank, the minister of finance and the prime minister are expected to produce an appropriate policy. The economy is the topic of debate between those in power and the opposition, the subject of incessant commentary, detached or partisan, always humming away to make up half the editorials in all the newspapers, among other reasons because it is supposed that it is the hurdle at which elections are won or lost.

All this has a certain logic given that Europe has had about 10% of its labor force unemployed for some years now (and in countries like

Ireland and Spain the figure rises to about 20%). Every European country has its own problems, but almost all of them seem to be particularly preoccupied about the future of their industrial apparatus and about what has been called, in recent discussions, the capacity of European countries to face up to 'the challenges of competitiveness and productivity'. The most widespread opinion assumes that this capacity is defective, especially in relation to that of others (such as the United States and Japan). But the outcome of this is to worry about finding an adequate economic policy, country by country and government by government. Among other things because, if this were not so, no one would quite know for certain what an elected government could be held responsible for, after such an abundance of enthusiasm and rhetoric every few years: or to whom businessmen should address their requests (and demands) with such tenacity and the unions with such vehemence.

The public life shared by all European countries revolves around the news broadcasts of their respective television channels, with their apparently detached explanations of the positions of political and social agents on these matters, and with their implicit invitation to spectators to adopt their own position. 'Unemployment, different solutions to unemployment, trust in different politicians to apply these solutions, persistence of unemployment': this is the mantra ritually invoked to the nation's gods which would metamorphose viewers into fellow citizens. If this mantra (or an equivalent) were to be interrupted, the vacuum would be deafening in its silence. It would be like finding ourselves in the soulless cosmopolis of the late Roman Empire: as if their gods had left the earth. (In such a way that perhaps now, anticipating this feeling, many people behave as if they still believed that these domestic economic policies are fundamental, although they suspect that they are not; and they do so for the simple reason that they want to retain the illusion of some public forums in which they can still recognize each other as fellow citizens of the same polity.)

In any case, for the moment, the vast majority of opinion in each country continues to insist on attributing responsibility to its own government for its economic and social policies. And here again we face a considerable problem: practically all European countries are trying to come to terms with the almost insoluble question of how to control and reorganize their heavily state-funded welfare systems which they have inherited from the past. This is a matter of enormous importance in the everyday life of the general public; and it is logical that it commands a large part of their attention.

In short, at this moment, the question of the construction of European unity takes second place to domestic matters such as the redefinition of relations between every nation's politicians and their constituencies, economic policies intended to 'overcome the economic crisis' or to 'make adjustments to the new conditions of the international markets' (depending on the phase of the economic cycle), and the impending revision of the welfare system.

Performative Contradictions in the European Arena: Integrative Political Discourse versus Divisive Politics and Policies

An additional difficulty in the development of a European public space arises from the double dimension of the political debate, and its very nature of being a conversation made out of speech acts and performative statements, out of rhetorical statements and substantive policy. In this respect, we observe that the European political class, which is supposed to focus attention on European matters, and which, so far, has been rather inclined to preach the gospel of the European political union, and to indoctrinate their domestic constituencies in the virtues of looking beyond the narrow horizons of the national interest, however, by their very deeds has been sending a much more ambiguous message.

Thus, we have a curious divergence in the structure of the scale of preferences, the centers of interest, and the background assumptions of political discourse between one sector of the political classes and the most cosmopolitan economic, bureaucratic and academic circles on the one hand, and the greater part of the public on the other. The former devote a good deal of their energies to managing problems in a trans-European context, distinct from that of their respective countries, and in their eyes this adds increasing plausibility to the hypothesis, or the suspicion, that national policies have a very limited effect on events. (Although it may also encourage them in the compensatory illusion that a supranational European policy would have a decisive effect on them: an illusion which could prove equally mistaken, but that is another matter.) The latter abide by their normally limited experience within a national frame of reference, and therefore they persist in making whichever government happens to be in power responsible to a large extent for what happens (to the desperation of those 'cosmopolitan' members of their respective governments).

However, there are some matters common to both these elites and the public which have to be resolved in a European political context, but which, paradoxically, only tend to reaffirm the prevalence of the national interest outlook. When discussing these, I propose to show a new source of difficulties for the creation of a European public sphere: which is, that actual European policies (her public policies and politics) may contradict pro-European rhetoric.

At this point I wish to introduce the concept of 'performative contradiction' which, taken in its widest sense, consists of contradicting words with deeds (or, strictly speaking, that certain behavior implies an existential affirmation whose content contradicts the content of the verbal proposition: Habermas, 1991). Let us take the European public policy *par excellence*, which is, of course, her agricultural policy. For a long time, taking care of this policy absorbed most of the energies of her civil servants and most of her economic resources: even in 1995 half of the Community budget was spent on subsidies to European farmers (Comisión Europea, 1995: 433). But the fact is that European agricultural policy is, above all, a policy designed to satisfy a few extremely important pressure groups on the domestic political front in the signatory countries of the Treaty of Rome, particularly France, Germany and the Benelux nations, which they then imposed on nations who were incorporated into the Community at a later date; and above all, it is a policy oriented towards maintaining what is supposed to be a fundamental, symbolic ingredient of the territorial identity of each one of the nations in question. As a logical consequence of this, when the time comes to admit a new member, agriculture has usually been the main issue determining the ease or difficulty of the negotiations. Thus, for example, the Community waxed lyrical about the incorporation into Europe of the democratic Spain which rose from the ashes of her Francoist past. However, although Franco died in 1975, and Spain applied for entry into the Community in 1977, she was only admitted in 1986; and not before our neighbors had made absolutely clear that the price Spain would have to pay for entry would be a substantial reduction in the competitive potential of her agriculture with respect to French agriculture. And in case the lesson should ever be forgotten, French farmers periodically take it upon themselves to express their popular fury against Spanish agricultural imports, in the best tradition of peasant revolts under the *ancien régime*; while French political parties of all shades look modestly away and calculate the foreseeable electoral results of their discretion.

All of this is naturally quite understandable. It is not a question of it being otherwise; it is merely designed to show, in the simplest way, the kind of feelings and interests associated with these practices which are no more than 'the national interest *über alles*' or, in other words, the triumph of self-interested nationalisms. As a result, it comes as no surprise that the same logic (which it is difficult to describe as pro-European) that considers Europe as an aggregate of self-interested nationalisms surfaces when the problem arises of what to do with the competitive potential of Central and Eastern European agriculture. It is obvious that the development of civil society, liberal democracy and a market economy in these countries requires economic growth and trade with Western Europe; and no less obvious that this implies opportunities for the exportation of their agricultural produce to Western Europe. However, with the logic inherent in her agricultural policy, Western Europe has refused to give these countries such an opportunity, thus contradicting her rhetorical declarations of concern for their fate with her actual behavior.

It is not difficult to see that a tendency exists for the logic inherent in the main public policy of the Community to be extended to other areas. The distribution of the structural and cohesion funds has always given rise to extremely tough and rigorous bargaining in which different national interests confront one another. The very idea of structural and cohesion funds responds not so much to a feeling of solidarity *per se* as to a compensatory mechanism (a side payment) in exchange for the overwhelming commercial penetration by the richer countries of Northern Europe into those of the South, which have made it possible for the former to capture a large share of the markets and (capital and real estate) assets of the latter.

In short, the everyday reality of European politics differs from unitary rhetoric and consists of an amalgamation of national interests. It is true that with sufficient reiteration it is hoped that in the very long term the line between 'what is yours, and what is mine' will become blurred, and a new Community will emerge. I do not say that eventually this might not happen, but it is clear that, after 50 years, it is not sufficiently advanced to prevent the European political game still being seen principally, though not exclusively, as a series of games played by agents and networks of agents of the different member countries. In many cases, in the short term, these are zero-sum games. This is how most play games for the distribution of places on the Commission, of headquarters, and of available funds; any attempts to project the long-term perspective of a wider, unitary project onto these games have to take into account the immediate, basic reality of short-termism.

On the other hand, such a wider, unitary project would seem to demand a stability of leadership that for some nations justifies their pretensions to be the leader or co-leader of all the rest. It is true that there have been recurrent episodes of joint initiatives, understanding and co-leadership by France and Germany. But, naturally, these two countries have tended to qualify their aim of collective leadership with that of satisfying their own particular interests. Perhaps owing to this, the other countries have only accepted this co-leadership at intervals, conditionally and with reservations; for the better when it has been discreet (meaning less leadership) and at worst with loud protests and clear ambivalence. This ambivalence was demonstrated in the early 1990s, for example, when it became German policy to transfer the consequences of her own fiscal irresponsibility onto the shoulders of the other European nations (when she wanted to avoid financing aid and subsidies to East Germany by raising taxes in West Germany for electoral motives, which brought with it inflationary tensions which, in turn, forced the Bundesbank to raise interest rates).

Thus it is that at the very heart of Community policy we frequently find the kind of behavior, and the discourse implicitly or explicitly associated with it, which reinforces a sense of the differences of interest and identity between the European nations.

Problems of Rhetoric, Language and Narrative: the Challenge of a European 'Community'

Finally, there is another difficulty for a European public sphere to develop. One of the basic topics of a civic conversation is the expression of sentiments of attachment for and commitment to a community, which may have religious overtones. A civic religion is a blend of two symbolic components: symbols and rituals connected to some basic ('civil') institutions, and those connected with the assertion of the particular community (a 'country', *patrie* or 'quasi-primordial' community) which those institutions belong to.

So we have a wonderful dream of European unity and a substantially more prosaic everyday reality in which, however, the dream has to find fertile ground where it can grow and flourish. And there is no doubt that this is happening, in spite of everything. Because the growing frequency of contacts and their intensity in all spheres of life encourage stimulating exchanges, positive-sum games, invitations for new meetings and opportunities for mutual understanding; and this is what some people hope will prevail at some indefinite point in the future. But high hopes need hard work on the ground and from this perspective it is of interest to weigh up the difficulties of development in another area of the European public sphere: in the rhetoric of persuasion.

The most obvious difficulty in this respect is that of language. In the United States, English functions as the medium of communication for all members of the community, on whom it imposes a 'spirit of language' which is far more than just words or syntax in that it embodies a repertory of cultural forms, thought processes and emotional expression which allow peoples of the most diverse origins to share the most elemental and everyday experiences as experiences which define them as members of the same nation. In Europe, we neither have nor shall ever have a similar linguistic medium. Whoever wants to live a 'European experience' will be obliged to learn at least three or four languages, including English, probably German, perhaps French, as well as their own language or regional languages. Most of which they will never learn in any depth; they will use them without ever becoming fluent.

The spread of languages throughout all our countries, given the stability of the majority of their populations, will probably take place along cosmopolitan routes where hybrid communities will settle. Languages will gradually extend in these communities as well as in the capital cities and the most dynamic cities. But it is unlikely that a plural society on the lines of the American model, where ethnic populations are scattered by geography, with no links to a particular territory with continuous borders in which they clearly predominate and venture to call 'theirs', will be achieved in the foreseeable future.

This makes it far more complicated to find the narratives, and the myths implicit within them, on which to build shared memories. In the United States, Americans share the narrative of the foundation of the old colonies, the saga of the War of Independence and the Constitution, and 200 years of (fundamentally) institutional continuity based on these origins. In Europe, nations tell stories which, familiar to one, are foreign to the next, stories that are like inverted mirror images. The glory of one led to the decline of another, the revolutionary expansion of one was the invasion of another, the divine Church of one was the scourge of heretics to another; the Enlightenment may be seen as imitation or banality; the dance of princes and territories, as a dance of death; the procession of heroes and victims to one is a line of scoundrels and sinners to another. Over time, the hostility and rancor have diminished somewhat; but it is doubtful whether they will ever disappear entirely because they are closely bound up with the founding or defining myths of identity of almost all the European nations. So we shall have to reconstruct our relationships with our respective histories in a metaphorical sense, by seeking the ('objective') truth of our origins in parallel with the ('subjective') truth of what our feelings are today towards those origins, the greater part of which the sensitivity of people today (apparently so reasonable) scarcely allows them to understand.

The part of our history which we understand best and which, to some extent, can unite us most easily, in spite of all its horrors, is that of this century. Even so, there are considerable divergences between some nations and others, especially between the greater part of Europe and the British Isles, since only the United Kingdom appears to have had a relatively continuous historical sequence for the last three centuries, leading to a civil society which is both a liberal democracy and a market economy, whereas no continental European nation can claim a history of the same continuity. Only during this century can the majority of nations in Western Europe claim a similar continuity, having undergone the *via crucis* of a fascist or fascist-inclined totalitarian or authoritarian state and an appalling war before attaining (or reviving), by diverse means, some variant of the democratic and market ideal, and having remained in this state of glory ever since. Therefore, it is this combination of passion, resurrection and glory, or ascension to heaven, if I may be permitted the religious metaphor, which has in some way unified a rather confusing and contradictory series of earlier historical trajectories in the case of Western Europe. As regards Central and Eastern Europe we should add the variant of a different totalitarianism prolonged over another 40 years, with a happy ending.

The problem with recent history is that at its center lies a disturbing narrative nucleus. Almost all these European nations underwent their totalitarian experiences as the result of processes which, to a great extent, were endogenous; so that without an external war or external military pressure, led (in one way or another) by the United States, it is not probable that they would have overcome them: Western Europe by means of the war and Central and Eastern Europe as a consequence of the strategy of containment. The most disturbing part of this narrative nucleus is that at the heart of the glorious experience of a new united Europe resides a horror of itself: left to themselves, these countries fell into a frenzy (to an almost inconceivable degree in some cases) which they were unable to overcome by their own efforts. This consideration is inseparable from a certain feeling of humiliation or shame on the part of most of these nations (which is almost beyond confession, because to confess to it would go against the sense of due self-respect which it seems essential to maintain on the world stage). The compensatory narratives of resistance in France or Italy, or dissidence under Francoism and Salazarism in Spain and Portugal, of the subsequent good behavior of Germany and Austria, to give some examples, are not sufficient, in view of the profound wounds to the self-esteem of all these nations produced by years or decades of cooperation or collaboration with political regimes which, retrospectively, have come to be considered as contrary to the minimum standards of decency or civilization. (And to this we could add other complementary feelings relative to the colonial experience of these countries, at least in some circles.) An analogous argument could be applied to nations of Central and Eastern Europe.

The totalitarian experience was, without question, fratricidal: the institutionalization of a permanent state of civil war as opposed to the coexistence proper to a civil society. It was a civil war of nation against nation, class against class, at times race against race, which required the exaltation of violence and the regimentation of society under the orders of 'men of steel' or 'men of iron'; and which led to a world war which was lived in Europe, logically and almost literally, like a civil war (of which Spain and Greece, as well as France and Italy, had their own particular, local versions). The Europe which emerged from that world war was a Europe obsessed by the traumatic memory of that fratricidal experience (as was the Spain which emerged from Francoism). Perhaps, as a result, part of the impulse of the European nations to involve themselves emotionally in the process of European unity resides in an impulse of flight towards the future, towards a future which will make up for (and bury) a doubtful past; whereas part of the emotional reticence of the British to get involved in this process may reside in the fact that they never underwent the experience. But let there be no mistake, this circumstance marks the impulse at the same time as it marks the limits of the impulse for unity. Because a process which partly responds to such an impulse is also a process which responds, to the same extent, to a sense of distrust and flight away from oneself.

Conclusion: Difficulties as Opportunities

A European civil society needs a public sphere, namely, a critical mass of concerned citizens who discuss European issues and will (eventually) be ready to support European policy, as a precondition for a responsible European public authority. At present, we have observed Europeans' tendency to focus their current debates on domestic political responsibility, corruption, respect for the rule of law, and socioeconomic policy. We also know that, in the post-Maastricht period (since 1992), many Europeans have seemed reluctant to accept wholeheartedly a process by which political responsibility is removed a step farther from the arena of domestic politics into the European scenario, where most of them would lose sight of the issues. This situation may be construed as a difficulty but also as a new and exciting opportunity to be able to build a European public sphere.

If, in many countries, the domestic politics of the last few years have revolved around the problem of the full implementation of the principle of political responsibility in the terrain of domestic politics, this may have put their publics on the right track if they were to extend its application to the larger European scene. Weber (1958

[1918]) suggested that political responsibility was the mark of a true political calling. There is, however, a disturbing side to Weber's assertions on the matter. He saw the plebiscitarian and charismatic leader as an active and responsible leader, who embodied decision and creativity, at the forefront of a mass of passive and (by implication) less responsible or (in the extreme) irresponsible followers. This ideal situation was, therefore, only a step short of a scenario in which a leader, who was barely accountable either to history or any god, would face a mass of subcitizens. This was a recipe for disaster, as the German experience demonstrated as soon as the nation had entered that age of 'icy darkness and hardness' of which Weber (1958: 128) himself had had a premonition. I think, however, that Weber's position, besides being dangerous, was inconsistent because a leader can only be responsible before responsible people. Only responsible people can oblige their leader to be responsible for his acts, because only people who are themselves responsible, and see themselves in this light, have the capacity to muster the inner resources needed for demanding responsibility from their leaders, and for accepting the costs and risks that such demands entail.

If applied to the current European situation, my reasoning suggests the relevance of questions such as the following. Which are the institutional mechanisms that guarantee the application of the principle of political responsibility to the European scenario? How are European politicians going to be accountable for their decisions and accept full responsibility for the foreseeable outcome of these decisions? Is there a public made up of concerned citizens who are able and willing to stand up and demand such accountability? Might it not be that, in the process of European construction, decisions are made in such a way that the moment of truth when politicians take full responsibility for them, has been, and is, systematically avoided? By pursuing the answers to these questions, it may be possible to place the proper limits of European public authority and its accountability to European citizens at the center of the European public sphere where they belong.

In sum, in this short essay, I have endeavored to set out some of the difficulties which Europeans have in developing a public sphere, although its existence would be highly desirable if they aspire to the construction of a European civil society. The main contents of such a public sphere should be politics (how to make politicians responsible), the economy (how to regulate the European economy) and the Community's identity. There are, therefore, three main sources of difficulties. Firstly, in difficult times such as the present, public interest and attention center on internal matters, and the greater the difficulties the more attention they attract, particularly when it is expected that, by their very nature, they should be dealt with by national governments. This is the case as regards the crises of credibility of political parties and government (especially in some countries), and the economic crises and revisions to which the welfare state is subject. Secondly, European policy is hampered by what we might call a severe 'performative contradiction' in which the political establishment's behavior contradicts its rhetoric, given that its everyday behavior tends to follow the logic of self-interested nationalism. This is demonstrated by what happens with regard to most public policies (starting with its agricultural policy), the political games (or politics) of the Community, and the distribution of power, money and influence within it. All of these are continually reactivating the self-interested nationalism of member states. Thirdly, grave difficulties of a rhetorical nature exist as regards Europeans ever being able to persuade one another of their mutual community of feelings. Language, remote historical narratives and, finally, the nucleus of their most recent historical narrative present them with serious problems to which there is not, nor will there ever be, an easy answer. This hampers the development of a feeling of European fellowship or co-citizenship.

In fact, the term 'European citizenship' is perceived as though it were a condition by which people from different nations should have similar rights to be asserted *vis-à-vis* the European public courts and public officials, but not a condition by which those different peoples should share a common destiny and a common burden (or duty) of civic responsibility, together with pride, memories, and the excitement and anticipation of future common endeavors. Far from being the cornerstone of a civic religion, European citizenship is seen as a vehicle for furthering private claims (to be put before the public authorities). This is why every new problem that Europeans face is perceived not as a common challenge but as a nuisance (or an aggregate of particular nuisances), while anticipating a new round of precarious tradeoffs between reluctant partners.

Perhaps this inventory of difficulties will cause the reader to feel that its author is sending a subliminal message of the undesirability of a European public sphere, and by implication, of the whole construction. Nothing could be further from the truth. I do believe that the difficulties are enormous, but I do not believe that we should be discouraged by them. In any case, and if I may appeal to my own local tradition, I can only add that I would share with Cervantes a certain fascination for seeing things as they are, for seeing improbable and extraordinary undertakings with some sympathy, and even for feeling the inclination, at best, to undertake them or, at worst, not to shrink away from them, whatever the result. (An inclination, if truth be told, perhaps more appropriate of Don Quixote than of Cervantes, and possibly not that sensible.)

In any case, we, Europeans, are faced by tasks which, though difficult, need not prove impossible. Development of the public sphere is essential for the creation of European unity protagonized by an active citizenry and not by a trans-European political class or establishment which, by a process of manipulation, drags a heterogeneous series of national publics, alternating between apathy and confusion, along with it. Firstly, this citizenry is capable of understanding by itself that a variety of domestic policies for confronting certain crucial problems offers a learning opportunity by means of comparing numerous public policy experiments. Secondly, this citizenry could develop a certain critical awareness towards performative contradictions in European policies, between actual behavior and appeals to principles, and it could deliberate on the extent to which it wishes to accept the implications of the self-interested nationalism which tends to dominate real policy-making (for example, in the form of protectionist trade policies). Thirdly, this citizenry could devote more attention to the problems of constructing a community of feelings and to the problems of reconsidering their remote and recent historical narratives which such a construction may involve.

Finally, I would suggest that, if my line of reasoning is correct, and the development of a European public sphere depends mostly on an active citizenry instead of on political elites, then some current misunderstandings over the way the construction of Europe is presented to public opinion should be avoided.

Thus, we observe that the European policy networks of politicians, civil servants, lobbies, experts and journalists quite often tend to trust the success of European construction to a process of muddling through. This is the result of endless national bargaining, the institutional inertia of meetings and timetables, and the spillover logic of the everyday activities of European civil servants and courts of justice. However, the muddling through is then *presented* as a goal-oriented process that corresponds to a definite strategy or grand design. The grand design is then *supposed* to be vindicated by the occasional referendum in which the European public is summoned, from time to time, to confirm the general direction of events. In fact, these interventions by the public are looked upon with the utmost apprehension by politicians who try either to avoid them altogether or to frame them in such a way that the policy networks will be left with the impression that things are under control. In addition, this combination of protracted politics with occasional outbursts from the European masses is then *mixed up and embellished* with two narratives. One of these suggests that we are witnessing the equivalent of a *sui generis* constitutional foundation of the European political system by means of a European quasi-collective decision. The other, that this quasi-decision is the result of a sort of 'dialectical relationship' between the core members (mainly France and Germany, plus the Benelux countries) and the peripheral members. The core nations would be the motor and the driving impulse, embodying the necessary will and determination, and the active principle: in short, the sacred center of the Union. In contrast, the peripheral nations would be wavering between resistance and acquiescence, between staying on the margins or being dragged into the process.

There can be no doubt that this exercise in myth-making fits the sentiments and self-perceptions of not a few people among the European political elites and in the core nations. I wonder if it has any chance of ever being accepted by the general public and by the peripheral nations. I wonder, too, if a European public sphere and the corresponding civil society can be, or should be, built on these misconceptions.

Notes

1 have discussed elsewhere another additional factor (Pérez-Díaz, 1995). It concerns the performative contradiction of many critical intellectuals between their explicit discourse and the messages which are implicit in their way of living (in friendly surroundings or ecological niches, universities for instance, provided for them by 'the system'; paradoxically, this would provide these thinkers with a practical illustration of the kind of living arrangements to be defended, or protected, against that very 'system' which was providing those arrangements to them).

2 Furthermore, I would argue that a polity of responsible politicians or politicians with a political calling (as Weber would put it) requires the presence of such a critical mass of concerned citizen, which should be placed in a continuum somewhere between Weber's (1958 [1918]) professional and occasional politicians, and that such a polity cannot be obtained if charismatic demagogues face an audience of (irresponsible) masses of followers. See below.

References

Alexander, Jeffrey (1993) 'The Return to Civil Society', featured essay in *Contemporary Sociology*, 22 (6) (November): 797–803.

Alexander, Jeffrey (1994) 'The Paradoxes of Civil Society'. Social Sciences Research Center, Occasional Paper 16.

Bailyn, Bernard (1967) *The Ideological Origins of the American Revolution*. Cambridge, MA: Harvard University Press.

Cohen, Jean and Arato, Andrew (1992) *Civil Society and Political Theory.* Cambridge, MA: MIT Press.

Comisión Europea (1995) *Informe General sobre la actividad de la Unión Europea.* Luxemburgo: Oficina de Publicaciones Oficiales de las Comunidades Europeas.

Gellner, Ernest (1994) *Conditions of Liberty.* New York: Allen Lane.

Gouldner, Alvin (1980) *The Two Marxisms.* London: Macmillan.

Habermas, Jürgen (1991) *Moral Consciousness and Communicative Action*, trans. C. Lenhardt and S.W. Nicholsen. Cambridge, MA: MIT Press.

Hayek, Friedrich von (1979) *Law, Legislation and Liberty. Volume 1. Rules and Order.* London: Routledge and Kegan Paul.

Keane, John (ed.) (1988) *Civil Society and the State.* New York: Verso.

North, Douglass (1990) *Institutions, Institutional Change and Economic Performance.* Cambridge: Cambridge University Press.

Oakeshott, Michael (1991) *Rationalism in Politics and Other Essays.* Indianapolis: Liberty Press.

Pérez-Díaz, Víctor (1993) *The Return of Civil Society.* Cambridge, MA: Harvard University Press.

Pérez-Díaz, Víctor (1995) 'The Possibility of Civil Society: Traditions, Character and Challenges', in John Hall (ed.), *Civil Society: Theory, History, Comparison.* Cambridge: Polity.

Thucydides (1972 [*c.* 404 BC]) *History of the Peloponnesian War*, trans. R. Warner. Harmondsworth: Penguin.

Weber, Max (1958 [1918]) 'Politics as a Vocation', in H.H. Gerth and C. Wright Mills (eds), *From Max Weber: Essays in Sociology.* New York: Oxford University Press.

Name Index

Adamson, W., 68, 74
Adler-Hellman, J., 31
Adorno, T., 167
Ahrne, G., 14, 84, 88, 90, 94
Alexander, J.C., 1, 7, 9, 32, 72, 79, 94, 96, 97, 107n, 109n, 112n, 119, 129, 133n, 134n, 138, 139, 140, 142, 157n, 162, 193, 212, 214, 215
Allen, W., 157n
Almond, G., 77
Althusser, L., 108n
Anderson, B., 158n
Apter, D., 111n
Arato, A., 67, 68, 115, 158n, 162, 163, 194, 212, 214
Arendt, H., 128
Aristotle, 6, 110n
Atkinson, A., 62n
Auyero, J., 72, 78

Bailyn, B., 108n, 111n, 217
Bakewell, D., 155
Banfield, E., 13, 21–4
Barbalet, J., 60, 61, 65n
Barber, B., 197, 198, 205
Barker, E., 110n
Barnard, C., 88
Barthes, R., 107, 108n
Bartolomé, J., 75
Bataille, G., 123
Bean, G., 63n
Becker, H., 118
Bell, D., 63n
Bellah, R., 108n
Benda, V., 194
Bendix, R., 163, 165, 167
Benjamin, W., 120
Bennett, W.L., 110n
Benz, W., 116
Berezin, M., 122, 125, 134n, 158n
Blok, A., 71
Bobbio, N., 10

Bodin, J., 125
Boissevain, J., 71
Borón, A., 69
Boschi, R., 26
Bosworth, C.E., 70
Boudieu, P., 109n
Boyte, H.C., 68, 69
Brain, P., 62n
Braithwaite, J., 63n
Brennan, J., 63n
Brown, E., 151
Brubaker, R., 7, 143
Bruckner, P., 116
Brunsson, N., 88
Buchanan, J., 51, 63n, 64n

Caillois, R., 110n
Calderon, F., 30
Calhoun, C., 12, 28, 67, 86, 93, 138, 162, 167, 185
Calvin, J., 169
Cardoso, R., 26
Carsten, F.L., 126
Castles, F., 64n
Cawelti, J., 111n
Chartier, R., 164
Chatterjee, P., 144
Cheibub, Z., 26, 34
Clapham, C., 72, 75
Clark, T.N., 78
Clinton, W., 199
Cobb, J., 9
Cohen, C., 122, 123, 125, 130, 131, 134n
Cohen, J., 67, 68, 96, 115, 158n, 162, 163, 166, 212, 214
Coleman, J., 97
Collins, R., 133n
Corden, 64n
Curti, M., 111n

Dahrendorf, R., 191
Dalton, D., 90, 91
Dandeker, C., 120, 123, 125, 127

Subject Index

adhocracy, 89, 93
African-American community, 145, 147, 148, 154
American Founding Fathers, 1
amoral familism, 13, 21-4, 31, 32, 34, 37
Argentina, 78, 112n
Australia, economy and politics, 41–6, 49, 51, 54, 55, 57, 60, 61
authoritarianism, 28

Bill of Rights, the, 102
binary codes, *see* civil society, symbolic dimension of
Brazil, 21, 34, 78

Canada, 77
Capitalism, 2
Catholicism, 134n, 194, 206
China, 77
Christianity, 6, 29, 134n
Christopher Commission, 156
Civil society: in Australia, 14, 40, 41, 45–8; in Brazil, 13; and capitalism, 3–4, 10; as capitalist epiphenomenon, 4, 5; and citizenship, 143, 144, 235, 236; as 'civic religion', 3, 216, 230; components of, 58, 116; and confidence, 57, 58, 59; definitions of, 1–4, 7, 40, 48, 49, 67, 73, 84, 86, 96, 115, 138, 191–3, 211, 212; and democracy, 30, 66, 68, 69, 70, 72, 77, 84, 107; as discourse, 102–6, 110n, 111n, 117, 118, 119, 138, 142, 143, 157; and economic reform, 41, 43; in Europe, 17, 211, 218–20, 230–237; as ideal-types, 2–8, 102; in India, 70; and inequality, 21, 25–7, 31–2, 34, 35, 37; in Iran, 70; in Japan, 70; in Latin America, 13, 25–36, 70; and the media, 67, 68, 97, 138; as moral force, 3, 97, 116, 132; and narrative, 140, 141, 157, 216, 230, 236, 237; and organizations, 84–8, 91–4, 97, 217; and

other non-civil spheres, 7–12, 48, 51, 56, 62, 85, 86, 97, 215, 218; and patronage, 14, 67, 71–80; in Poland, 16; and public opinion, 7, 16; and the public sphere, 30–31, 35, 67, 68, 69, 139, 162, 211, 212, 213, 219, 234; 'real' versus 'ideal', 1; and rights, 102; in Russia, 70; Scottish moralists' definition of, 3, 211, 212; as semiotic system, 99, 139, 140; and social movements, 66, 86, 90, 91, 93, 97; as solidary community, 7, 32–3, 35, 72, 96; and the state, 5, 68, 90, 94; symbolic dimension of, 97–105, 118, 140, 142, 146, 156; and trust, 195, 196; and voluntary associations, 30–31, 36, 68, 70, 86, 89, 90, 91, 97, 192, 217
civility, 71, 84, 142
clientelism, *see* civil society and patronage
collective identities, 29, 30, 33, 34, 36, 37, 77, 131
colonialism, 45, 46
Communism, 117–119, 127; and rationality, 128–30
community, 215, 216, 217, 221, 230; as *Gemeinschaft*, 52, 120, 191; as 'imagined', 158n
confidence, 57–61
corruption, 222, 223
critical theory, 186
culture area analysis, 117, 134n
Czechoslovakia, 191

democracy, 2, 99, 101, 108n, 117–19, 125, 128; constitutional democracy, 71, 74, 77, 78; industrial, 88
Democracy in America (A. de Tocqueville), 75
Dreyfus affair, 141

economic efficiency, 47
'economic rationalism', 41, 42, 44, 45, 46